HANS NIELSEN HAUGE

The Apostle of Norway

Hans Nielsen Hauge

The farm-boy from Thune parish, Smaalenene Amt, who roused the people of Norway from a prolonged spiritual slumber and industrial inactivity to a vigorous awakening that culminated in the Declaration of Independence of May 17th, 1814

By

A. M. ARNTZEN
Author of "Historical Sketches" and other writings

WIPF & STOCK · Eugene, Oregon

Wipf and Stock Publishers
199 W 8th Ave, Suite 3
Eugene, OR 97401

The Apostle of Norway
Hans Nielsen Hauge
By Arntzen, A. M.
ISBN 13: 978-1-61097-348-9
Publication date 3/3/2011
Previously published by Lutheran Free Church Publishing, 1933

PREFACE

The "Progressive Genius," Hans Nielsen Hauge, was a genuine Norwegian, born at a time of religious darkness and industrial dormancy in Norway. It was an act of Providence that a genius was born to stir the people. Hauge was typically Norwegian, as John Bunyan was typically English, and Luther typically German.

The following pages will acquaint English speaking peoples with this remarkable pioneer of the progressive movement in Norway.

H. N. Hauge was so thoroughly convinced of his mission that he would rather go to jail than compromise. Hence, he was arrested ten times—and the last time he remained in prison ten years.

In presenting the following sketches of H. N. Hauge, the main sources of information are: His autobiography with letters from his contemporaries; Klaus Tolvsen's *Efterretninger;* Mikkel Grendahl's *Memoirs;* Prof. S. F. Stenersen's *Life of Hauge;* and Court Records from 1797 to 1814. Later: *Life and Time of Hans Nielsen Hauge* by Bishop Dr. A. Chr. Bang, J. B. Bull and others.

Upon the request of progressive people this volume is published in memory of this noble son of Norway, who stirred the people from the North Cape to the Naze, and from the North Sea to the Swedish boundary, into a spiritual awakening that bore the nation successfully to liberty even while he still remained in prison.

ARNLIOT M. ARNTZEN.

Minneapolis, Minnesota, 1933.

CHAPTER I

Springtime in Norway

It is in the early spring of 1771. The warm water of the Gulf Stream exerts its influence upon the ever-changing currents of air, creating balmy zephyrs gradually wafted north, eventually persuading King Boreas to retire in favor of a milder season and seek a rest in his ancient lair of Ultima Thule.

The sun is climbing higher and the days are lengthening. The waves of warm air are slowly moving north. The heavy blanket of snow covering the landscape must be removed, and the wonderful forces of nature awakened to new life and activity.

The snow is melting. Little streams of water begin to appear here, there, everywhere. On the mountain-side they merge and form turbulent rivulets dashing from crag to crag down to the plains below. Here they meet with others and join the larger streams, breaking up the ice and carrying things away to the distant sea.

Patches of bare ground appear on the hillsides facing south. On the undulating surface of the lowland plains, hazy vapors rise from the bare patches, showing the underground forces at work thawing the frozen soil. Nature is awakening to proclaim the glad news that spring is coming to visit the "Land of the Midnight Sun."

The winter has been very severe. Man and beast in confined quarters have suffered more or less from poor accommodations and intense cold sweeping in great waves from the northern mountains. The supply of fodder for cows, goats, and sheep is dwindling away, and the coast-people gather kelp and seaweeds at low-tide to help out the shortage, while the upland people away from the coast go into rifts and vales at the foot-hills to cut twigs, shrubs and bushes to mix with the fodder to tide them over until grass-time.

Spring is coming to make everybody glad—nature is awakening everything, everywhere. The weasels, rabbits, and ptarmigans shed their winter coats of white as the snow melts, and soon they will have new and seasonable dresses in brown shades mixed with gray.

The grouse family will soon be mating, and their turbulent love-making is heard in the distant woods. Wolves and foxes are preparing for spring, refurnishing their lairs for an eventual increase in the family. The mole, the groundhog, and "old bruin" have awakened and are coming out to enjoy the change of air.

The mild air is wielding its influence by shading the distant woods in a haze of delicate blue to match the blue sky and the far away rim of the ocean. The white shroud of snow is lifting, and out of the cold sepulcher a new life is emanating, even as last year and every year before—a life persisting in its myriad forms from season to season—always renewed and yet the same.

The winged nomads of the air begin their annual pilgrimage to the Northland to spend the summer in a delightful climate while raising and training the offspring. The advance guard of crows and starlings is already crossing the blue water of Skakerak to begin their work as scavengers, where the ground is bare.

Other winged tribes will soon follow to greet the barren landscape with lovely music from the Southlands and enliven the perspective of dark fields and naked woods with their gay and beautiful colors.

* * *

For many long, long years Norway had suffered under an alien and precarious government. Socially, politically, and spiritually the people had been buried deep under the winter-snows of mental torpor and dormant souls. They had lost all ambition above getting something to eat and a place to sleep. Prone to despair and sunk in hopeless despondency they meandered through a dark and dreary life of drudgery without purpose, aspiration, or strength to rise out of a base and servile existence.

After the Reformation (1537) "community schools" were introduced to supplant the monastic schools of Catholic times, but had not been well received by the lay-people. "Book-learning" was looked upon as a sorcery to aid the king's officers, vassals, bailiffs, and constables; and for more than a century the new school system vacillated between being tolerated or rejected.

Yet education had strong supporters in the cities and the more cultured rural districts. They secured competent teachers and the "3 R's" were rigidly drilled into the children. The most potent factor in education, however, was their religion.

In 1737 Bishop Dr. Erik Pontoppidan of Bergen published his famous S a n d h e d t i l G u d f r y g- t i g h e d. This explanation of the Catechism, and Bible history were made compulsory requirements in preparing for confirmation. This study necessitated a greater skill in reading, and the boys and girls read and read to commit these books to memory until they became quite able readers.

Thus the laity became a reading people in spite of illiteracy, bias, and prejudice, and the reading-habit developed in after years a desire to read periodicals and books. Eventually, illiteracy yielded to education, and newspapers began to flourish when people were able and willing to read. Statistics show that at the close of the eighteenth century, 80 per cent of the population of Norway could read.

With the reading of newspapers and pamphlets came knowledge of the outside world. New ideas crept in to undermine accepted opinions and doctrines. Pietism was supplanted by rationalism and materialism, and the worldly pastors followed the trend to preach about economical and social topics instead of the ancient and old-fashioned Gospel.

Then came years of poor crops. Many districts were facing a famine, but the hardy race managed to live through the years of starvation on barkbread and fish, when luck was good.

Yet all these adversities did not bring about any spiritual awakening or any higher ambitions to improve or to seek a better standard of life socially and politically.

Dancing, drinking, fighting between families, feuds between neighbors, and frays and brawls between various contending factions, political and otherwise, prevailed at public gatherings.

Such were the conditions of the people, especially in the backwoods districts and the slum districts of the cities, while in other localities there were found devout Christians praying for spring and relief from this dreadful winter of perverted minds and intellectual depravity.

CHAPTER II

Birth of a Genius

In Thune parish, 75 miles south of Oslo (then called Kristiania) and 12 miles northeast of Fredrikstad, there is a farmstead called Hauge, at that time owned by Niels Mikkelsen and his good wife Marie, with four children: Bertha, 8 years old; Ole, 6; Mikkel, 4; and Karen, about 2 years old. They were robust and healthy, of dark complexion, blue eyes, ruddy cheeks—overgrown for their age, but nevertheless active and cheerful.

The weather is fine and they want to play outside, but mother says: "No! The ground is so wet and muddy."

Their sad and solemn faces are glued to the window panes to watch everything going on outside. The housemaid has told them many extraordinary tales and funny stories about the little fairies, and the children want to see how the fairies took the snow away.

* * *

The house-cleaning was all done. The floors had been scrubbed until they fairly shone, and the men had brought small branches of spruce cut into small bits and spread thickly over the floors as a carpet. This helped to keep the dirt off and gave them a touch of nature, besides filling the rooms with a fresh and sweet fragrance of the evergreen forest in the uplands. Preparations were made for expected company by baking and cooking things toothsome and pleasant enough even for the taste of the fastidious.

Hospitality in the farming communities was not

only common, but most liberal, and during the holidays at Easter, Pentecost, and Christmas there were general rounds of visiting. The more prominent farmers would "hobnob" with officers, doctors, and pastors of the district.

The democratic tendency of liberal hospitality between peer and peasant acted as a powerful agent of cultural progress. The farmers were Odelsbønder (freeholders) even on small farms, and usually out of debt and quite independent. Only the larger farms had Husmen, who rented a few acres with a cabin on it for their families, and paid the rent in manual labor to the landlord. As a rule they were invited with their families to the festivities at the farmstead. Mingling with different people gave them a wider range of thought, and the reading of borrowed newspapers expanded their mental horizon. Thus the lines of caste were often lost sight of, and a democratic spirit was fostered.

The population along the coast also enjoyed the freedom of the sea as fishermen or sailors. Importers and wholesale merchants had their own fleet of ships going to the various countries for supplies, and thousands of young men were trained on their ships going to distant lands. Strenuous training gave them efficiency, and eventually they learned foreign languages.

The young men shipped in foreign vessels, especially English, or joined the navy, and continued until, tired of a seafaring life, they landed on their native shores to marry and settle down in a home of their own, perhaps inherited.

These cultural agencies had a strong influence upon the development of habits, customs, fashions, tastes, styles and manners of the populace in the seaboard-towns, and it spread into the interior farm districts even to the uplands and mountain regions.

This progress in civilization, like the forces of

nature, will give fair warning of an upheavel or a revolution in due time, and a single man can furnish the spark to explode the dynamic forces.

* * *

Easter is close at hand. At the Hauge farmstead there is unusual hurry and excitement. The children are brought over to Grandma and Grandpa, and it makes them happy to know that they can stay, perhaps several days. The hired man is racing over to Glemminge with horse and K a r i o l (carry all) to get a midwife, and the rest of the family are making preparations for a new arrival.

The sun has set and the shadows of evening deepen. The farmer and the chore-boy are looking anxiously towards Glemminge for signs of the hired man and the expected midwife, wondering if the muddy roads have stalled him. No, there is a speck away off in the darkening shadows; it is coming nearer. There are two. The midwife must be bringing a nurse or a helpmaid to assist her.

* * *

The farmer helped the ladies off the K a r i o l and bade them enter. They took off their wraps and went into the sick-room.

"You are doing fine," the midwife said, after a brief examination and words of greeting. "You have a little fever and your temperature is up, but the pulse is normal. The condition of your body is excellent, and you will come through real fine. Yes," and she smiled roguishly, "your rosy cheeks tell me that you are going to have a boy."

"That's fine," said the farmer, and smiles twinkled on every face.

"Supper is ready," the maid announced, and they followed her into the dining-room and sat down at the table.

"Now let us thank the Lord for His grace and the good things that we receive out of His hand," said the farmer, as he bowed his head and repeated a Scripture passage with a short prayer.

"The Lord is certainly good to us to give us what we need and supply our daily wants. We read about war clouds and hear of nations preparing for war, and when the storm breaks, we'll see harder times than these. The English have trouble with their colonies over in America, and France is watching for an opening to have a tilt with England. War will certainly come sooner or later, and the smaller nations will suffer the most, because they are not able to defend their neutrality.

"Perhaps I ought to apologize for the plain food and simple fare on our table, but you will understand how infinitely better it is for us to have plain food than no food, and I refrain from apologizing, hoping that the Lord will remember us and help us, when the wrath of the nations are upon us, looting food supplies and taking the bread away from widows and orphans."

* * *

The evening meal was finished; the maids carried things away and retired. The midwife followed the husband into his wife's room and said after a brief examination: "Nothing doing before midnight, so I may as well have a little nap," and the farmer showed her the guest-chamber. Soon the house was hushed into a solemn and peaceful quietude. Only the wall-clock kept on ticking loudly.

The farmer remained at his wife's bedside and whispered an occasional word of comfort and cheer.

He read from Psalm 130: "Out of the depths have I cried unto Thee, O Lord! Lord, hear my voice; let Thine ears be attentive to the voice of my supplications."

The words fell as balm upon his wife's distressed and troubled soul and had a wonderful power to soothe her mind, reaching the innermost recesses of her heart to give her a firm belief in God's promises and His willingness to fulfill them.

The clock on the wall kept on ticking. The hours passed, and now twelve strokes announced midnight. Both midwife and nurse came into the sick-room and ordered the farmer to go and get some sleep.

*   *   *

It was five o'clock in the morning on the 3rd of April, 1771. The farmer, Niels Mikkelsen Hauge, had had quite a nap when the midwife came to the alcove with a bundle in her arms and said:

"It's a boy! Congratulate your son!"

"A boy!" he said rather incredulously.

"Yes, and aren't you glad?"

"Of course I am glad, but I did not expect it would be a son."

"Well, didn't I tell you so last night?"

"Yes, but how did you know?"

"Oh, that's a secret of our profession."

He took the bundle rather awkwardly, and peered into the red face of a wee bit of humanity with rather wondering eyes. "The Lord be praised, how wonderful and perfect He molds us! Is—is he all right?"

"Most certainly!" said the midwife, "he is as fine looking a baby as I ever saw, and weighs nearly ten pounds."

"What a chunk," said the father as he weighed it upon both arms. How is the wife—the mother?"

"Oh, she is doing fine after the severe labor she had, and she is awake now, so you may come in."

He carried the bundle very carefully into the bedroom and laid it in the arms of the mother, who had a sweet, angelic smile on her face. It gripped his heart in such a wonderful way that he knelt by the bedside with a heart full of thanksgiving for the precious gift God had given, praying that the boy be favored in grace to grow up a God-fearing man and a good citizen.

The group made a beautiful picture. By and by the others came in to look at the baby and voice their compliments to the new arrival.

It was a holiday for the household. The farmer wanted something extra for breakfast in commemoration of the happy event, so the maid set the finest of the Easter baking on the breakfast table. A merry family they were, cracking jokes at the husband, who busied himself carrying choice dishes to his wife. She drew his head down and whispered in his ear, "What a prince of a husband you are!" And of course he snatched a kiss, while waves of laughter came from the guests.

After breakfast the midwife was taken back to Glemminge, while the helpmaid was left behind to care for the mother and baby a week or so.

In the afternoon a few days later several of the neighbors' wives came to see the baby boy and the mother. They brought d e l i c a t e s s e n and savory dishes like R ø m g r ø d (cream pudding) G o r o cake, F a t t i g m a n, etc. They talked and talked of all the babies that had come during the past years and commented on their cute ways, while the mother rather enjoyed their prattle and idle talk. Anyway, time passed so fast that evening was upon them before they knew it, and they had to hurry home.

* * *

The first Sunday after Easter was an ideal spring day. The sun shone brightly and the air was warm. At the Hauge farmstead the convalescent mother felt strong enough to go to church, and they decided to have the baby christened. The snow-white baby dress of enormous length, in which the other children had been baptized, was brought, and today it was going to serve again for the new baby.

They were ready to go. The sorrel had a shining new harness, and the K a r i o l was washed and polished. Mother should ride in state, and the husband himself took the reins.

At the church the many relatives and friends came to pay their respects and congratulated the parents with another son, and "such a fine boy!" After a little while the parish clerk came and they went into the sacristy to have the baby registered for baptism.

After some preliminaries the clerk asked of the parents, "What name is the boy going to have?"

"We have agreed," answered the father, "to name him Hans after my uncle, and as my son it will be Nielsen. Born on the Hauge farm, his surname will be Hauge," and the clerk wrote in bold letters:

HANS NIELSEN HAUGE

After services the parents invited some of the nearest relatives to a family reunion and a celebration in honor of the day. Quite a number came to the "barselgilde," as it was called. They feasted and drank coffee (looked upon as a luxury), and late in the evening the host asked permission to have a short devotion.

They arranged themselves in groups, (as hymnbooks were few) and sang with hearty voices the old favorite Thanksgiving Hymn:

> *Now thank we all our God,*
> *With heart and hands and voices;*
> *Who wondrous things hath done,*
> *In whom His world rejoices;*
> *Who from our mothers' arms*
> *Hath blessed us on our way,*
> *With countless gifts of love,*
> *And still is ours today.*

The farmer read one of David's Psalms and prayed the ever bounteous God to accept their humble thanks for His blessings and benefits, His guidance and care, to lead them out of darkness into light, to preserve them from evil, and to remain true in His grace and peace.

Then they sang:

> *All praise and thanks to God,*
> *The Father, now be given;*
> *The Son and Lord who trod*
> *This earth to gain us heaven.*
> *And Spirit from above,*
> *Whom earth and heaven adore;*
> *For thus it was, is now,*
> *And shall be evermore!*

* * *

Two years later a baby girl was born into the Hauge family, and she was christened Anna, for her grandmother. As Anna grew up, Hans was her steady companion and took good care of her. Hence, they were always together and seemed to be almost inseparable.

When they became old enough, they went to school together, and Hans helped her with her lessons. Hans, although the older, had all he could do to keep ahead of her, and the school days saw the two diligently plodding along into new fields of knowledge, where they were drinking of the fountain of wisdom in liberal draughts.

CHAPTER III
Midsummer Happenings

Several years have passed. It is a summer evening in July, and haying is in full swing. The work is finished for the day, and the rakes and scythes are hung on knobs or resting upon the walls of the tool-shed. The family has gathered for devotion, and they are singing.

After the song, the farmer is heard reading a chapter out of his beloved Bible, followed by a short prayer. Then they sang the ever-beautiful, old evening hymn, by Paul Herbert:

Now God be with us, for the night is closing;
The light and darkness are of His disposing;
And 'neath His shadow here to rest we yield us,
For He will shield us.

Let pious thoughts be ours when sleep o'ertakes us;
Our earliest thoughts be Thine when morning wakes us;
Remember Thee, in all that we are doing,
Thy praise pursuing.

Father, Thy name be praised, Thy kingdom given;
Thy will be done on earth, as 'tis in heaven;
Give daily bread; forgive our sins; deliver—
Us now and ever!

The singing ends, the house is very quiet. A soft summer breeze sighs in the trees. A few belated swallows skim through the air, soon to seek their nests under the rafters for the night. The scent of new-mown hay comes from the meadows, and the poplars and birches whisper to the night-wind the secrets of nature.

* * *

The hired man came out and sauntered toward the barn, and the boys, Ole and Mikkel, followed. Going inside, where the chore-girl had begun milking, he asked, "Are you going over to the Braaten dance tonight?"

"I don't know," she answered. "I haven't thought of it."

"There'll be a lot of people there. Kristen Gleng will fiddle, and you know there'll be some fun when he's around."

"Sure it will be fun," she said. "Kristen Gleng is full of fun."

Mikkel slid inside to hear better what they laughed at.

The hired man resented this and asked, "Where is Hans?"

"Oh, he is reading," answered Mikkel demurely.

"Hans is always reading," said the man. "He ought to make a good preacher."

"He surely will be a preacher," the girl said, "that's the opinion of Pastor Seeberg. He praised Hans at the last Sunday examination."

"He will take his death at reading so much," said the hired man.

Ole came inside to get the benefit of the conversation.

Then they all suddenly started, as the stalwart farmer appeared in the doorway. They wished to get outside, but couldn't.

A dead silence followed. The hired man pressed himself farther into the darkness of the stall. The maid bowed her head and milked fast and furiously; the boys stood still and felt embarrassed.

He slowly questioned them, "Any one here going to the dance tonight?" His voice was calm and dignified.

No one answered. They were all stricken dumb.

He looked at the hired man, who was still visible,

and said, "Can you, who have prayed to God this evening, go and dance without sinning. Then go, but—take the Lord with you!" He spoke mildly yet firmly, then turned to walk back to the house.

* * *

At the chamber-window upstairs Hans was reading in the twilight. He was tall for his age, but slim. His hair was turning darker, but his eyes were mild and large and very deep. Occasionally he looked out of the window and let his eyes roam over the woods and fields.

The book rested on the window-sill—a leather-bound volume, old and worn—the family-Bible of the Hauge ancestors. Inside the front cover was written with pale brown ink: Ole Hansen Hauge, Anno efter Christi Byrd (birth) 1721, and underneath, the words: Gud er min Styrke; mig skal ey fattes! (God is my strength, I shall not want.) Below was written in plain black ink: Marie Olsdatter Hauge, Anno 1760.

As Hans read this on the front cover, his thoughts went back to his forefathers, who had read this book, thumbed its pages, and found peace, comfort and happiness in the Word.

His mother came up the stairway.

She came over to him, stroked his hair lightly and lovingly, and softly said, "Close your reading for today, my dear; it's bedtime."

He looked up at her longingly and said, "Yes, I will, only it's interesting to read what God can do with men."

"Yes, yes, I know," said his mother, "I have often thought how wonderfully God does all things. But —where are the other boys?" she added.

He looked out and confessed that he had not seen them.

The mother was going down but turned and said, "Go and fetch the boys in, and urge them to go to bed. We have to be up early now that the weather is fine and there is a lot of haying to do."

* * *

Midsummer night had settled over lea and vale, but it was not dark. A mellow light permeated the darkness and revealed the hazy outlines of neighboring farms. Far over the fields the grasshoppers and crickets chirped their nocturnal chants and the bats flew around.

Upstairs in the Hauge home the three boys were in bed, Ole and Hans in one and Mikkel in the other bed alone. Apparently everybody was sound asleep when the clock struck eleven.

Mikkel woke up, and then slipped out of bed very quietly.

He hurriedly dressed, grabbed his cap and shoes and moved towards the stairway in his stockings.

Then Hans sat up. "Where are you going?" he whispered.

Mikkel stopped short, but did not answer immediately.

"Just a step outside," he managed to say and went down the stairs.

Hans sat and stared. He went over to the window and looked out. The light of the summer night was sufficient to reveal objects at some distance. Over by the tool-shed he saw the hired man and the chore-girl. The white kerchief on her head shone conspicuously.

They started on a by-path across the meadow in the direction of Braaten, and some distance behind Mikkel sneaked after them.

Hans saw it from the window, and hot blood shot through his veins, as he whispered, "All three going to the dance."

At once he felt a great sadness filling his heart. He folded his hands and sank on his knees beside a chair with his head pillowed on his folded hands in continued prayer. A faint noise reached his ears. Some one was coming up the stairs. It was his brother Mikkel.

The kneeling boy felt a wave of joy flooding his heart, and tears came fast and silently, but they were tears of joy. Then he went over to Mikkel and threw his arms around his brother's neck.

Mikkel whispered: "What a queer boy you are!"

Hans was too happy for words, so he turned and went to bed, as did his brother, and soon both were sleeping.

* * *

After breakfast next morning Niels Mikkelsen started for the meadows with the hired man and Hans.

The Glommen river ran high. Heavy rains in May and June had caused a great rise, and the current ran strong and heavy.

Niels unlocked the boat and the three stepped in.

The hired man was drowsy and rowed in a listless way. He had returned from the dance at five that morning, but no one had mentioned anything about it. They at length reached the other shore, pulled the boat up and fastened it.

They walked towards the hayshed, carrying their rakes.

"Were you at the dance last night?" Niels asked.

The hired man, Peter Thoresen, bit off a piece from a roll of tobacco, chewed, spat and then said, "No, I wasn't!"

The boy, Hans, who had come up behind, turned red as fire when he heard it, as if he had been the guilty one.

"Thank God for that, Peter!" said Niels Mikkelsen. "I was afraid you had been there, since you look rather worn out today."

"Oh, one can be tired anyway," said Peter as he spat in his hands and began to rake. He said no more but raked hard, piled the hay into heaps, and carried it down to the boat.

But the boy, Hans, went about trying to hold tears back, swallowing hard, as he raked together what the others spilled.

They stepped into the boat. Hans sat down behind while the two men rowed. On the other side they saw his brother Mikkel, with horse and wagon ready to receive the hay when they came across. Near the landing the current ran swift and strong.

"Now make a strong pull for the shore," said Niels Mikkelsen to the hired man, as the current caught the boat.

The hired man started to spit in his hand when the oar slipped and fell into the water. He arose and grabbed for it, but, dizzy from a night's fatigue, he lost his balance and went into the water.

The man came up near the boatrail. Niels Mikkelsen caught hold, and the man pulled himself up on the rail, but the weight of the two tipped the boat. The boat came near enough so Mikkel could reach it with his rake, and the two men waded ashore with thankful hearts. But where was Hans? His father looked around. "Hans!" he shouted.

Father and son ran along the shore.

The motionless body of the boy swirled into a little bay.

Mikkel, pale and haggard, ran the swifter, and came to the spot with rake in hand. He ran out in the water until he reached the body with his rake.

A minute later the apparently lifeless body lay on the sand in the sunshine. The father bent over and felt of the heart.

He lifted up the body—turned it over to drain

the water. He held him over his knee to force the water out of the lungs.

He lay the body on its back, and worked the arms up and down to compress and expand the chest until he was rewarded with a gasp for breath and then a sigh. A spasm ran through the body.

"Our merciful Lord be praised," he said. "The boy is breathing."

Hans, wrapped in a robe, was placed on the wagon and taken home.

* * *

His father and brothers stood by the bed while his mother sat with his hand in hers.

The boy opened his eyes. He looked at them in surprise. He did not understand why he was here, or how he happened to be in bed.

His father bent over him. "Thanks to God, we still have you with us," he said in a low and pleasant voice.

Then the boy at once remembered everything. He lay back with eyes half closed as if collecting his thoughts.

His mother pressed his hand and said, "Did you pray to God?"

"Yes!—but it was so cold—and it was so dark—and I thought. I thought—maybe I could not—come to heaven."

After a while the boy again fell asleep.

"Wonderful that we were permitted to keep him!" She looked up at her husband and continued, "There is significance in that."

CHAPTER IV

The Boy Carpenter

It is late in September, 1787. The sheaves of harvested grain have been placed on poles set in the ground.

The nearest fields on the Hauge farm have been cleared and the sheaves hauled into the sheds. The cattle are let in on the cleared fields, and the daughter, Anna, with her knitting, is sitting near the gate watching them.

She is plying her knitting needles industriously and glancing occasionally at the cattle, now lolling peacefully. She is fair, with a sweet face and a serene look, indicating a kind disposition untrammelled by worldly cares.

Hans, her favorite brother, was nearly a grown-up man now in his 16th year, and preparing for confirmation. He had promised to make a cabinet for the minister and have it ready within a week. Being handy with tools, a cabinet was not beyond him. He came out to have a chat with his sister.

"Well," Anna ventured, "perhaps you intend to make the pastor a present of that cabinet?"

"No, I do not. A laborer is worthy of his hire," said Hans.

Anna continued, "How much will you get for that cabinet?"

"Two dollars," he answered readily, "it is quite a job."

She smiled up at him and said, "If you have promised him to have it ready in a week, you must do it."

Hans walked slowly back to the shop and began work with a good will. "Do it," she had said. "Yes, do it, that is the word."

* * *

On the road west of the Hauge farm, a man came walking south carrying a pack. He wore a shabby coat and a dilapidated hat. His nether garments were patched, and his shoes had seen better days. Yet, you could not call him a tramp. He looked a man of the world, worn threadbare.

When he came to the fence near the turn in the road, he spied a flat stone by the hedge and sat down. He unstrapped a big knapsack, and took out bread and butter. He was hungry because no one had invited him for dinner, but the buttered bread with slices of dried beef sufficed. He was the well known fiddler, Kristen Gleng.

He carried a small stock of goods—laces, handkerchiefs, thread, needles, buttons, knives and other articles, as a side line to better his acquaintances with people.

After the meal there came a faint tone. At first it seemed far away but soon it grew into a loud, penetrating whine. Kristen Gleng was tuning his violin. One needs music to help digestion after a heavy meal. First a short prelude, soft, smooth and serene, to interpret the peace and calm of an autumn day.

Then suddenly, as a western storm, it broke into a wild and frenzied tune, embellished by fantastic flourishes, indicating a mad race of freely swarming rhythms—the outpouring of extravagant melody. Faster and faster, wilder and wilder came the volume of sounds. Like a whirlwind, the turbulent melody leaped from the strings of his violin and flew away over the fields.

Hans came to the door of the tool-shed. He

walked over to his sister and asked, "Who is he?"

"I think—he must be—Kristen Gleng," she answered.

After a while the wild playing broke into one of his "Halling" dances. It came thundering on and on, as a veritable A a s g a a r d s r e i, or, as we would call it, a regiment of rough riders.

Hans was rather taken aback by this turbulent music, and with his hands on his back he walked over to the hedge.

The bow made an extra flourish, and the playing stopped.

"Hello! And you don't dance?" said Kristen in a teasing way.

"No, I do not," answered Hans.

Kristen laughed immoderately. "Ha, ha, ha! But calves will dance, so will kids and pigs dance—everything dances," said Kristen with a wicked leer.

"Well, I don't," said Hans. "I am neither kid nor pig nor calf nor maverick, and have no desire to dance, or eat grass as they do."

Somehow this angered Kristen, and he began to swear at Hans.

"Why do you swear?" Hans said, "do you think it is right?"

"That is good. Thou shalt not swear," roared Kristen, as he wrapped his violin in the old rags and hugged it.

Hans turned to go back to the tool-shed.

Kristen jumped up and cried: "Hold on! Wait! You must stop and look at my goods, and do some trading."

Hans turned back rather dubiously.

Kristen lifted his pack to the flat rock and opened it.

Hans came closer to look at the goods. Maybe he would want some if he could strike a good bargain, so he asked for prices.

Kristen named prices, so high that Hans turned to go.

"Oh, wait!" cried Kristen. "See here, my son! Twenty for the knife, fifteen for the kerchief and ten for that bright self-hooking buckle for your belt, is dirt cheap."

Hans turned back and examined the things more closely.

"I will give you one ort" (25 cents).

Kristen spat and began swearing that this was the limit of insolence and browbeating.

"If you do not stop swearing, I will not buy at all," said Hans.

Kristen answered as to himself, "Oh yes, do not swear."

Hans ventured, "Will you take an ort for the lot?"

Kristen spat again, then laughed, "I dare say, I'd rather take two." His dark-brown eyes danced with mischief.

Hans drew out an old purse from his pocket, opened it and fingered the money, found a silver ort, and said, "Here you are."

Kristen spat again and said, "Well, have it your own way, but you have to set up the drinks on the purchase."

Hans took the knife, buckle, and kerchief, as he handed Kristen the money, rolled them up and dropped them into his pocket and said, "Yes, I can give you a glass of milk."

"Milk! milk, did you say! Well, I am no calf," and Kristen laughed.

"Water, then," said Hans.

"Water! Do you take me for a cow, to drink water?" Kristen's tone was angry. "To offer me water, when I want whiskey!"

"Whiskey?" said Hans. "A hog won't touch it, and I haven't any."

"You are a funny bird," said Kristen, as he tied up his pack, and lifted it upon his back together with the violin.

Hans suddenly asked, "Where are you going now?"

Kristen blew his nose violently, then said rather briskly, "Oh, well! I am going to the auction in Glemminge, where I have big trade, plenty of customers, card parties and dancing."

He gave his pack another jerk and started down the road.

Hans met his father near the front steps of the house.

His father asked, "What kind of a fellow was that?"

Hans felt ashamed but said, "It was Kristen Gleng."

His father had a solemn face, and looking straight at Hans, he said, "What did you want of him?"

Hans looked up, blushed and replied, "I made a good bargain."

Then his father said, "Three weeks from tomorrow you will be confirmed." The voice was mild and a little sad.

Hans felt the reprimand in his father's words, and went over to work in the tool shed. He took out of his pocket the articles he had bought. He looked them over very carefully, and placed them in the remotest corner of the old tool-chest.

* * *

A few days later, Hans helped his father bring a cow to the auction in Glemminge, and was surprised at the great number of people. It was a regular market day for bartering or trading anything saleable.

Hans watched the motley crowd eagerly, as they

were drinking noisily, browbeating and cheating each other. He felt sad, as one sang:

> *When they his goods have taken,*
> *As skinners fierce and bold,*
> *They carry home "the bacon",*
> *And jolly revels hold.*
> *They drink and feast and scurry,*
> *To theater and ball;*
> *Blood-money is no worry—*
> *The farmer pays for all.*

Hans sauntered over to the auction-stand. A farmer was leading up a yearling colt to sell. It was well fed and curried. Auctioneer Klaus Lundeplads remarked that the nag looked wise, and— "How much am I bid?—No doubt she is of royal blood and culture, and comes real high. How much?"

"How do you know that she is of royal blood?" one asked.

"Why, her name is Queen, and queens are always royal! How much?"

"Twelve skilling! .... One ort! .... Ort and twelve!" ... from several.

"Can she dance—dance on one laig?" was heard from the crowd.

"Of course she can—same as you when you're drunk. How much?"

"And throw kisses at the audience?" another ventured.

"Most certainly! And swift ones too, with a pair of heels!"

"How much am I bid for the critter? How much? How much did you say?"

"Five dollars! (riksdaler) That's a decent bid! Five! Who says six?"

"Can she sing?" came from the laughing rioters.

"Sure! Sings like a nightingale in January! Six! Seven! Speed up!"

"Seven. Who said eight? Eight I have! Now say nine!"

"Does she sew and spin?" was heard from the crowd.

"Yes, she sows wild oats and spins like a top."

Roars of laughter greeted each sally, and Hans felt disgusted. He turned away to find his father, who was trading his cow for a plow-horse. They evidently had reached an agreement, as his father was making ready to go home when Hans came so they left immediately.

CHAPTER V

Debating Theology

A single cart drawn by a single horse came up the lane to the Thune parsonage. Hans was bringing the new cabinet.

The lane was cool and refreshing. The shade trees and well kept grounds gave a pleasing impression. The old parsonage with its many niches and corners at present housed Rev. Gerhard Seeberg.

There was also a smaller, modern residence on the other side of the gardens for the curate, at present Rev. Chr. Hammer.

The pastor and the curate were coming around a turn on the gravel walk, and were evidently engaged in a very deep discussion.

Both had acquired the fashionable pastime of smoking, and just now they puffed vigorously to fill in a lull in the conversation.

Pastor Seeberg held, at arms length, a venerable old meerschaum with a long stem through which the burnt air of mellow tobacco cooled delightfully. The curate, on the other hand, sported a rather modern "cowhorn" of the English type, with a short curved stem and a bell-shaped bowl.

"As I said before," began Pastor Seeberg, "it is a veritable fact, my dear brother Hammer, that the good deeds cannot save. Only through faith may we gain salvation. It is faith—faith alone!"

The curate held out his cowhorn, looked at it intently, as if to get an inspiration. He felt the mild warmth of the bowl, and caught a whiff of the sweet burning "salmagundi", as a wisp of blue smoke curled lazily upward, then said:

"V e r b a l i t e r   d i c t u — Your Reverence is right; but, r e a l i t e r — 'Faith without works is dead,' says the apostle James (2:26)," and the curate resumed smoking.

Pastor Seeberg swung around, as Hans neared the gate with a salutation. And the pastor called to him, "What is your errand?"

Hans opened the gate and came in.

"Ah! I see! It is my good boy, Hans Nielsen Hauge, bringing my cabinet," said the curate.

Hans took off his cap and shook hands with the pastor and the curate; then they went outside to look at the cabinet.

"That is well, my boy," said the curate with a kind smile, "that you have it finished."

Pastor Seeberg stepped around to feel of the jointing, the polishing, and general finish.

Then he turned to the curate and said, "That schoolboy of yours is quite a carpenter, and I promised myself a minister of him."

"Oh, but he knows his books just as well," said the curate.

Hans turned red from embarrassment.

Pastor Seeberg turned to the cabinet again. Then asked, "Who made the lock and hinges?"

Hans looked up and said quietly, "I did."

"Well, well! You are a blacksmith also?" said

the pastor with new interest, for the things were neatly made and well polished.

The curate had taken a puff from his cowhorn and now asked, "Well, Hans, how much are you going to ask for that cabinet?"

Hans took courage and named the price, "Two dollars as it is."

The curate drew some heavy puffs from his cowhorn and said, "Two dollars! Hm! Two dollars?"

The pastor smiled indulgently and said, "I believe, Hans, that you are a commercial man as well as a craftsman."

Hans turned red again, but said in his quiet way, "The curate mentioned two dollars when I agreed to make the cabinet."

"One dollar fifty must be sufficient," said the pastor patronizingly, "one should not ask too much."

Hans looked rather bewildered, then said, "The curate may pay whatever he likes."

The curate exchanged glances with the pastor and said, "I had the idea that one dollar was sufficient, but since you have done a fine job, I will make it one dollar and a half to you."

Hans nodded and turned to the horse.

"Take the cabinet over to my library," the curate added, "and I will settle for it afterwards."

Hans drove around to the curate's home, while the two went inside the gate to continue the discussion.

The curate lighted his cowhorn and proceeded, "As I said, Your Reverence—r e a l i t e r—faith is dead without deeds—and, salvation cannot be obtained without faith; but faith is only the hand that grasps the grace of Providence. To live, to attain happiness and enjoyment from it—is dependent upon and subject to the will of man."

Pastor Seeberg drew some strong puffs from his meerschaum, then he began in a dignified manner:

"In this, Brother Hammer, thou dost err greatly. True happiness is found exclusively in faith's devotion to the Lord's service, in the joy it brings to work in His vineyard. Without faith our work and the best deeds are worthless."

"Assuredly," began the curate, "but—"

Just then Hans came back from delivering the cabinet.

"Assuredly—" he waved his hand at Hans to come inside.

Hans tied the horse and came in.

The curate had opened the purse and counted some money.

"Assuredly," he mumbled with the stem of his cowhorn between his teeth. "Here you are, Hans," counting into his hand, "one dollar, one ort, ten, five, five, three, and two skillings (cents) makes a dollar and a half."

Hans took off his cap, bowed his thanks to the curate, and added, "I say thanks to you, Parson, for the privilege."

"No thanks for what you have earned," returned the curate.

He shook hands with Hans, and bade him good bye! Pastor Seeberg took his hand and said, "Farewell, my boy. I hope to see more of you."

Hans untied his horse and started for home.

"Assuredly—" the curate began a fourth time; but his cowhorn had gone out, and he had to re-light it once more.

"Assuredly—it is as you say, dear Reverend Pastor. I admit it, l i t t e r a v e r b a t i m, but—thus says Christ: 'Unless ye keep every Commandment of the Law, ye cannot enter heaven's kingdom.'—Item—"

"Seeberg!" called a lady from the porch.

It was Mrs. Seeberg calling her husband for dinner, and when she saw the curate, she added, "And

—may I ask the Reverend Brother Hammer to join us? We have broiled lamb, eel fricassee, fruit salad, and pickled cucumbers. Oh, yes, we also have excellent soup, sliced tomatoes, green peas, and fresh dewberries and cream."

"Thank you! My respects to you, dear Lady Seeberg, I shall certainly avail myself of such a tempting invitation, to feast upon the sumptuous delicacies in such excellent company, and will accept, as your humble servant, with thanks!"

The lady courtesied and stepped inside.

The two turned to the library entrance.

As they mounted the steps, the curate began once more, "I t e m—It is good common sense, and it stands to reason—"

"Common sense! Reason!" interrupted Pastor Seeberg. "Our reason is darkened! Darkened from being steeped in sin. A darkened reason is our inheritance from our forefathers back through the ages to Adam and Eve!"

The pastor waxed warm and belligerent, but cooling off a little he added, "It is only the Word of God that has the power to enlighten a darkened reason."

Just at this moment the door closed upon the controversy, and the gentlemen soon came to a new field of conquest.

CHAPTER VI

Confirmation Day

It is a bright and beautiful Sunday morning. The Thune Church is decorated for confirmation service, and the bells are ringing in happy harmony for the festive occasion.

These bells had rung for centuries in that ancient stone tower, calling generation after generation to the house of worship for the various festivities—weddings and funerals, as well as Sunday and holiday services. The powerful tones floated over hill and vale in the clear and calm morning with a glad ring, echoing a requiem for departed generations.

The autumn sun shone brightly on the multicolored landscape. All nature was decked in a most wonderful manner with colors of many shades artistically blended as if to rival even the rainbow.

The cattle are browsing and the tinkling of many bells is heard; but over all float the powerful tones of the church bells, with a message to old and young, to men and women, to rich and poor alike: "Come, come! Come to God's house of worship."

* * *

Hosts of well-clad people are on their way to church. Even old folks seldom seen out of doors are out. The weather is fine.

A venerable, white-haired veteran comes walking with a cane in his right hand and his left hand on his back. He is sweating, and he stops to get his breath.

His wife, also white-haired, keeping step with him, unwinds a kerchief wrapped around the hymnbook and hands it to him, that he may wipe his face. Gallantly he thanks her, and with a smile she again wraps the kerchief around the hymnbook that he gave her years ago, when they were young.

Niels Mikkelsen Hauge is standing in his front yard, and he bows to his old neighbor and his wife as they pass by. He is waiting for his family to get ready.

* * *

Hans was not ready. If Hans could have had his own way, he would have dressed as usual; but his mother and sister insisted that confirmation comes only once in a lifetime, and he must dress accordingly. So he took the new suit, tailored for him the previous week, and put it on.

Hans looked into the mirror and drew a deep sigh as he murmured to himself, "Would that my soul were clothed as well."

Anna ran to her room to fetch her things, and soon they were upon the highway, wending their way to church in the wake of their parents and the other members of the household.

As they neared the church, there were groups here and there shaking hands, exchanging the customary greetings and remarks about the weather and other generalities. The Hauge family came up and shook hands with the various groups in the same manner.

The groups drew together near the church door. It was customary not to enter until the pastor came and walked up the aisle at the head of his congregation—an old-fashioned custom.

The church bells had ceased ringing, but when the pastor came, they rang again, and the men uncovered their heads as they entered the church portals and went up to their respective seats.

The curate with the confirmands had entered the side door to the sacristy, where he gave them a few instructions before they went into the church and sat down with their respective families.

The precentor arose and led in prayer; then he gave out the hymn.

Pastor Seeberg himself preached the confirmation sermon.

In closing he said: "And you, my young friends, who upon this day shall renew the baptismal covenant—pray to God from your innermost heart that you may remain steadfast. Cling to your Savior in the dark days of trouble as well as in the bright days of life's sunshine. When the race on earth is ended and death is overtaking you—what is better than the strong arm of Jesus to cling to, when crossing the river of death! He will lead you into the mansions of heaven that He has prepared for you. May God bless you, for Jesus' sake, Amen!"

* * *

As the congregation began to sing the confirmation hymn, Hans and his companions took their places (according to the numbers given) to be examined by the curate in the books they had learned.

Hans felt diffident at first, but the curate asked such simple questions that his courage gradually began to rise, and he gained more confidence.

— — —

The examination drew to a close. The confirmands gathered around the altar, as the whole congregation arose and sang the well-known hymn: "O, let this day be blest."

Then one by one they repeated the confirmation vow, renewing their covenant with God in baptism —to renounce the devil and all his works and all his ways. They confessed their faith and belief in the triune God, the Father, the Son, and the Holy Spirit, then gave their hearts unto God, and their hand to the pastor to bind the vow.

When the turn came to Hans, the vow was given in a trembling, low voice, but it made the venerable pastor's heart warm to hear it.

The congregation arose and sang the closing hymn: "Let me be Thine forever," and Pastor Seeberg pronounced the benediction.

The precentor read the closing prayer, and three strokes upon the large bell announced the close of the confirmation service. The people came out and thronged around the bailiff to hear the announcements, and then hurried homeward.

CHAPTER VII

Going to the City

In the years that followed, it happened many times that Hans saw the finger of the Lord indicating the way for him.

He worked in a logging camp, and barely escaped a falling tree. He had been on a river-drive, floating logs on Glommen, and twice he had gone under, but was saved as by a miracle.

He was strongly reminded of the nearness of death on land and water wherever he went; and if he failed to walk the narrow way, he would share the judgment of the world.

Some years later, to get away from these temptations and from military service that he considered very un-Christian, he took a position as assistant or deputy with his brother, Ole Nielsen Hauge, who had been appointed sheriff in the Thune district. This occupation did not agree with him either and he finally tendered his resignation and went home to work on the farm.

He was pondering what to do next when he heard that there was work to be had in the near-by city of Fredrikstad.

It was in the early spring of 1795. His parents, brother Mikkel, and his sisters, Karen and Anna, were wishing him good luck and God-speed as he said good-bye, ready to go to the city.

Traveling afoot was customary, but Hans obtained a ride with a neighbor farmer who helped him to find a lodging in the city.

Hans had been recommended to Madam Kruse, a widow of a former officer in the king's army. He found her in her small combination shop and store in which she made her living. She offered him a position as clerk in the store, but the wages were so small that he hesitated to take it. He went to his lodging and pondered it for a while, but finally decided to accept the place.

The work was not to his liking, but there were so many things to learn about habits, people and the peculiarities of city life, that he put up with it. The weeks passed very fast. Madam Kruse had furnished him a room in the attic, and he took his meals at a cheap boarding house, where people drank, played cards and gambled.

Kristen Gleng was among them.

He noticed Hans standing near and hailed him: "Come on, boy! Get into the game, and make some extra money to help along. You are not getting a fat salary; that we all know."

"No, thank you! Really, I do not play cards," Hans answered.

"You do not play cards?" Kristen began to laugh immoderately. "That's a good one—ha, ha, ha! This overgrown boy, never played cards! Ha, ha, ha!"—and the others joined in the chorus.

Hans looked very sober indeed.

"Hans is very saintly, isn't he?" a sergeant in uniform said.

"Oh, no!" Hans answered quietly, "but I wish very much that I were, and I would be far better off."

"Well, you w o n' t be at Madam Kruse's!" Kristen said rather spitefully, "however much you may read your Bible," and he laughed again.

The cards were cut and dealt, and the bidding began.

"You lead this time, officer," said Kristen, as the others gave in on the bids and waited for him to play.

The cards came, clap, clap. Some thumped the table with dramatic flourishes—slap, slap! The players became excited, clash, crash! Kristen yelled; but the officer had the best hand, and Kristen lost.

He jumped up and swore, as he paid his bet, that he should never play such a rotten game again.

"Stop swearing, Kristen!" said Hans in a quiet manner.

Kristen flew into a rage and swore horribly with fire and brimstone in every oath and told Hans to shut up.

Hans answered: "I will gladly do so if you will stop swearing."

"I will do as I —— please," Kristen roared defiantly.

"Are you sure of that?" said Hans.

Kristen swore again.

"Suppose," said Hans, "that the Lord takes you in hand?"

"What can He do about it?" Kristen sneered with an ugly grin.

Hans straightened himself. His eyes became darker as he said, "Kristen, in time you will see! Or the devil will get you."

"The plague of old Beelzebub take your reasoning," Kristen spat after him; "you have read yourself crazy."

Hans could not but smile as he said, "That's what you and others blindfolded by the devil will argue, that the Bible will make men crazy; but what about the devil that makes men card-crazy, dance-crazy, sex-crazy, stage-crazy, whiskey-crazy, and dollar-crazy? No, no, Kristen Gleng, it is such as you that fiddle, dance, drink and gamble, that are crazy. Many have done so before, and many will do so hereafter."

Kristen attempted a coarse laugh as he said: "What do you know about such things?"

"Well, yes, I do know!" Hans answered, "and if you read the Bible yourself, you would learn to know what I know."

Kristen said: "If I am a poor sinner neither holy nor learned I am just as God has made me."

Kristen arose rather satisfied with himself.

Hans said: "You maintain that you are as God made you, but you should not say that, for God is not to blame for what you are."

"Who should I blame then!" snarled Kristen rather visciously.

"Blame yourself," said Hans. "It was not God but yourself who let the evil grow to dominate you."

"I have not—" Kristen began.

But Hans interrupted him, and said: "Maybe you have not, or—maybe you have. Some things are inherited, but most of your ways are acquired. Search diligently, and you will find it so."

Kristen was painfully irritated, and he reached for his violin and started to play. But he broke off in the middle of a strain and said, "Hans, you are making it far worse than it really is!"

Hans repeated: "Worse than it is! O Kristen! suppose you changed about and began trying to do better—would that hurt you?"

"Hold your tongue, you, you—saintly Hans, I won't listen!"

The others loudly laughed at this sally.

Hans stepped forward and said with some force: "Think it over, Kristen! Think of your death!"

"Why should I?" Kristen broke in.

"Because it may come sooner than expected," said Hans.

Kristen forced himself to laugh as he said: "We shall all die."

"Would you die now?" Hans asked.

Kristen remained mute. He did not know what to answer.

Hans continued: "I have been near death many times, and I know what it means to face death."

Kristen said: "Why think of these things? It makes my nerves creep."

"That is exactly what you want to think of," said Hans, "otherwise, you will not only be going astray, but you will be lost—lost for all eternity. You might die tonight, Kristen. This night thy soul is required of thee—then you will find it urgent to read God's Word."

Hans turned to the door and walked out.

For several minutes no one spoke. Somehow they could not rid themselves of this idea about death.

CHAPTER VIII

Hans and the Girl

In that cheap boarding-house facing the harbor, our young friend Hans continued to eat cheap meals. His weekly wages were so small that he ate sparingly. He always felt hungry. The robust country boy became thin and lanky. He had no real friends. The young men that he met with were rather unfriendly because of his set ideas and his way of speaking his mind to everybody regardless of station. They pitied him, however, on account of his lowly occupation. In pity they invited him to drink with them to forget his troubles. Hans only smiled at this show of friendliness and refused; but it worried him.

It was Saturday evening, and the girl that waited on the tables was not busy just then. She sat down to have a chat with him, seeing that he looked worried and lost in sad thoughts.

She was neat and well formed. Her warm complexion and robust health made her quite attractive, especially when her lustrous eyes and fascinating smile dimpled her rosy cheeks. She told him she had come from Ness in Romerike and was now eighteen. She kept on talking at random, trying to find what would interest him, but he was hopelessly taken up by his own thoughts. Suddenly she thought of something and asked abruptly: "Hans, don't you ever go to dances?"

Hans was rudely awakened from his day-dreaming trance.

"What? What did you say? Do I go to dances?"

Hans stared — stared at the girl. The question seemed so absurd to him. He shook his head and slowly said: "No! I do not like it."

"Not any liking for dancing?" she repeated. "That is very remarkable for a young man like you." Her right hand passed involuntarily upward to some stray curls that evidently needed attention.

After a little, she asked: "Really, but don't you care about dancing? Don't you think it is fine to dance, when you have a nice partner, and plenty of good company?"

Hans turned to his bowl and did not look up, nor did he answer.

The girl continued: "Hans, you have missed a lot of good things in life, and this is one of them. You have plodded along in irksome slavery looking glum and dreadful. Your shoulders stoop, and you bend over, making a sorry figure. If you learned to dance, the ugly kinks would disappear; you would look straight as an arrow, and step gracefully to delicious music."

Hans smiled: "Yes, but don't you think other things could do that?"

The girl returned the smile, and asked: "What other things?"

Hans felt confused, so he said: "That is not easy to tell."

The girl laughed. A white row of sound teeth added zest to her delightful way of laughing.

Hans felt cheap. "Was she—was she laughing at him?"

She saw that he was embarrassed, and continued kindly: "Oh, but you should tell why you have not made use of those other things."

Hans felt more and more a bewildering sensation of something warming his blood until it was racing in his veins and a blush suffused his face. He had a feeling of gratifying content.

The girl laughed again, and somehow Hans laughed too, although he did not know why he laughed.

"Oh, but you are funny," she said.

Hans did not understand her merriment.

"Have you thought of those other things?" the girl said again.

Hans sobered immediately. "The other things. God's Word can tell us about the other things."

She sobered, too, and her eyes expressed the surprise she felt. "Yes, God's Word on Sunday, but what of other days and Saturday evenings?"

Hans answered: "Why not use God's Word the other days and on Saturday evenings?"

The girl's smile broadened into a laugh as she said: "Preaching to us every day, and on Saturday evenings when we want to dance? Oh, but that would be rather too much of a good thing, would it not?"

"No, no!" said Hans. "Of the good things there can never be too much; and the preaching of God's Word can never hurt us. If we really observe, follow, and do what God's Word teaches us, we should be far happier and lead better lives, and brighten the surroundings of our home and the community where we live, with the blessing of God upon all our undertakings. We should not have frequent fights and drunken brawls and obscene talk. We should not have this ever-present card-playing and wicked gambling."

The girl sat waiting and asked: "What more?"

Hans looked up, and continuing his thoughts, said: "With clean souls, clean lives and God's Word to guide us, our talk and actions would be clean, with no cursing and swearing to soil our mouths, nor rough-house squabbles and neighbor-quarrels to destroy domestic peace, no foul gossip, vile slander and wicked lying to poison our souls, no jealousy, bad faith and horrid family feuds to wreck happy homes."

The girl sat demurely listening as he talked, then suddenly said: "The porridge is getting cold, shall I get you a warm dish?"

"Thank you," he said, as she brought the dish.

She sat down and said rather musingly: "So you think we must not seek amusements, nor enjoy the good things."

"On the contrary," Hans replied, "we should get the best there is."

The girl's face brightened into a warm smile as she naively said: "That's what I have wanted all the time."

"Yes, but we are often badly deceived," Hans answered.

"Deceived!" she cried, staring at him with wondering eyes, "how deceived? Sugar is sweet, and cake is good—no deceit at all."

"Yes, that's so," said Hans, "but too much of it will make you sick, the same as worldly pleasures may taste sweet, but they will make your soul sick with uncontrollable passions."

"Oh, but I am not hoggish," she answered.

"No, I do not think you are," Hans answered, "but we are easily deceived just the same, thinking that we can gauge our appetite and desires, control ourselves and choose what we think is good."

"How is that?" she asked as if she did not fully grasp his meaning.

"Why, we are so conceited," said Hans, "and have such good opinions of ourselves that we do not heed what God tells us in His Word."

"God's Word, yes! God's Word," she said musingly. "That's what the pastor told us of God's Word in the confirmation class."

"Assuredly!" said Hans; "and God's Word is the

light from heaven to guide us and shed light upon our way. It is so much brighter than the world's glitter that we should not be blinded by earthly glory. We should then be able to see the lurking evil behind worldly pleasures, the so-called innocent pastimes; innocent games and wanton behavior; innocent sport bordering on scandal; innocent dancing and noisy frivolities, hilarious carousing and drunken brawls—"

"Oh, please, do not say any more," the girl interrupted.

"But don't you think it is?" Hans said as he looked at her and saw that she was rather displeased.

"I don't know what to think," the girl answered quite resentfully.

"Well, but you can see the great difference between the joy of God's children and the joys of the world," said Hans.

"No!" she said; "I do not think that God's children have any joy whatever or c a n be happy."

"Why do you say that?" Hans replied; "even you, perhaps not a child of God, felt real happy the other day when you saved that little girl from being run over; and, I dare say, far happier than you were at the seamen's dance a week ago."

"That's different," the girl said, but she flushed with pleasure as she remembered how she had hugged the little child after she had got her out of harm's way and crooned over her in happy possession until the parents came and took her away.

Hans had finished the evening meal and bowed his head saying grace.

"Thanks for the food," he said to the girl.

She came immediately to gather the dishes, and as she bent over him she said: "God's Word is good, yes! but there are other good things. "And her voice had a delicate inflection as she drew a deep sigh.

Hans felt warm and swallowed hard, yet he managed somehow to say: "That may all be, but it is not for me."

She placed the dishes on a tray and sat down again.

After pondering she suddenly said: "Maybe you are married?"

Hans looked at her again as he arose from the table and said in his slow manner: "No, I am not married."

She looked up at him with an admiring smile; then she arose and came close to him, as she said: "What are you going to do with yourself this evening?"

Hans did not know of anything particular to do.

She fingered the lace of her apron rather nervously as she said slowly: "I do not half believe what you said about dancing." Her eyes were downcast as she hesitatingly asked: "Hans, don't you dance? You m u s t know how to dance, but maybe you do not like me."

Hans felt more and more bewildered. Something that robbed him of his normal sense possessed him, and a mysterious element held him in a trance. He was under a spell of some influence that he was not able to analyze, but he struggled to free himself from it.

He did not answer immediately, but after a little he managed to say: "No, no! It is not that, not at all; but I truly believe that dancing is sin, and that is why I never learned to dance."

"Dancing is sin," she repeated; "Oh, but why is it sin?"

Hans sobered, then answered with conviction: "Dancing is sin because of the evil it fosters. It leads away from God instead of leading to Him. Every disobedience to God is sin."

"Sin?" she questioned again, "then everything is sin."

"Yes, everything that comes from our sinful nature is sin," said Hans, "but God's Word can change our nature and make us avoid sin."

She smiled at him as she teasingly said: "Really, Hans, you talk like our pastor; maybe you will be a preacher."

Hans turned quite red at this last sally, but said: "No, no! I am not fit for that."

"Anyhow, you are a queer one," she said, as she picked up the dishes and carried them into the kitchen.

"Queer one," Hans murmured to himself; "has it gone so far that people think I am queer? And queer because I believe in God's Word?"

The girl returned from the kitchen to set another table.

Then she turned to Hans and said: "I don't want you to be angry with me, Hans, for what I said to you, because—really I am not bad. Some of my folks were like you, but their world was so dark and gloomy, and they were so strict. I wanted something more cheerful. I wanted to be glad, to laugh and have fun, so I came to the city."

Hans was not thinking of her. He was wrestling with his own thoughts, how he should prevail in so many temptations, to remain true to his covenant with God. His line of thought tumbled again. He heard: Cheerful and glad. No, he could not be angry with her.

So he said: "I am not angry with you for what you said, but I rather like the way you said it. I like to hear people speak openly and freely without reserve, because it reveals an honest character that has nothing to hide."

"Yes, that's what I always wanted to be," she said, "and I know you are honest too, for otherwise you would have said nice things to me that you never meant, instead of telling me those horrible things."

Hans pondered hard. He wanted to say something, but it was not easy to speak to her about her soul's salvation.

"Here come the other day-boarders," she said; and she ran to the kitchen to prepare the dishes.

CHAPTER IX

Temptation and Downfall

Hans was reaching for his rather old-fashioned cap when the others came into the dining-room.

"Don't go, Hans, you are not in such a hurry," said one.

"It is Saturday evening," said another.

"We need cheering up," said a third.

"I should say Hans does, staying with that ancient Madam Kruse," drawled the sergeant.

They sat down at the table as the girl brought in the milk and porridge. They dipped their spoons in the milk and ate in silence until one said: "This needs moistening."

"What! is there no more milk?" the girl said as she surveyed the table. But there was plenty of milk, so she added: "Isn't the milk moist enough? Maybe I should pour some water into it?"

The others laughed, and even Hans had to smile.

"Yes," said the other, as he laid aside his spoon and began to fumble at his inside coat pocket. The result was a good sized whiskey bottle. He took a swallow and handed the bottle to the sergeant.

The son of Mars took it and held it to his mouth. He leered at Hans, and said: "Here goes to your health and prosperity."

The next one took the bottle, and performed the same ceremony. "Skaal, Hans! and good luck!"

The sergeant took the bottle and went over to Hans, saying:

"Here, Hans! take a good drink to stave off the starvation at Madam Kruse's. Compliment your friends who drank to your health."

Hans looked hard at the sergeant and politely refused.

"Why, Hans, why don't you drink when you can drown your troubles and all your worries," the others chimed in.

Hans felt really weak, and his system craved something to give him strength. He did not realize that it was the lack of "good meals" that robbed him of strength and courage. He must have entertained the ever popular idea that this strong extract of grain contained the same amount of nourishment for the body as the grain itself.

The sergeant kept on teasing him in very oily tones. His flattering words almost convinced Hans of the beneficial use of strong drink.

Hans had seen and heard how doctors freely prescribed wine, rum, and brandy for sick people; and he was feeling sick. Even Pastor Seeberg had said: "A dram in need is good indeed," and now he felt the need of it more than ever.

He finally took the bottle and tasted the firewater. It burned his tongue, and he spat and handed the bottle back to the sergeant.

"Oh, that's nothing," said the sergeant; "that's not even a baby drink. Take a drink, a real drink, a man's drink."

Hans shook his head and spat to get that burning off his tongue.

"Oh, you must drink," said the other men, "you must drink to our health, as we drank to yours, Hans, drink!"

"Yes, come now," said the sergeant; "get over your scruples and drink. It will make you feel more like a man—a real manly man—" and the son of Mars smiled as if Hans cut a sorry figure beside him.

"Come on, Hans! Take a drink. We are wasting time," said Gypsy Lasse, as he took the bottle from the sergeant and sampled the liquor with a grin. "Here goes to our valorous sergeant, the king's officers and my partners."

Kristen jumped from the table and jerked the bottle away from Lasse. "It is my turn now," he said, "and I drink to the health of the king and all his officers and everybody else, Gypsy Lasse and myself."

He started again: "I—hic—dri- hic (he had swallowed the wrong way)—drrr— -ink—hic."

His partner, Kaat-Ola, sprang up and grabbed the bottle. He drank to the health of so many that the sergeant became alarmed. The contents of the bottle were reduced very fast, and nothing would be left for him.

"Hold on! Kaat-Ola," the sergeant cried. "You cannot have all." He caught Ola by the arm and took the bottle away from him. He took three heavy draughts, and between each he managed to say: "Good stuff! As good as any made this side of Drøbak" (A wet town).

The bottle was nearly finished when Lasse called loudly: "Hans, Hans! Don't go! Hans! Wait!" Lasse and Kristen caught him and led him back to his chair where they held him.

The sergeant looked again at the bottle. There was a little left, and he decided to compel Hans to drink whether he wanted to or not.

"Here, Hans, drink this, and we shall be good friends again." But Hans shook his head. The sergeant insisted that he must drink, or they would never be friends any more. But Hans remained stubborn in his refusal. The others smiled and winked at the sergeant most vigorously. He finally saw what they meant.

"Why won't you drink?" the sergeant roared, and as Hans opened his mouth to answer, the sergeant jabbed the neck of the bottle into his mouth. Hans swallowed a mouthful of the vile liquor before he knew it, and Lasse tickled his throat so he had to swallow again.

Hans sputtered and strained to get his breath. He was all afire inside, and the burning raged on. Flames shot before his eyes. Was he in the sea of fire and brimstone already? Was this hell, and were they devils? Gypsy Lasse found another bottle. "Here, Hans, take some of this. The whiskey has paralyzed you, but this old rum will bring you back. You may be sure it will."

Hans tried to refuse, but when Lasse put the bottle to his mouth he drank. The quartet laughed at the saintly Hans, but their throats went dry, and they had to pass the bottle around.

The bottle came to Hans. "Drink, now," said Lasse.

"You can stand what we can," said Ola.

"Hans, we are ashamed of you," said Kristen.

"You big fool!" said the sergeant.

They circled around and harassed him in fiendish glee.

Hans felt bad and worse, the worst he had ever felt.

They came with another bottle, and they made him drink.

Hans hardly knew what was going on now. The noise in his ears, the veil over his eyes, the something weighing down his body, the swaying of everything made him dizzy, and he wanted to vomit.

The sergeant shook him and said: "What's the

matter, Hans? Brace up and be a man. You're no baby."

Hans lifted his weakened head a little, the tears streaming from his eyes.

"Hans! Oh, say Hans! what are you crying for?" the others chimed in. "Maybe you cry for your mamma? You forgot to read your Bible."

"Yes, Oh, yes, go home and read your Bible." And the quartet now began to laugh until the tears flowed.

The girl had finished washing in the kitchen and came in.

She saw what they were doing and told them to leave Hans alone. Then she went over to Hans and helped him to his feet. He staggered and would have fallen if the girl's strong arms had not stayed him.

She led him to the door and out on the street. The evening air was cool and crisp and braced him wonderfully. She led him on towards his lodgings. Somehow his staggering steps became steadier and she said: "Can you make home alone, now?"

"Yes, Oh yes, thank you," he managed to say, as he staggered on, and the girl watched him until he reached the door of Madam Kruse.

The quartet had also come outside and howled in ghoulish glee at Hans' tottering walk.

The girl turned on them angrily: "Now you get!"

And the quartet started arm in arm zigzagging down the street to the dance-hall, singing a wine song.

CHAPTER X

A Bitter Awakening

Hans was crawling up the back stairs in Madam Kruse's house. From far away he sensed a voice: "Hans, you are drunk."

He clung to the railing and pulled himself one step at a time, subconsciously upbraiding himself: "Woe unto me! Woe, woe unto me!"

He reached the landing and came to his room in the attic where he threw himself on the bed and wept bitter tears of remorse.

A flood of evil was swallowing him, just as the dark, cold waters did when he was drowning in the Glommen river years ago.

A cold fear froze his heart, now indeed he was lost. As a last effort he tried to say the Lord's Prayer, but he could not remember a word. He was floating about, sinking lower and lower, deeper and deeper into a state of lassitude, finally fading away into oblivion.

Hans slept—the heavy stupor of a body overcome by liquor.

His soul still struggled on in a world of horrible dreams that revealed the fury of devils having possession of his soul.

* * *

It was Sunday morning. The bells of the various churches in Fredrikstad were ringing for the morning service.

Sunshine and a clear sky made it a lovely morning, and the people enjoyed the walk to church.

Children, dressed in their best, walked with their parents, evincing a desire to show off their finery with an occasional laugh, although the parents repeatedly warned them to remember that it was Sunday.

The sun shone in through an attic window upon the face of one still asleep. The rays beat down on his face till it began to burn. At last he awoke and realized that he was lying across the bed with his clothes on.

He heard the church bells calling, but could he go to church?

Then like the publican he prayed: "God be merciful unto me."

And a voice within him said: "Go, Hans! Go, and sin no more."

Hans felt hope springing up, and he hurried to take off his work clothes and change into his Sunday apparel.

He sat down to read his Bible. The church bells had ceased ringing. The people were in church and the service had begun. Hans felt the quiet of the hour. He was alone with God, and he read and prayed. Everything else was lost to his senses.

People were returning from church, but Hans was so absorbed in reading that he did not hear them come. He did not even hear that some one was coming up the back stairs, until a knock on the door stirred him.

Hans called: "Come!" and turned in haste to see who it was.

"Good morning!" said Kristen Gleng, and closed the door.

"Good morning!" said Hans, and a flush of shame suffused his face, as he remembered the tragedy of the evening before.

"You are already up," said Kristen.

"Yes," said Hans, "and God be praised. I did not die in my sin, but I may have another day of grace."

Kristen leered and said: "That was a stiff one last night."

Hans paled and then turned fiery red. "It was an evil deed."

Kristen looked embarrassed, but smiled.

Hans continued: "It was very wicked, and yet I thank you for it."

Kristen was greatly surprised but said, "Nothing to thank for!"

"Yes, I do want to thank you for it," said Hans; "I had need of it, and it gave me a lesson that I always shall remember."

Kristen laughed loud and long.

"No, you need not laugh," said Hans; "it is a serious matter, and it has taught me the curse of sin."

Kristen looked at him and said: "I wonder if you are full yet?"

"Yes," said Hans; "I am full of sorrow for my great sin."

Kristen looked down and said: "You aim to be a saint, Hans?"

Hans stood up resolutely. "That I am not! I am a sinner, the same as you, but here is a Book where we find the way out of sin."

Kristen answered: "I say, Hans, you read too much; it makes you stupid, distracted, confused, and crazy."

Hans smiled and said: "No, you do not seriously believe, that—that God's Word will make people crazy? How can you believe it?"

"Think of last night, Kristen, how crazy we all were, and will be again when we drink the vile stuff. And yet you lay it to God's Word. That's the craziest of all, when we must know that it is God's Word alone that prevents sin and gives us healing for our many sins."

Kristen arose to go. He was short on argument and excused himself.

Hans held out his Bible to him and said: "Here is the fountain where we find the waters of life. You cannot deny that this is a better fountain to drink from than your pocket flask."

Kristen went out and slammed the door.

* * *

Late in the afternoon that same Sunday there was a knock on Madam Kruse's door.

"Good evening!" she said, "come right in."

"Good evening!" said Hans, as he walked in and followed her to the sitting room. She motioned him to sit down. "Was there something that you wanted?"

"Yes," Hans answered; "I want a talk with you."

Madam Kruse stiffened preceptibly and stared hard. Was he going to ask for a raise in his wages?

Hans felt uneasy and said: "I came to ask if I may go home."

"Go home," asked the Madam; "for how long? Is anybody sick?"

Hans turned on his chair and coughed a little as he responded: "No, there is no one sick at home, but I feel very sick."

"But you do not look sick," she said. "You look as well as ever."

"Yes, in my body," answered Hans, "but not in my soul."

Madam Kruse again stared hard at Hans and began to wonder if he really was getting "queer" or "loony."

Hans wanted to explain, but Madam Kruse did not want any more and said abruptly: "How many days do you want to stay at home?"

Hans was embarrassed but said: "I did not mean it that way."

"You did not mean it that way; what did you mean then?" she asked.

"I wanted to leave for good," he answered with a trembling voice.

Madam Kruse, turning red of face arose in a dignified manner, as she said: "What reason can you have for wanting to leave?"

"I have an urgent reason, the safety of my soul," said Hans.

"Ah! Well, well! So you are of that kind," she said. "You are afraid to risk your soul here, with a church only a block away."

Hans flushed to a deep red as he managed to say: "Yes, I am—of that kind—as you call it."

Madam Kruse became very angry and retorted: "You may as well go; really I have no use for such a queer person in my employ."

"Thank you!" said Hans, "and thanks for the time I have been here."

Hans arose and turned to go.

Madam Kruse stood perplexed. Was he really going to leave? He had done good service for small wages, and he was so dependable. She pondered and said: "Hans, wait!"

Hans turned back with questioning eyes: "Was there something?"

"Yes," said Madam Kruse; "you have three dollars coming on your wages, maybe you want a raise?"

"No, no!" said Hans, "I never thought of that. And you need not pay me the three dollars. I did not give you sufficient notice."

Madam Kruse thought again and said, "I will give you the three dollars now, and possibly I may raise your wages after a while."

Hans looked at her as she faltered: "No, no! that was not what I came for. I was satisfied, and had no thought of it."

Madam Kruse frowned and shook her head: "You cannot go like that."

"But I must," Hans insisted.

"Must, must!" she cried; "Why must you? Is there any reason whatever, that you must leave?"

Hans was rather taken aback at this, but determining not to yield, he said: "I have given you the reason and must go!"

Madam Kruse felt shocked and sank back into the old armchair. She stared at him in wonder. "What a freak this is anyway," she thought.

As she remained silent, Hans held out his hand to her and said: "Good-bye, Madam Kruse, good-bye! You can easily find a better clerk!"

Madam Kruse had lost her ever-ready tongue. Automatically she extended her hand and whispered: "Good-bye, Hans, and thank you!"

As the door closed after him she shook her head and sighed: "What a pity that Hans should be like that. He was a promising young man, and he might have become something, a real somebody, but religious fantasies will spoil his future. May Providence preserve his reason."

CHAPTER XI

Homeward Bound

The next morning Hans was ready for the journey. He went to the postoffice and found there a letter from his father. He broke the seal and read as follows:

"Dearly beloved son, Hans!

"Your last letter I have received, and I have read it with some concern. I see that you are worried over your associates, which are worldly and wicked people, and you have many evil temptations. It is only what you must expect, that the city is infested with these things that bring about the downfall of the unwary. Therefore you must watch for pitfalls, and guard yourself against snares that are set by evil-doers to trap the inexperienced youth. Pray to the Lord for safety. God will permit temptations, that our faith may be tested, but when we pray to Him for help and strength to struggle against the evil days, we shall in the end become victorious, and our faith shall prevail.

"Really we need you very much at home to help with the haying and the harvest and the gathering in of the grain, which is giving promise of a bountiful yield.

"For this and various other reasons we are longing for you. It is our wish to have you come home, if you have not the courage now to remain in Fredrikstad. Perhaps we may expect you home, God willing! Your father, mother, sisters, and brothers, one and all, send you their love and greetings. May the Lord's manifold blessings rest on you.

Your loving father,
Niels Mikkelsen Hauge."

Hans folded the letter carefully and placed it in an inner pocket. He wanted to think, and he sat down on a bench in the lobby.

He was looking toward the ever creaking doors where people came in continuously and lined up before the delivery window to get their mail, then hurried out through another door with nervous haste.

He closed his eyes and saw the great throng of people come—to heaven's postoffice—the church—to get their messages, and then hurry away. He thought of the flowing stream of people racing into the turbulent rapids of worldly life, where thousands upon thousands of lives are wrecked and lost forever.

Unbidden tears welled up in his eyes as he saw a certain figure, not exactly a derelict, but careworn and sorry looking. He looks like me! Yes, indeed it is I, Hans, and going back to my home, a prodigal.

His day dreaming was not disturbed until the large bell in the town hall droned out eight long strokes.

Hans came to with a start.

It was eight o'clock already and he had quite a journey before him.

The stream of people that had come for their morning mail was still hurrying through the corridors, and Hans mingled with the crowd until he came outside.

Home, home! his heart was singing, and then a thought came to him: "How would he feel if he had no home?"

Again he thought of the prodigal son that had plenty of money, and yet was a homeless wanderer who did not find a homelike place in all the wide world.

Hans began to see a number of prodigals who were much poorer and in a far worse condition than he was—thousands and thousands having no home at all, perhaps not even a chance to get one.

What pitiful lives, what unspeakable tragedy!

No temporal home—no church home—vacillating from bad to worse, and drifting as derelicts in the siwash of a rotten world.

Oh, the pity of it! They plunge on even though they hear the cry of lost souls in the sea of fire and brimstone calling to Father Abraham to send Lazarus with a drop of water.

Hans felt a chilling sensation and shuddered as he again remembered the fearful results of the firewater that he took that dreadful Saturday evening.

CHAPTER XII
The Homecoming

Toward evening a lone traveler came to the gate of the Hauge farm. He was tall and thin, and he looked very tired.

As he came to the gate he straightened up, and a smile flitted across his face as he thought: "Home, at last."

He lifted the latch and went in, turned around slowly and closed the gate carefully. He looked over the well known fields bathed in the rays of the sinking sun and giving him a smiling welcome.

His sister, Anna, coming from the hen-coop with a basket of eggs, saw him and ran to meet him with a real happy smile of welcome.

"Hans," she exclaimed and took hold of his hand.

"Yes, sister Anna, it is Hans."

She set down her basket and grasped his hand with both of hers and said: "Welcome home, Hans —how glad I am to see you!"

"And so am I," Hans answered, "even more than you may think."

"And how glad mother will be. She has fretted and worried about you; and now she will be so glad," Anna continued.

"Is mother well?" Hans asked.

Just then her father, Niels Mikkelsen, came to the door and called, "Anna." But he stopped short, when he saw the two.

"Yes, father," Anna answered, "and here is Hans!"

"Well, I believe," he muttered—.

The two hurried up to him, and Hans clasped his

father's hand, as he said: "Good evening and God's peace I wish you, father!"

"Good evening, and welcome home," his father answered.

"Is everything well with thee, Hans?" his father continued.

"Yes, in body I am quite well; but my inner man is frail and needs some rest and comfort," Hans answered.

As they turned to go in, the mother came out and embraced her son with a hearty hug. "Welcome home! Hans!"

They went in, and Anna brought a tray of rolls and milk.

"You must be starving, Hans, having traveled so far. Father and mother, you have some food too; you had no lunch."

The three began eating, and Hans said: "I was not homesick, but I had to come home to get away from bad company."

"Yes," said his father, "I thought it would be that way."

"Yes," said his mother, looking intently at Hans, "we understand."

His older sister, Karen, who had been over to a neighbor, came in and was much surprised to see Hans; but when he arose she grasped his hand and cried: "Oh, welcome, Hans! Welcome home, my big brother."

"Thank you! sister Karen!" he responded.

"And you did not like the city?" Karen continued eagerly.

"No," said Hans somewhat slowly, "the city did not particularly agree with me, and I came home."

"Were not people nice to get along with in the city?" she asked.

"Well, they pretended to be polite," said Hans.

"Did the people wear Sunday clothes on week days?" she asked.

"I was not particularly interested in clothes," Hans answered, "but I saw many people wearing nice clothes on week days."

"Did the women wear hats like men folks?" she continued.

A broad smile flashed across Hans' face at this rapid fire questioning, and then he answered slowly: "I gave so little attention to the women that really I do not feel competent to say what they wore."

"No, Hans," she said, "it is not important, but plain curiosity makes us ask about things we never see."

Hans rose and said: "I did not mean anything unkind."

He picked up his luggage and went upstairs to his room where he found his mother busy fixing up and tidying.

"Oh, I am so glad, mother, to be home with you and all the others," said Hans as he sat down. "And now I shall begin work in earnest."

"Yes, I am glad too," said his mother, "and I shall have more peace of heart when I know you are safe with us."

"The work in the city was quite easy," said Hans, "but it felt heavy on account of the wickedness and evil surroundings."

"That I can understand very well," said his mother; "but now that you have come home, it will be different."

Hans had laid his handbag on the bed. Opening it he picked out a small package and said: "Here is something for you, mother," as he handed it to her. She took it and sat down, too surprised to say a word.

Sister Karen came up just then, and Hans held

out a package for her and said: "This is for you, to go with the clothes you named."

Karen blushed a deep red as she took it and thanked him for it, but was unable to say any more. "And here is something for Anna," Hans said, holding out another package.

Karen ran out to find Anna, and his mother said: "What makes you so extravagant, Hans? You were saving before."

"Well, one may change his mind and live differently."

Karen came up with Anna, and Hans handed her the package.

"How can I thank you!" Anna exclaimed as she took the gift.

Karen had opened her package and found a cream-colored kerchief with a fancy border. She spread it before them to see, and rolled it between her hands to feel its soft finish.

"Oh, I thank you ever so much, my good brother," she said, as she tried it on. "I believe it is real Orleans silk," she added.

Anna opened her package and found a kerchief of light pink with a flower border. She turned to her mother to see if she approved; then turned to Hans and whispered: "Too fine—it is too fine for me."

But Hans would not listen.

Then Karen broke in: "Yours is not finer than mine."

Anna hung it on Hans and said: "You keep it yourself, Hans."

"No," answered Hans, "I bought it for you, and you must keep it."

"But won't it make me vain," she said, "to wear such nice things?"

"No, the nice things that we wear," said Hans,

"should indicate what we are in mind and soul, clean and sweet, chaste and good."

"And," said Anna, "did you really want me to have this?"

Hans nodded.

She grasped his hand, and a deep look came into her eyes as she said: "I will remember what you said, Hans, and thank you for all."

Their mother sat with the package in her lap and looked at them admiringly as she noticed what influence Hans had over his sisters.

Karen went over to hang the kerchief around her mother's neck. She noticed the package, and she asked: "What have you got, mother?"

"I do not know," her mother answered.

"Don't know?"

"Why, it smells like coffee," Karen said.

"Yes, it is coffee," said Hans; "it is for company. And here is a package of amber crystals (rock candy) to go with the coffee, at the winding up of a house-party."

His mother smiled her thanks, and the girls broke into a laugh as they chimed in: "Thank you, thank you, Hans, now we can celebrate."

The girls started down the stairs, and Hans followed them with something in his hand that he gave to his father as he came down. The girls saw this and wanted to investigate.

A smile brightened his father's face as he noticed their eagerness, and he proceeded very slowly to unwrap the mystery.

It was a "dragonhead" meerschaum with a long cherry stem and a flexible extension to the mouthpiece.

"Hans," said his father, "are you getting to be a spendthrift?"

Hans felt ashamed and looked down.

"Well, never mind! I appreciate your lovely intention," his father said, holding out his hand, "and I thank you for your fidelity."

Hans pressed his father's hand but felt too bashful to reply.

Later in the evening when supper had been finished, the girls were busy clearing the table, while their mother sat in her armchair knitting.

She looked at her son Hans, who sat by the window looking westward, where the sun had just set, leaving a red glow in the sky. He turned to his mother and said with a happy smile: "We are going to have fine weather tomorrow."

"Yes," his mother answered, also smiling, "it looks that way."

Through the open window they heard the father talking with the older brother. Hans arose and strolled out to greet his brother Mikkel, who just then had come from Graalum.

After a while they all came in and sat down. His father took down from the shelf the family Bible, and they all bowed their heads while he read from God's Word and gave thanks to the Lord for His many blessings.

They said good night to one another and went to bed.

CHAPTER XIII

Working on the Farm

The next morning Hans was up early and strolled over into the out-fields, while the others were doing the morning chores. He came to the brook where he had so often fished.

He sat down on a fallen tree and thought of how often he had been here to try his luck with the wary trout.

Then he noticed that there was quite a strip of waste land along the creek. It was a tract where timber had been cut in previous years, and there was a heavy second growth.

Then an idea of clearing came to him, and he mumbled to himself, "That's something I can do;" and he started for home. He came to the house and washed, and they all sat up to the table as the head of the family took down the family Bible for morning devotion.

Hans felt a new joy in his heart as he listened to his father's simple prayer, and a blissful sense of peace came into his soul.

This was different from the carousing at the boarding house in Fredrikstad, where they rushed to the table as hungry wolves.

He always knew that he had a good home, but never before had he appreciated his home as much as he did now.

After breakfast he went with the other menfolks into the fields and helped along with the work.

The work was hard, and his muscles rather flabby and weak, so he felt tempted to give it up and go home; but he had a strong will, and that gave him greater endurance. When dinner came he was surprised to find that he had hoed as many rows of potatoes as the hired man.

Meanwhile his mind was very busy trying to solve what he should do in the future. He wanted to serve God. But how?

One day he asked his father about the waste land along the creek, if he would let him lease it.

His father looked at Hans as if he were an enigma. Finally he said, "Hans, I wonder what you can do with that waste land? There are so many stones and even large boulders, besides stumps and new growth that the land is not worth clearing. I have had some experience of what clearing will cost."

"Yes, I know of what you have cleared, father," Hans said, "although I do not know of your experiences; but that is one reason why I want to try it. I want some of the experiences that you have had."

His father smiled as he heard this, and said: "Hans, you will try what others won't try, but do not ruin your health in doing it."

"And if I promise that, father," said Hans, "will you let me lease the land on somewhat easy terms?"

"Yes," said his father, "I can make easy terms. You may have everything that you raise or make on it."

* * *

Hans began to work. He piled up great stacks of brush and stumps; and when they were sufficiently dry he set fire to them, and when partly burnt he covered them with earth and made charcoal.

He dug and spaded, and raked and dragged the ground smooth, pulled out the stones and planted the ground with beets, for they always brought a good price.

His mother felt sorry for him, that he should waste his energies on this work, but he would say:

"Stump-pulling and stone-breaking to conquer the wilderness is not easy. It is only through very severe labor, that a wilderness will yield anything."

"So is the work of the Holy Spirit to break stony hearts, to uproot the stumps of sinful habits, to cut away the rank growth of evil desires, to clear the branching briars of wicked thoughts, and cleanse the heart and soul from worldly rubbish, filth and garbage. That is the gigantic work of God's Spirit, and He never tires; why should I, the merest atom in creation, peeve and worry over a little clearing work that gives me needed experience."

Thus Hans was musing while he worked, and sometimes said as much to those who teased him; but they would shrug their shoulders and say: "Nutty! I should say he is nutty."

CHAPTER XIV

Spiritual Waste-Land

It was midsummer, and the haying season was at hand.

Hans had cleared most of the tract, and now he had a near view of the king's highway.

One day as Hans was resting after digging out a stump, he saw two men coming. One was "Schoolmaster Ingbrit," sometimes called "Woodshoe Ingbrit," one who lived a fast life; and the other was the well-known fiddler, Kristen Gleng.

"Why, here is our friend Hans home again," said Kristen.

"Yes, I came home," said Hans.

"So are we, coming home," said Woodshoe Ingbrit in a rusty voice, and added: "To our heavenly home."

Fiddler Kristen said, "To rest in the Savior's wounds."

Fear assailed Hans; he wanted to be glad, and yet he felt sad when he thought of former days.

This schoolmaster Ingbrit, who had led a dissolute life and lost his position—how could he sing hymns of praise of God?

Woodshoe Ingbrit said, "You also need conversion, Hans!"

Kristen chimed in; "Yes, you must be converted, Hans."

"That is good of you both to say that," Hans answered.

Ingbrit took his hand, saying, "That's right! Wash in His blood!"

And Kristen added, "I am washed in the blood of the Lamb."

Hans asked, "And you have begun a new life in God?"

"Yes," said Kristen, "I hide in the wounds of Christ."

"Saved by Him," added Ingbrit.

"So, you have turned away from your sins?" queried Hans.

Kristen clasped the hand of Hans and said: "Don't ask me about my sins; God hath taken them away."

"For us He died," said Ingbrit, "and He is a rock against Satan."

Hans was getting more and more bewildered. "Who converted you?" he asked.

"He who is persecuted," said Ingbrit.

"The stone that the builders rejected," said Kristen, and whispered in Hans' ear: "It is His Excellency, Pastor Seeberg."

Hans was shocked. "Pastor Seeberg, who was discharged for conduct unbecoming a church officer?", he exclaimed.

"Yes, discharged by scribes and pharisees," said Ingbrit.

"Discharged for the wounds of Christ," added Kristen.

Then Woodshoe Ingbrit caught the spirit and said: "As in the days of old, they listened to Johannes, so shall they listen to us; and now I bid you farewell, Hans."

"Farewell, Hans!" said Kristen, and turned north with Ingbrit.

"Farewell to you both," said Hans, as they left him.

The two men could not have a true acknowledgment of sin, because their talk was so shallow, like riff-raff before wind and wave.

Hans began digging around another stump with renewed vigor, saying to himself: "If these men had ever dug a stump, they would know how deep the roots go."

After a while the next stump was up. He sat down and mopped his face while he still pondered on the problem. God had set man to work from the beginning, even before he had fallen into sin. Hence, work was not the penalty of sin, but a healthful exercise that God had set Adam to do in Paradise while he was yet innocent.

After the fall in sin, the curse of thorns and thistles proved the evil fruit. But God's Word, "In the sweat of thy brow shalt thou eat," proved to Adam that manual labor was a blessing.

Hans brought to mind the talk with the converted travelers.

They were scattering seed by the wayside for the birds to pick, they threw seed on stony ground without removing the stones, or seed among brambles without clearing. What, then, would the harvest be?

Hans was beginning to learn another lesson of

the analogy between physical and spiritual life. He saw how man must be fully aware of his sins and recognize how deeply sin is rooted in the heart before he knows what to confess.

Hans followed this train of thought, and he had never thought so deeply before; yet he had not found the solution he wanted.

CHAPTER XV

Typhoid Fever

God had better use for Hans than making him a "dime novel" hero; therefore, He gave to Hans a far better training—a very severe training—to prepare him for the spiritual grubbing and stump-pulling and stone-breaking that he was to do in Norway.

Hans will be a bright example for our boys and girls to emulate.

* * *

The harvest was about finished. The season was dry, and water was scarce. Hans had a bad headache for several days. The doctor was sent for, and he pronounced it typhoid fever of a very malignant nature. The fever had so much of a start that the doctor's medicine did not break it, and the fever raged on.

Hans was out of his head and did not recognize anybody. Even the doctor began to have doubts about his recovery.

His mother went to relieve Anna, who had sat by his bedside all day. Anna's tears were flowing as she bid her mother good night.

Hans stirred, and his mother hurried over with a glass of water to moisten his parched lips. He was trying to say something, so she bent her head and heard him whisper: "I shall die, mother!"

A tear fell on his face, and he whispered again: "You must not cry, mother!" But how could she help crying when he was dying?

His mother bent over him and asked: "Are you in much pain?"

After a while she heard him whisper as if to himself: "If I could be with God I should have no sorrow, no pain. Pray for me."

His mother knelt by the bed and prayed with an aching heart: "Have mercy upon me, O God! Wash me from mine iniquity and cleanse me from my sin. Create in me a new heart, O God, and renew a right spirit within me. Restore unto me the joy of Thy salvation."

Hans' eyes closed and his breath was faint.

"Read a hymn to me," he whispered; and his mother opened the hymn-book and read from "Last Preparation":

> *Oh, this world, it is so cold,*
> *All its lights are passing shadows,*
> *And our vanities so bold*
> *Soon are dead, as frozen meadows,*
> *Just like fog they disappear,*
> *And no sign of heaven near.*

She looked across at Hans. His lips moved as if in prayer; "Read me some more," he whispered.

And his mother read to him the next verse:

> *Farewell then, thou earth of clay!*
> *False the hope we from thee borrow:*
> *Let me go in peace away,*
> *Every joy on earth is sorrow;*
> *From deceit and empty show*
> *To the dawn of day I go.*

She looked up again to see if he understood what she read.

But Hans was so unnaturally quiet. He lay with folded hands, his breathing very faint.

She felt cold all over. This, then, was death—coming. Death—stealthy and quiet. She called the others, and soon they were all gathered around the bed where Hans lay.

They looked at one another.

Then Niels, his father, found his voice, and spoke: "God has been very gracious unto us this day. This is not death but a healing sleep."

"We will kneel and thank God."

The family knelt around the bed in thanks to God, for Hans slept.

He slept on until late the next day. His youth, vitality and healthy constitution had carried him through this battle of life and death.

He awoke with a smile on his face; and his voice had come back.

"It looks to me as if God has a special mission for you, Hans," said his mother.

"God has called me back from death many times, to give me one more chance, to keep my covenant with Him," he added.

Hans thought and pondered until he fell asleep thinking of the words of Jesus: "Ye cannot serve two masters; for either ye will hate one and love the other; or else ye will hold to one and despise the other; Ye cannot serve God and mammon."

CHAPTER XVI

Spiritual Revival

Weeks passed, and Hans was gaining strength. To be out in the fresh air, doing what work he could was excellent medicine.

His evenings were spent in reading the Bible, and with the deep interest came also a better understanding of what he read. The most important verses and passages he committed to memory, so his stock of Bible knowledge was constantly increasing.

He felt the necessity of knowing these Bible passages by heart, so that he could feed on them and better meditate on their truths.

He made several efforts to write a book but postponed the task. It was nearing Christmas with lots of extra work to do, preparing for winter and the holidays. Christmas came with the usual round of social functions and general festivities.

Meanwhile he studied over and over again what he really wanted to say. He studied his sentences intently to discover what was lacking.

In this way he kept on training during the long months of winter. He gradually gained efficiency, although he had no one to help him, and later on in the winter he began to realize his pet idea of writing something that people would read.

* * *

In the meantime the Seebergians had begun their revival meetings in the neighborhood. Somehow it created quite a stir. The people flocked to these places in wonder, as they always do when something excites their curiosity. A number of people had been stirred by the preaching of Pastor

Seeberg, who was an eloquent man. Then he was called to Oslo on summons from the bishop; but his followers kept right on with the revivals.

There was schoolmaster Ingbrit, who could talk on any subject under the sun in a general way, so to speak.

There was Kristen Gleng, the fiddler, who had peddled goods and gossip from parish to parish all over Smaalenene.

There was the exceedingly humorous wit, Klaus Lundeplads, who for years had been assistant bailiff and auctioneer of the district, and whose salacious stories always found willing listeners.

This triumvirate became leaders after Seeberg went away, and their hobby was the exaltation of Pastor Seeberg as the innocent victim that suffered like Christ and His apostles at the hands of the scribes and lawyers; and, playing upon the sympathies of the people, they found quite a following.

Next to the unjust treatment of Pastor Seeberg was the new Gospel that they preached: To come and wash in the blood of Christ and become converted just as they had been converted.

This was different from the small catechism of Luther, beginning with Moses, teaching the commandments to convict us as sinners before we realize that we need a Savior. The Seebergians recognized sin as something Christ had washed away, and which was, therefore, past history.

Thus it was that the preaching of these laymen came to many as a message of inspiration in the spiritually dead times. For, aside from meetings like these and according to custom, everybody went to church on Sundays and listened to lengthy sermons by rationalistic pastors on sub-soiling, potato-planting, vaccination, cattle raising, innocent pastimes, deep plowing, social etiquette, hemp cultivation, etc.

Sometimes the people tired of these discourses

and stayed away; but the bailiff was wide awake, and the guilty had to pay fines.

* * *

A week after New Year's day, 1796, Hans had made a trip to Varteig, and on his way back he saw men and women dressed in their best coming up the highway and heading toward a farmhouse near the edge of the timber. As Hans came up, he also turned in.

So far he had not paid any real attention to these people, but the rumors were many, and he felt a strong desire to hear for himself. When he came up the house was already full, but the doors were open and the people were standing outside on the porch.

Hans nodded to some people that he knew, but seeing the doorway crowded he remained outside. The people inside were singing a well-known church hymn, and when the song ended a voice that he well knew began to read. It was the newly converted Seebergian, Kristen Gleng.

He began to preach in a strident voice, sometimes rising to a shriek, and then falling back to a whisper.

He told how he had confessed his many sins and had renounced the world.

Hans was warming up inside to hear this confession.

Again the voice rose, so that those outside could hear the words: "As He was persecuted, so shalt thou be persecuted."

The voice lowered and Hans could not hear any more. Then suddenly the words came loud and strident: "Friends! let us join hands and follow this leader who has been persecuted.

"Let us follow him, though they took away from

him the parsonage he lived in, and the pulpit in which he was called to preach."

Hans felt a chill in his soul as well as in his body, standing outside in the cold. He bowed his head in shame as he realized that they took Pastor Seeberg to be the good shepherd who had led them to the green pastures and living waters.

He shuddered as he thought of how blind they must be to accept this as the true gospel. Christ was the Good Shepherd, and not a sinful man like Seeberg, who had been convicted of several things unbecoming his station.

To Hans it was revolting and nauseating to hear the exalting praise of a man whom he knew to be erring and arrogant.

He heard the benediction pronounced, and as the people began to come out he turned back to the road and went home, but his heart was heavy. Darkness had settled upon his soul, and he did not see his way.

He went to church on Sunday as usual; he read his Bible and prayed, but God seemed to be far away. He was assailed by a great doubt; he could not harmonize the Gospels and the Epistles of Paul, Peter, James and John with what he had heard at this revival.

* * *

Weeks passed into months. Hans had little by little found peace of heart and soul, but it was only a calm before another storm.

Towards spring Pastor Seeberg came back from Oslo where the trial had again gone against him. The final decision deprived him of his office, official robes and insignia, and the deposed pastor was angry indeed. He began a series of so-called revivals, and the people flocked to hear him. But instead of preaching Christ, the crucified Savior, he preached about his own martyrdom, the unjust treatment at the hands of his colleagues, and the unreasonable decision of the courts that deprived him of his rights.

He continued this "revival meeting" throughout the home parish and the neighboring parishes, to set the people against the alleged evil of a tyrannical government.

The excitement increased, and people argued pro and con. Instead of a spiritual awakening there was a continued wrangling about "guilty" or "not guilty" in regard to the deposed pastor.

Hans had been occupied with his own troubles, but now he made up his mind to investigate. With a few men he made a call on Pastor Seeberg, but the pastor refused to see them or hear what they wanted.

Later Hans wrote a letter to Seeberg that ended as follows:

"Therefore we appeal to you, to make amends before God and man for the uncharitable words and actions towards neighbors, and the transgressions against the Law of God and the laws of the land. Only conceit has led you to believe yourself innocently suffering as Christ and His apostles, when you received due penalty for your uncharitable deeds."

This letter to Seeberg, sent by a messenger, was never answered.

CHAPTER XVII

The Boy Convert

Spring had come with the season of plowing and seeding. Hans had reached his twenty-fifth birthday, but worry and anxiety had plowed deep furrows on his sad face, and he looked years and years older than he really was.

He had plowed for several days, but his mind

was more intent on salvation than on plowing. The Bible verses and chapters committed to memory kept on arranging themselves into connected thought.

He rather felt than understood the influence of the Holy Spirit to bring new light upon God's Word. He began to think of the new life that soon would come out of this dead and dark soil, the plowed field. It was like quickening into life a dead and darkened soul; and a prayer went up from his heart that God would create in him a renewal of life and a stronger faith.

Somehow he felt a vibrant joy and happiness as he pictured to himself what such a life must be. There was a longing in his soul for a closer communion with the Lord, and he began to sing:

Jesus, I long for Thy blessed communion,
Yearning for Thee in my heart and my mind;
Draw me from all things that hinder our union,
Take me to Thee that new life I may find.
Show me more clearly my hopeless condition,
Show me the depth of corruption in me,
So that my nature may die in contrition
And that my spirit may live unto Thee.

Mightily strengthen my spirit within me,
That I may learn what Thy Spirit can do!
O take Thou captive each passion, and win me;
Lead me and guide me, for weak I am too!
All that I am and possess I surrender
If Thou alone in my spirit may dwell;
All will I yield Thee, my Savior so tender
Take me and own me, and all will be well.*

Hans' spirit arose; his soul seemed to be lifted towards heaven, and there was peace and joy in his heart. It passed all understanding, and his inner man experienced a Pentecostal day. For Hans it was a spiritual Baptism, a renewal of his spirit and inner life, and with profound wonder he lifted up

---
* German, 1712, Tr. P. J. Hygom, (Danish) 1740, Tr. G. T. Rygh (English) 1908.

his eyes to heaven and prayed. He went home with heart and soul filled with song.

The following days and weeks Hans seemed to walk on air. Everything was so wonderful, although he never could tell how it happened. But one thing he felt above everything else: "God had wrought a miracle within him, something that was beyond human power."

* * *

Hans had finished the spring work, and he was planting the Haugebraaten, near the king's highway. Three men, arm in arm, came sauntering along. Hans immediately knew them and saw that they were quite intoxicated.

Hans turned away in shame, but they shouted: "God's peace to you, Hans," and then Kristen Gleng came forward to shake hands.

"Awake, Hans, and be converted," said Kristen, "and (hic) ... be converted ... (hic) ... that your sins ... (hic) ... may be washed away!"

Hans paled, something seemed to freeze within him; he was speechless. Kristen tried to say some more, but the others grabbed him by the arm saying: "Come, brother, don't waste any time on Hans!" and they sauntered on down the road towards Fredrikstad.

Hans finished planting and went home more sick at heart than ever.

During the winter he had written down many things that he had thought of and had experienced. These papers increased in bulk, and it was difficult at times to find what he wanted; so Anna suggested that he should group his writings and arrange them in systematic order.

This he did, and soon they formed themselves into a book that could be printed. This work interested him so much, and he was so anxious to have it well expressed that he read chapters and portions of the book at family gatherings to hear their opinions of it.

Then his father or his brother Mikkel would occasionally put in a word and bring new thoughts, while his mother would sit and wonder how Hans could think of so many things.

The title Hans had given to the book was T h e W o r l d's F o l l i e s, but here he had come to the "follies" of the pastors, and he had put it rather strongly because there were so few converts and so many church members not living a life according to the Word of God.

His father shook his head and said: "Those are very severe charges."

Hans admitted that they were, but not so severe as God's Word in Matt. 23.

His brother Ole, the sheriff of the district, also shook his head and said: "They will put you in prison for such harsh words!"

Hans had a determined look as he said: "Be it so! Even the disciples of Christ were cast into prison for speaking the truth."

Hans pondered. Should he, for his own safety, and to save his work waive this, which he knew to be the truth? He decided to think it over, but after pondering for weeks he let it stand.

* * *

Hans was on his way to the city of Oslo.

He was happy and contented. His first attempt at writing a book was accomplished, and he had decided to have it printed.

At noon he stopped to rest and have lunch. When he opened the pack he was surprised to find that the manuscript was missing.

The smile on his face and the joy of his heart were gone. Where could the manuscript be? How did he happen to lose it?

All that hard work spent on it had gone to waste. But—on second thought—maybe it was God's will that it should not be printed. To make sure he walked back several miles, but he found no trace of his beloved manuscript.

He turned off the highway to visit a farmer that he knew.

Hans told about the lost manuscript and what was written in it, and the farmer was very much interested.

Towards evening a traveler arrived, footsore and weary, and asked for lodging over night.

He was welcome to that, and came in with the pack that he carried. He opened his pack and took out a package of papers that he had found.

Hans became interested, and when he saw the package, he knew immediately that it was his. He told the stranger of his loss and what was in the package. When they opened it, there was the manuscript. Hans was overjoyed to get it back, and offered a handsome reward for its recovery, but the stranger refused to take it.

Hans thanked him heartily for his generosity.

After supper Hans read passages from his manuscript. He even read whole chapters of what he thought would interest his friends, and he was amply rewarded by the interest of his listeners.

The question of practical Christianity was viewed from various angles. This led to the question of presenting the Gospel, and who was to blame when there were so few conversions and so little of real spiritual life among the church people professing Christianity.

Hans read another page from his book, how every true Christian should live according to the Gospel and should preach it with his daily life. Deeds speak louder than words.

"I have heard," Hans continued, "that talk is

cheap, and it certainly is cheap talk that we have from the pulpits when the subjects are farming fishing, dairying and like occupations that people know far better than the preacher. That's just killing time." The others agreed very readily to this.

Before they went to bed Hans found a Bible, read a chapter, and prayed in a manner that was new to the listeners. He thanked God for His great love, His unlimited grace, the Holy Word, and converted souls. He thanked God for His great patience with sinners, and prayed that their sins and failings would be forgiven. He concluded by asking God's blessing upon this house and family, friends and relatives far and near, and that they be kept steadfast in faith, even unto the end of life.

Hans afterwards shook hands with each one as he bade them goodnight and went to bed.

CHAPTER XVIII

Happenings on the Way

Next morning Hans arose quite early and continued his journey.

He felt refreshed and animated, walking briskly along the highway, so happy because he had recovered the precious papers that meant so much to him and the work he wanted to do.

After some hours, Hans stepped over into the shade of some nearby trees. He sat down on a convenient stump, then bethought himself, and kneeling, gave thanks unto God for the many gifts received, and for the returned manuscript. And as his heart was yet full of fear for his calling, he prayed fervently and long, pleading with our Father in heaven to help and sustain him in his arduous task of wakening the people.

A man came walking along the road. As he came near and saw a man kneel by a stump, and heard a murmur, he concluded that the kneeling man was sick, and offered to help him.

Hans arose slowly and thanked the man for his kindness, saying: "No, I am not sick. My body is well, but my soul is in trouble."

The man no doubt thought that Hans' mind must be unbalanced, so he simply said: "Yes, that is bad!"

Hans caught the inflection of unbelief and said: "If you were sick at heart and soul, you would pray to God, would you not?"

The man shook his head as he said: "You should not go alone upon these highways when you are sick."

"But I am not alone," said Hans, "God is always with me."

The man looked at Hans sadly and thought: How sad that such a fine young man should have lost his reason in this way.

Hans said nothing, but he wondered how he should be able to convince this man and make him understand.

They had turned back to the highway and walked on in silence quite a distance. Then Hans asked: "Do you live anywhere near here?"

"Yes," said the man, "I live only a few miles north from here, and I am on my way home now."

"Maybe you are a farmer," said Hans.

"Yes," answered the man, "I was raised on a farm."

"Perhaps you own a farm?" said Hans.

"Yes, I am a freeholder," said the man with a touch of pride.

"Then you have much to look after and a lot of

work to take care of everything and farm successfully," said Hans.

The man looked at Hans very keenly as he heard this. That sounds rational; he cannot be so very much out of his mind, he thought.

"The fields look good this year and may yield well," said Hans.

"Well, they are not bad," said the man.

"Especially the barley," said Hans. "It is coming out early."

"Yes," said the man, "the barley looks good."

"And the potatoes are fine," said Hans, "and may yield a good crop."

"I think so," responded the man.

"And the hay is heavy this year," said Hans, "it will be hard to cure, if we get rainy weather."

"Yes," said the man, "especially the clover."

"Well, I think timothy should be sown with the clover; it would stand up better and cure better and give more milk," said Hans.

"Do you really believe that?" said the man with some surprise.

"I am sure of it," said Hans, "because we have tried it for several years and always have had good results."

The man looked more surprised and said: "Are you a farmer?"

Hans answered that he was.

"And where do you live?" the man asked.

"I live on the Hauge farm in Thune parish, about twelve miles northeast of Fredrikstad," Hans answered.

"And where are you going?" the man asked.

"I am going to Oslo," Hans said, "to get a little book printed, if I can find a printer willing to do the job."

"To print a book," said the man, "have you written it yourself?"

"Why, yes," said Hans, "the idea came to me gradually, while working on the farm." Then he quoted:

The seasons come, and seasons go,
To house and home in weal and woe
The people race upon the main,
From place to place—an endless chain.
They plow and seed a waiting field,
They hoe and weed for better yield.
Then harvest they the golden grain,
And house it well from snow and rain.
In early springtime they begin
A grist of hard work—grind again.
From year to year, crop after crop,
Until we hear death calling, "Stop!"
Then rest their bodies 'neath the clod;
The soul must stay to meet with God.
But is the soul prepared in love
To reach the goal in heaven above?

"That is the index to my book," said Hans, "and indicates what I had on my mind and wanted to write."

The man stood dumbfounded and speechless with wonder.

Hans ventured, "Is all your land cleared, or under cultivation?"

"No," the man said, "I have some acres that I want cleared."

"Well, yes," said Hans, "I have cleared a few acres of stones and stumps, brush and bramble, but cleared land will yield good returns."

"That is very true," replied the man, "but sometimes the work of clearing may be beyond your strength."

"Yes," said Hans, "I believe it; and yet it is still harder to tear up stumps of evil habits and break stony hearts, or weed the inborn wickedness and plant the seed of God's Word therein."

The man looked at Hans and asked: "Excuse me, but are you a preacher?"

"No," said Hans, "I am not."

The man was silent, and Hans continued:

"It all depends upon whether or not you are willing to let the work of clearing and weeding in your heart be as thorough as it is upon your farm. And you know it will be a wretched yield without weeding; nothing but distress and misery will follow if all the evil within us is allowed to grow like rank weeds."

"Yes," said the man, "there are plenty of weeds, and I don't see how we can get rid of them."

Hans smiled and said: "Would you get rid of them if you could?"

The man felt uneasy as he answered: "Who would not?"

"Oh," said Hans, "God knows how to weed evil from the hearts of men."

"But," said the man, "how can you believe such a thing?"

"Because," said Hans, "belief in God's Word will weed out evil deeds."

"Oh," said the man, "but that is difficult."

"Yes," said Hans; "it was that way with me. The Lord must begin plowing in your soul, and tear up evil roots and weeds and stones."

"I do not know how to pray," the man interposed.

"We shall see," said Hans; "you know the catechism, do you not?"

"Well, a little," said the man.

"The first part contains the ten Commandments. Read them," said Hans, "and ask: Have I kept them both in letter and in spirit?"

"I know without reading," said he, "that I have not kept them."

"The next part," Hans said, "tells you what to believe, and the third part tells you how to pray."

"I shall look up my catechism," said the man.

"Thank you very much. Here is my farmstead. Won't you come in and rest?"

Hans could not stop just then, but he promised to call on his return from Oslo, then bade him goodbye, and left.

CHAPTER XIX

Nearing the Capital

Hans continued his journey. He felt happier after meeting with this man, because somehow it strengthened his faith in the mission he had in mind —to help his fellowmen find salvation.

Mile after mile he tramped. He tried to find a solution of the trying task to bring people to Christ, for the Conventicle Act of 1741 forbade laymen to preach. He prayed for light.

Toward noon he was very warm and perspired profusely. The road was dusty and his thirst increased. Then he saw a man at a well near the highway, and he hurried to get a drink of water.

After quenching his thirst he began questioning the man about the people in the neighborhood, and the man in turn asked Hans for his name and where he came from.

The man happened to know Hans' father, so he invited the traveller to the house. Here they found the noon meal ready, and the good wife got an extra plate for Hans who was very thankful for the hospitality.

The man was well read, so conversation never lagged. Both enjoyed exchanging ideas. Soon they drifted into spiritual matters, and Hans showed the man his manuscripts and read some passages.

As Hans read the man nodded his approval, until Hans came to the part containing the criticism of the priesthood, when he suddenly shook his head and said: "That will never do! It will displease the church authorities."

Hans was well aware of this, but he insisted someone must speak of it—wake people from their lethargy, when their spiritual welfare was in the hands of arrogant priests and pompous prelates.

Hans picked up his traveling bag, shook hands with the good people, thanking them for their kind hospitality, and said good-bye, while they in turn wished him God-speed.

* * *

Hans was nearing the capital. He could see the towers and turrets and the high roofs of large buildings.

His pace had slackened. He began to think how Martin Luther, the monk from Wittenberg, must have felt when he came in sight of Worms to meet the emperor and the prelates.

The spires and steeples in the city of Worms did not intimidate him. We hear him say: "Even if there are as many devils as there are tiles on the roofs, I shall go."

Hans felt a flow of warmth sweep over him. Assuredly, Luther followed the footsteps of his Master, who walked up the hill of Calvary carrying the cross, wounded, bleeding and dying.

Hans sensed the fearful agony of Jesus as He walked along Via Dolorosa, leading to Calvary, followed by "a great company of people, the women wailing and lamenting."

Jesus, turning to them, had said: "Daughters of Jerusalem! weep not for me, but weep for yourselves, and for your children! For, behold, the day shall come when ye shall cry to the mountains, 'Fall on us, and to the hills, Cover us'."

"Wonderful Savior," thought Hans, "even walking to His death He was thinking of the sinful men and women who in pity He warned of the coming calamity that would destroy Jerusalem and the whole nation; yet He says not a word about His own suffering."

Hans found great relief in this meditation, and now he felt how God answered his prayers in a most simple manner.

Hans felt happier. The burden of his soul was lifted, and his tired limbs began to quicken. It was evening but he happened to find lodging in the suburbs.

CHAPTER XX

Tackling the Printers

Next morning the capital lay before him. The confusing tangle of streets and avenues extended in all directions, regardless of compass or cardinal points. He saw warehouses, stores, shops, offices, churches, residences, and small dwelling houses promiscuously scattered.

Hans continued along the Bishop's Lane around the Oslo harbor and Bjorwick to Gammeltorvet (Old Market). Here he began to inquire if any one could direct him to a reliable printing office.

Yes, there was one over in Raadhusgaten (Court Street) opposite Hotel d'Angleterre, and they pointed toward the castle.

Hans walked a few blocks along Strandgaten, and came to Raadhusgaten. Here he turned to the right and soon found the hotel; and across the street he saw a sign that read: Jens Orbeck Bergs Bogtrykkeri (printing office), and he hastened over.

He felt nervous as he reached the door, and it was with a trembling hand that he opened it and went into the printing office.

A number of men setting type turned their questioning eyes on him—eyes that plainly said: Another "rube" with a poem!

The proprietor, Mr. Berg, sat at a large desk by the window.

Hans stepped up to the desk saluting: "A blessed day and God's peace," he began, "Have I the honor to speak with Mr. Berg?"

But the proprietor, looking up across his spectacles, cut him short and said: "No! We are very busy today."

As Hans did not go, the proprietor, Mr. Berg, looked up again over the horn-rimmed glasses and said: "No, we do not print such things, and—I have no time to talk with you."

He gathered up a bunch of papers and stuffed them into a roomy pocket, put on his hat and left.

Hans did not know what to do. He looked at the printers—then became fascinated by their quick way of picking up type and clicking it into the composing stick.

One had just finished a galley, and locking it went to the proof press. Hans was interested and he went over to see how it was done.

He wanted to ask if they printed books that way, but refrained, as he thought they would laugh at his ignorance, so he just said: "You are printing a lot of things here?"

"Yes," said the printer, "we do that; otherwise we could not make a living in these hard times."

"Well, perhaps you could print this for me," said Hans, as he unwrapped his bundle of manuscript.

The printer was examining his proof-sheet; then

he turned to Hans and said: "Is it verses that you have written?"

"No," said Hans, "it is not verse."

The printer hung his proof on the file and took the proffered manuscript. He read the title page: "Meditations on the World's Follies, in nine chapters, written briefly by an unlearned boy, Hans Nielsen Hauge from Thune parish."

The printer smiled as he read this and said: "That sounds great! Are you going to be a Ludvig Holberg?"*

Hans felt the sarcasm but managed to say: "No, I do not aspire to such heights of celebrity."

The printer turned the leaves, read a sentence here and there, and then exclaimed: "Why, it is a religious book! It will not pay to print this. People won't buy it!"

"And I believed this to be a Christian country," said Hans—"and I hoped to find Christian people."

"Well," answered the printer with a peculiar grin, "you are in a print shop for the time being."

"So I am," said Hans, "and here I hoped to get my book printed."

Hans gathered up his manuscript, arranged it in proper order, wrapped it up and started to leave.

The printer noticed that Hans was well dressed, and—perhaps he had money. So he said more politely: "Call again tomorrow when the boss is in, and he may agree to print it for you."

* * *

The next morning Hans called early, he was so anxious about the printing; but Mr. Berg was not in. He would be back in the evening.

Hans was greatly disappointed; he left and wandered about. In his rambles he came up to the

---
* Norway's Shakespeare.

castle, but as he started to enter the grounds he was turned back by a sentry pacing back and forth.

Afterwards he came upon a hill where he had a fine view of the bay, dotted with islands and vessels of many kinds. He looked across the Piperviken harbor, past Tyveholmen, Brandskjær and Bygdø, far out in the bay. Hans was so enraptured by the sight that he forgot about his unpleasant experience of the morning.

After looking long and well he walked up to the park to look at the rare plants and flowers brought from some foreign country. He was greatly interested and forgot everything else.

Towards evening the cravings of hunger became so strong that he broke away to get something to eat, and then he remembered the appointment to meet the boss at the printing office.

He hurried over, but Mr. Berg was not in—had been away all day; but he would be in next morning. The men had gone, but the head printer was there to straighten up things and check up work before leaving.

He had an intelligent face, and just now a winning smile. He was measuring the galleys. The work was above the average. He turned to Hans and said: "Well, what is on your mind?"

Hans was very thankful for this favorable opportunity, and so he said: "I see you are a trusted man of experience in charge of responsible work, and I thought perhaps you could give me advice on some delicate questions that I have raised in this manuscript."

"Yes," said the printer, "perhaps it may not be beyond me."

Hans had opened his manuscript and was turning the pages: "Here, read this," he said, as he pointed to a certain passage.

The printer took up the pages and read, and it

dawned on him that this was not a "fool hayseed"; aloud he said: "Those are rather strong assertions."

"Yes," said Hans, "but every word of it is true, and truth must prevail." The printer admitted that it should, and read some more.

After reading a while he looked at Hans and said: "That certainly is stiff talk, and you are rather headstrong to say it."

"Oh, as to that," said Hans, "you may think me headstrong, but whatever is right and true should be said."

The printer looked at Hans rather admiringly and said: "If this be true, as it looks to me, it does not hurt to make it strong."

"It is true," said Hans, "every word of it, and I want to say it, even if I have to go to jail for it."

The printer liked his frankness, and—mentally seeing big sales of a book causing a sensation—he read some more, then said: "You are a stubborn fellow; yet I do not think you will get into trouble, because there are no names mentioned."

Hans was greatly relieved at hearing this and said: "That is quite true, and maybe I can get this book printed in spite of objections, now that you have seen what it is."

The printer looked away and said: "No, I cannot promise you anything, but call in the morning and see the boss. He may decide to favor you, although it will be quite expensive."

"Yes, I suppose so," said Hans, as he picked up his manuscript and bade the printer good evening.

CHAPTER XXI

Contracting for Printing

The next morning Hans took an early stroll down to the wharf and around the castle to get a breath of fresh air, and another view of the harbor. Besides, he wanted his mind clear, and he did not like to appear overly anxious, it might spoil what chances he had.

About the middle of the forenoon, Hans came to the printing office and Mr. Berg, the proprietor, was at his desk very busy.

However, when Hans came in he looked up and smiled with a friendly: "Good morning!"

Hans felt encouraged; and he too smiled, as he said, "Good morning," and handed the manuscript to Mr. Berg for inspection.

"Yes, let's see what you have," said Mr. Berg, as he surveyed the bulk of closely written pages. "This looks like a big job!"

Mr. Berg thumbed the pages, read a few lines here and there, sometimes a little interested—sometimes his face wrinkled. He turned some more pages, read a line or two with a smile, then he sobered—looked glum and shook his head, but said not a word.

Hans stood alert watching the changing features of the great man, and waiting rather anxiously for the final verdict.

"Well! — — —" Mr. Berg began, then stopped—he arose and went over to the head printer for consultation; but they talked too low to be heard, and Hans began to fear that there was little chance for his manuscript. Mr. Berg returned to his desk, took a sheet of paper and began to figure an estimate.

Hans began to hope again. The boss' figuring meant business.

"Yes," Mr. Berg said, but broke off again as he began to count the pages. He was intently absorbed in the figures.

Hans remained standing. He was staring fixedly at every change in the features of Mr. Berg.

At length Mr. Berg finished the intricate calculations and went over to the head printer again to compare figures on the various items. Obviously these were weighty matters that must be considered carefully.

Finally he turned to Hans with a smile. Hans brightened as Mr. Berg nodded and said, "Yes, I think we can print the book for you, but it will cost considerable money to print a book of that size."

Hans' buoyant hope fell again as he heard this. Considerable money meant "lots of money"—more than he could ever think of raising, even with the help of his friends.

Hans felt greatly embarrassed—yet he managed to say: "Thank you! And how much will it take?"

"Well!" and Berg looked over to the printers, as if estimating what they could do and how cheap they could do it—"Yes," he said, "everything is expensive, and this will cost at least thirty dollars."

A wave of relief swept over Hans. He had thought of a much larger sum, compared with the value of the manuscript. However, his native instinct of barter was wide-awake, and the chance of driving a bargain made him say in a subdued manner: "That—that is very high."

Berg looked at the manuscript, counting the pages once more and looking over the figures, as if trying to find some error.

Hans edged up a little closer as he ventured to ask: "Could it be done for twenty dollars?" He felt a strong urge to bargain.

"No, no!" Mr. Berg shook his head vigorously with a hurt look, "that is utterly out of the question!"

Hans looked crestfallen.

Mr. Berg looked sympathetically at Hans and ventured: "Perhaps it may be difficult for you to raise the money." Hans nodded in the affirmative and revolved in his mind how far he could go.

Mr. Berg arose and went to consult the head printer; then turned to Hans and said: "Well! seeing that it is your first venture and a losing one our lowest possible figure will be, let us say, twenty-five dollars." And Mr. Berg looked charity personified.

Hans observed the finality of the tone in which it was said, and, considering that further bickering was of no avail, he finally said: "Well, I suppose your word is final, and I shall have to pay twenty-five dollars to get this job done; but I can pay only half of it now."

Hans took out his wallet and counted out the money. "Here is thirteen dollars," said Hans, as he handed Mr. Berg the money, "for which you will give me a receipt upon the contract; and the rest of the money I will pay when the job is finished."

Berg wrote the desired contract with a receipt and handed it to Hans, remarking that Hans was lucky to get it done for that price, and that he hoped for prompt payment.

Hans assured him it would be promptly paid if the book was as promptly printed. Berg was glad to hear this, and smilingly remarked that he had his hands full of jobs, but work on the book should begin immediately.

"And how soon will it be off the press?" Hans asked; his voice trembling with eagerness.

"It is very difficult," answered Berg, "to give any definite time for work in this line, but, barring accidents, let us say about five or six weeks, if things run all right."

"Thank you, Mr. Berg," said Hans. "I shall be back by the first of August. Goodbye!"

"Goodbye! Goodbye," answered Mr. Berg, "and a pleasant journey."

* * *

Hans was homeward bound, and he walked on air. Things had gone smoothly, far better than he had anticipated.

His heart was filled with joy. His first mission was accomplished. He would have his book on the "World's Follies" by the first of August.

But what would people say about the book! And the Danish officers that ruled Norway, what would they say? But worst of all what would the clergy and the church officers say?

CHAPTER XXII

The Pastor's Dilemma

There was a hearty welcome at the Hauge farm when Hans came back.

The girls and father and mother felt a tremor of excitement as Hans came up and shook hands with them, and the girls began firing questions so fast that he could answer only in a general way.

But the youngest, Anna, was not satisfied with this, so she teased him with questions until the whole story was told in detail. The book was really to be printed so that it could be read like other books.

Their venerable father sat with an indulgent smile as he listened to the animated conversation. Then, as it lulled, he asked Hans if he had called upon any of the government officials or the magistrate to hear what they had to say, or if they had given him any advice.

Hans admitted that he had not, and this rather put a damper on their enthusiasm. What will the king's cabinet do? How will the bishop and the clergy take it? What will be the outcome of it?

The girls consulted their mother and she said: "Sufficient unto the day is the evil thereof. Do not worry about the evil of tomorrow."

Hans said quietly: "Let us bow our heads and thank God." And he prayed with the fervency of a pent-up soul.

* * *

A new pastor had come to fill the vacancy after the suspended Pastor Seeberg in the Thune parish. He was rather illiterate, yet quite conceited and quick tempered.

The conditions in the parish were tangled, owing to the recent "revival" by Seeberg and his friends; and now the new pastor faced a wrangle of contending parties that he had not bargained for.

He found the Hauge family quite influential, and, hearing of Hans printing a book, he fancied that the family must be in some way connected with the Seeberg movement.

He sent word to Hans, asking him to come to the parsonage.

Hans was surprised. It was best to know the worst though, so he went.

He was ushered into the pastor's study, and as he saluted the great man arose from his ponderous armchair with the dignity of a high prelate. Then he nodded, giving Hans three fingers for a handshake.

"This is Hans, the son of Niels Mikkelsen Hauge?" he inquired.

Hans admitted that he was.

"And you are now printing a book?" queried the pastor.

Hans answered, "I am trying to."

"And is this book of the Seeberg propaganda?" asked the pastor.

"No, sir, it is not," Hans answered; "the book is about the 'World's Follies'; how foolish people are pretending to be Christians and yet live a worldly life—pretending they worship God when they worship Mammon."

"And I suppose," said the pastor, "that you accuse the ministerial fraternity of being Mammon worshippers who lead a worldly life?"

Hans admitted as much, but only as he could prove it to be true.

The pastor immediately cut off further remarks by saying: "I have your own word of it now, that you admit having done this terrible thing, you—you overgrown farm-boy with no education or anything else to recommend you—you have the arrant audacity to assume the exalted station of a super-critic, to wield the lash of caustic cynicism over the clerical fraternity and civil authorities, perhaps the king's cabinet or the king himself."

Hans tried to explain.

The choleric pastor kept right on, working himself into a vehement frenzy as the hysterical language frothed from his mouth.

Hans, feeling the hot blood of anger surging up, was barely able to hold himself in check. He managed, however, to remain calm and courteous, and as the storm abated and the pastor tried to get his "second wind," he bowed his thanks and left.

On the way home he felt glum and blue and hot by turns, realizing that this was only a foretaste of what was coming.

As he came to the home-gate, Anna came out, and she could see on his face that something had gone wrong; so she led him to a shady arbor and made him sit down on a bench and tell her what had happened.

Hans was reluctant to say what happened, but Anna somehow wormed it out of him until she had every detail. Then she began to cry in a subdued manner. Hans felt ill at ease and said: "Oh, please! Do not cry, Anna! It is not worth it!" But she began to cough.

She turned her face to him to say something, but another coughing spell came and Hans noticed with concern how her face changed, how thin and pale and drawn with pain it was.

A great fear seized him as he looked at her: Was he going to lose his sister, his boon companion from childhood? That severe cold last year—was it eating away her lungs? His fear increased. The pastor's scolding was as nothing to this. What had he to live for if she died?

After the coughing spell Anna looked up and tried to smile. She could read her brother's face like a book, and she said: "Yes, we've had a lovely time together—life has been sweet and full of joy; but do you know, we shall find something far better beyond?"

Hans felt the tears coming as he looked at his sister. He felt sick himself and began to hope that he might die too.

The thought came so strong to him that he cried aloud: "Oh, Anna, maybe our heavenly Father will let us die together, as we have lived together; that soon we shall be ready to leave at His calling."

"Oh, no!" said Anna: "No, Hans, God will need you to bring a Gospel message to our people that will show them true Christianity, and how to live a true Christian life. It is your life-work."

CHAPTER XXIII

A Progressive Youngster

It was midsummer. The chores were finished. The family was gathered in the big room for devotion.

The head of the family read and prayed from "Daily Meditations." They all joined and sang the old, old evening hymn by S. O. Bruun:

> *The sun has gone down,*
> *And peace has descended on country and town;*
> *The songbirds in silence have flown to their nest,*
> *And flowers are closing their petals in rest;*
> *So closes my heart from annoyance and care,*
>   *In homage and prayer.*
>
> *I praise for this day*
> *The Father in heaven, who prospered my way,*
> *Who shielded from danger, protected from harm,*
> *Promoted my labor, and strengthened my arm;*
> *For hours that passed lightly as birds on the wing,*
>   *Thanksgiving I bring.*
>
> *Forgive me, O Lord,*
> *My sins and transgressions in deed and in word.*
> *Thou knowest my heart and my innermost thought,*
> *The words I have spoken, the deeds I have wrought,*
> *My errors and failings I deeply regret,*
>   *Forgive and forget.*
>
> *I ask for no more,*
> *My light I extinguish, and fasten the door,*
> *And seeking my chamber, betake me to rest,*
> *Assured that my slumber this night will be blest,*
> *I fondly confide to Thy care and control*
>   *My body and soul.**

Several minutes passed in silent prayer; then Hans arose to add a few words to the Scripture les-

---

* S. O. Bruun, 1695. Tr. (Eng.) O. T. Sanden, 1908.

son just read. His heart was full of contrition for his many failings and short-comings.

He repeated verse one and two of Rom. 12, and stressed the words, "a living sacrifice" and to live "holy and acceptable unto God." He continued, "All true believers must present themselves as living sacrifices, holy and acceptable to God, our Father, in spiritual service—a consecration of their lives to work that they will be assigned in the great harvest fields here on earth.

"Be not conformed to this world," that means, we must not conduct ourselves or live as people of this world, but live as God's children, obedient unto the Lord.

"Our lives must be a living witness, testifying unto the glory of God. 'And be ye transformed by the renewing of your mind, that ye may prove what is the good and acceptable and perfect will of God'."

All of a sudden Hans stopped. He did not seem to notice the very sober faces around him. He looked straight before him.

His own past life came before his vision, and he forgot to say any more.

The others sat waiting for him to continue, but his eyes were downcast and he was lost in meditation. No one ventured to say anything; they were so busy with their own thoughts. Those simple words of the apostle: "That ye present your bodies as a living sacrifice"; what did they imply?

The aged father, reading again the opening verses of that chapter, pondered: Did Paul ask of them more than accepting the Lord Jesus as their personal Savior?

Anna was leaning over father's arm to read the verse herself. She pondered a little and said: "I haven't been a living sacrifice."

The father looked at her, the fairest in the family, and felt a strong love for this daughter.

The others also understood and felt in their hearts how empty it would be in that home if Anna should pass away. Tears came unbidden as they looked at her frail face.

She looked at the passage in the Bible and finally read aloud: " 'Holy and acceptable unto God'—how I wish I were holy and acceptable!"

A coughing spell interrupted her confession.

After a while the cough abated and Anna breathed more easily, but she said no more. A hush fell upon the family. Hans fell on his knees and prayed —prayed with the fervency of an overburdened heart that God would cleanse their souls and make them holy and acceptable.

* * *

The evening had been a spiritual reunion for the family, and God's blessing rested upon their devotion.

Almost daily some of the neighbors came visiting in the evening, and they were asked to join their devotion. It happened often that some were moved by God's Spirit to confess their sins and seek Christ.

Thus, from time to time this praying family was augmented by neighbors that began to pray, and Hans was often asked to come over to some neighbor and give a little talk on Christian life.

At first he did not give any lengthy talks, but as his audience increased and more and more people came to these gatherings he made more careful preparations and preached real sermons.

These meetings and their visible results gave Hans new thoughts and new ideas to work upon. In leisure hours he began writing extracts of his sermons and arranged them into regular series that in time grew into a book with consecutive chapters and paragraphs.

Hans found that the thoughts of the worldly

wise did not begin to compare with the revealed Word of God and the wisdom found in the Bible. He therefore gave his second book the title "God's Wisdom."

God created man in His own image, and willed that all men should be eternally happy, having God's wisdom and truth. Adam's falling into sin is a falling into darkness, where truth is lost.

Again, God revealed His wisdom and truth through His Son and gave it to us in the Gospel. The Gospel shows us the salvation of man.

Salvation is simplified through the inspiration of the Holy Spirit. The ignorant as well as the learned may understand how to become a true Christian, and the Gospel contains the fundamentals of Christianity.

Hans finished the book in less than two months, and in the closing chapter he predicted a great future for Christianity in Norway, when lay people should become converted into real Christians.

CHAPTER XXIV

Conflict with the Pastor

During the summer Hans was invited to speak at various gatherings in the neighborhood. These gatherings were growing larger and larger until they reached the proportions of public assemblies.

The Conventicle Act of 1741 forbade laymen to preach in public unless the local pastor or a king's officer was present. A brother of Hans, Ole Mikkelsen Hauge, as sheriff, notified the local pastor of these meetings, but he refused to come.

Then one of the influential neighbors, Iver Graalum, invited Hans to speak at his home and invited the local pastor also. The news spread quickly, and people from every part of the parish came to hear and see what was going to happen.

It was early in August. The day was warm, the windows and doors were wide open. Mr. Graalum and his boys were busy carrying blocks and planks to arrange seats for the people inside and outside the house.

More people arrived, and finally the pastor, Stevelin Urdahl, his assistant, Hans M. Schiott, and the king's marshal, Johan Radich, came in the pastor's new equipage.

As they alighted Mr. Graalum escorted them to a place of honor opposite to Hans who was standing, giving out the hymns to be sung. Immediately the singing began.

After the singing Hans read a "text" from the Bible and began to talk. At first the words came slowly and carefully weighed on account of the dignitaries present; but as he warmed to his subject, he waxed eloquent, and the fiery words struck home everywhere.

Hans saw neither pastor nor marshal nor chaplain, who stoically sat and stared at him with stony faces. Hans saw only a number of wretched, lost and condemned sinners, that, more than anything else, needed salvation and the betterment of miserable lives.

He pictured sin, depravity, and the prevailing excess and iniquities in such strong colors that even the hard-hearted began to flinch, as if they wanted to hide their faces.

Hans made them see their lost condition and how much they were in need of a Savior. He showed them how Jesus was standing with open arms to receive them—to save them, if they had the courage to break with the world and give up their sinful life.

His sermon was inspirational, full of striking illustrations from daily life and illuminating Bible verses to verify the facts presented. He closed with a strong and fervent prayer for the awakening of slumbering people and the success of God's Kingdom here on earth. Another hymn was sung, and the venerable old schoolmaster closed with prayer.

Many faces were wet with tears, and even the worldly-minded had sober faces and were deep in thought. This sermon was entirely different from the loud harangues of the Seebergians.

The pastor arose, and the many faces looked at him intently, wondering what he was going to say. With an air of authority and a frown upon his face he swept the audience with a look of scorn and began, "I have listened to the talk that Hans Nielsen Hauge hath given, because I was requested to do so, and in accordance with the duty of my holy pastoral office it is entailed upon me to see that the Word of God is presented pure and undefiled from the Scriptures to prevent any confusion within my parish.

"Hence, I forbid Hans Nielsen Hauge in the future to hold such meetings within this parish that is under my supervision and care; and if this offense is repeated, he shall incur the penalty of the law."

The situation was growing tense; but Hans in his calm and unpretentious manner arose and said, as he looked at the pastor with a steady eye, "I hear the pastor according to his official trust and duty now forbids me to hold these meetings; but this I believe he cannot do so long as I keep to the Word of God and admonish my neighbors and fellowmen to live according to His Word and its teachings. Therefore I will ask the worthy pastor if he, in my talk, has found anything that is not in accordance with the Word of God?"

The pastor did not deign to answer, nor did he

look at Hans; but he turned to Marshal Radich and said: "I beg of you, Hr. Marshal Radich, to inform these people who are here present what the law says in regard to the matter at hand."

The marshal turned to the principal men in the audience and said in a rather freezing tone:

"The matter in hand is correctly stated by our worthy pastor. The Conventicle Act of January 13, 1741, forbids such devotional assemblies, and parties conducting such services shall be turned away from the parish."

Hans arose again and said: "I have a copy of this Conventicle Act of 1741, and"—he drew a document from his coat-pocket—"let some one here read it before these people, that they may know exactly what the law demands." Hans turned to the head of the house and said: "Here, neighbor Graalum, read this," and he handed him the document.

The pastor jumped to his feet and reached out his hand as if to grab the document: "No, Master Hans! No such reading will be permitted." His voice was peremptory, cold, and commanding.

"Not permitted!" said Hans in surprise; "why is it not permitted?"

Several of the farmers arose on hearing this and stood beside Mr. Graalum who was intently reading the document.

"No, it will not be permitted," repeated the pastor with a strong voice. "It is not for these people to read and construe when they have the authorities to interpret the law. Is it not so, Hr. Radich?"

Marshal Radich nodded and added: "The worthy reverend is right, and the Conventicle Act of 1741 will not be read; that's final."

Hans made no answer to this, and as neighbor Graalum handed him the document, he placed it in his pocket and sat down while he said quite audibly: "All government derives its power from God."

Meanwhile the farmers began to murmur about injustice to peaceful people, and Mr. Graalum stepped up to the pastor and asked:

"What complaint has the pastor against this young man, Hans Nielsen Hauge? What harm has he done reading the Scriptures and asking people to live according to God's Word? Everybody knows that many of them that drank and swore and committed outrageous abominations have reformed and amended their ways—because Hans has had conversations with them.

"Why shall this be forbidden when other gatherings with drinking, dancing, gambling, and carousing are tolerated by the authorities? Yes—if this be so, we must say to you, Hr. Pastor, that we as Christian people will not stand for this."

The murmur grew louder and louder, and several went before the pastor to make a formal protest against his ruling.

Some said, "We will go to the King to get this law abolished."

Quite a number voiced this sentiment: "Yes, that is what we will!"

The pastor and the marshal looked at one another. These people were influential; it would not do to stir them into heated action; so the pastor arose and said to the marshal: "We have no more to do here. This shall be reported to the bishop and the magistrate, and we shall see who is right."

The marshal and the chaplain departed with the pastor in a courly manner, perhaps a little more politely than usual.

* * *

A few days later the pastor, Rev. Stevelin Urdahl, invited Hans for dinner. When he came he was received and entertained very pleasantly. After the courses they had coffee and "pretzels" and then the pastor invited him into his own study or library to join him in a bowl and a pipe of choice "Salmagundi."

Hans begged to be excused, as he neither drank nor smoked; but he wished to explain a few things and hear the pastor's opinion of it. After talking a while, the pastor requested of Hans to give him a written copy of the sermon he had given at Mr. Graalum's farmstead, when he was present. Hans readily agreed to this and took his leave.

A few days later the pastor received the requested sermon from Hans, and forthwith he sent it to the bishop in Oslo together with his own report of the meeting at Iver Graalum's home. In this report the "disturbance" Hans N. Hauge had caused was looked upon as very serious. Such meetings were against the law and therefore a nuisance that must be stopped—and stopped at once. If allowed to spread it would have evil results, perhaps cause a revolution, sedition and high treason.

CHAPTER XXV

Second Trip to Oslo

In the following weeks Hans refrained from speaking in public, but kept himself busy writing the closing chapter on his second book, "The Wisdom of God."

Then the answer from the bishop came; but it was not to the pastor's liking. The bishop held that "the followers of this layman, Hans N. Hauge, were a quiet sect of peaceful nature and law-abiding and should not be persecuted. It would be far better to let the Conventicle Act rest in this case where public safety is not threatened. Let it rest rather than prosecute such visionary dupes or stir them up to make trouble. If left alone, this movement would die out."

The pastor evidently pondered on this until he yielded to the suggestions of the bishop, for afterwards he did not molest Hauge or his friends when they gathered for devotion and spiritual edification. Thus it was a decided gain for Hauge.

In the following weeks the demands upon Hauge increased, and the number of adherents to this laymen's movement gained accordingly; thus, when Hauge left for Oslo in September, it was said that "Thune parish bloomed as the Lord's vineyard." To Hauge himself it gave more faith in his work and a will to continue as he had begun.

When Hauge came to Oslo his first book, "The World's Follies", was not half finished, but when he showed them some ready cash, the printer found reason to hurry the work, and by November the book was ready for the bookbinder.

Meanwhile Hans had not been idle; he had helped in the printing office and begun to learn the printer's trade. By the end of October the printing shop was literally swamped with jobs of every description, and Hans was the "handyman" that could do most anything. He helped in the book-bindery and soon learned how books should be bound. Thus he earned a living while he was waiting. He set in type a goodly part of the second book himself to offset the many delays. When the rush was over Hans packed up his belongings and started for home.

He reached home on the twenty-third of December, and on Christmas Eve they had a family reunion at the Hauge farmstead. The home folks were greatly impressed by the work he had done and wondered how he had been able to get out a real book.

After the holidays he made some primitive

presses and began binding the books that were in flat sheets. It was tedious work to fold the sheets and sew and cut them by hand for the covers that he had previously prepared during his prolonged stay in Oslo.

At the same time invitations to "come and give a talk" were numerous. He bound books all day, but in the evening he was wanted here and there "to talk," and very seldom he had an evening free.

People flocked to hear him, some perhaps out of curiosity to hear a man that had actually written a book, but most of them forgot this when they heard him talk.

He gave them something else to think about; he showed them how foolish it was to busy themselves with temporal things and stand idly in the market place in spiritual matters.

Even a hog will root for his food, but the idle people in the market place do not even root; they come begging for a "handout." What a life to live and then die with an unsaved soul! Will any sane man ever do that? Even the prodigal son had more sense. When reduced to eating husks he thought of his father and the home he had left—where even the servants were well fed and had good beds—he decided to go to his father and confess: "I have sinned against heaven and against thee, and I am not worthy to be called thy son, but make me as one of thy hired servants." And he came home to stay.

"How about you? Will you do as he did?" This was something to think about, and they came to hear more. It kept Hans very busy that winter, and the spiritual awakening spread to the neighboring parishes.

Often he had to make extended journeys to reach the outlying districts, and in most of these places there was no trouble.

In the Glemminge parish he found many friends,

so also in Raade and Varteig, where the pastors befriended him; but in the Rygge parish, Rev. Wilhelm Schnitler made all kinds of trouble, although he did not succeed in having Hauge arrested.

Hauge returned home and continued binding his books, and his brother Mikkel helped him. Many of his friends came visiting and took some books to sell for him. He prospered beyond expectations.

Later he journeyed to visit his friends in Fredrikstad. One of these, Nils Barso, obtained a permit from the local pastor, Rev. U. G. Feierman, for Hans to conduct meetings in the parish. Several meetings were held, but no one started any trouble and Hans left without being molested.

Hans then sailed across the fjord to Holmestrand and visited Tønsberg and Drammen, where he met some members of the Zinzendorf Brethern who welcomed him with open arms. He remained here a week, and then continued eastward through Asker and Lier where he found many willing ears and open minds. His books sold readily everywhere.

A week later he arrived at Aker (suburb of Oslo), where many converts gladdened his heart and made it a pleasant stay. He continued the journey southward to Moss and other places and came home to work on the farm about Easter-time.

In his home parish he was always welcome, and going to church regularly every Sunday he gained the friendship of his pastor, Rev. Urdahl, who began to notice improvements in his church members.

Hans did not make any long trips, nor did he preach much that summer, as he worked on the farm for his father during the whole season. However, he found time to form a Bible class for the converts that wanted to join. They met two evenings a week at the farmsteads to which they were invited.

Thus he gained more Bible knowledge for himself as well as for the members who had joined the class. They sang and prayed, and read—comparing the text with parallel verses in the Bible as the references indicated, thus gaining a treasure-chest of Bible knowledge.

The members of this class who later attained some prominence as evangelists were the two brothers of Hans, Ole and Mikkel, their cousin, Paul Gunderson, the brothers Iver and Torkel Gabestad, Gunder Viuldsen, Kr. Ramstad, Elling Hoidahl, the brothers Peder and Soren Roer and several others not named.

It was a profitable summer for these young men, spending the evenings studying the Bible and other sacred books and preparing themselves for the work that the Lord wanted them to do. It was quite different from going to dances and card-parties, night-reveling, drinking and carousing, yes, quite different; and they felt very happy because they had not yielded to these temptations.

Hans had secured a considerable number of books that helped them in their studies of the Bible —of Luther and others of Reformation times, also Dr. Bengel's "Treatise on the New Testament," that had been translated into Danish.

In the omgangsskole (circuit school) they had learned the "three R's" fairly well, and, supplied with note-books, they jotted down important thoughts and wrote outlines and sketches for short sermons.

As they became better acquainted with the Bible, the conviction grew that it was the book of sacred truth, that the 66 books contained in the Bible, written by 40 or more authors of the most varied calling during a period of 1500 years, between Moses and the apostle John, proved that these writers were of one mind and inspired by One—the highest of all authorities—the Spirit of God.

Some blamed Hans that he became lax in preaching, but somehow God led Hans to do the right things at the right time, and instead of one lone and solitary messenger, there were now at the beginning of the winter twelve young men ready to enter the great field as Gospel messengers.

At this time Hans was often assailed with doubt, whether his calling was in accordance with God's supreme will.

This had worried him more than anything else. He prayed and waited anxiously for an answer from God, but no answer came.

Late in the fall it happened that a copy of "The Conversion of John Tauler," translated into Danish, came into his possession. He read it with great interest.

A learned Dominican monk, John Tauler, was converted through a Waldensian layman, Nicolaus of Basel, who taught him the wonderful way and real virtues of true Christian life. This was an unusual story, telling of a layman teaching a learned man.

On every page Hans read a living recognition of the simple truth that salvation does not depend on profound learning, but on the experience of a true Christian life, reaching peace of soul through faith in Jesus as a Savior.

The learned Dr. Tauler found the humble layman with his experience a source of wisdom far above the wisdom of this world.

The reading of this book had a decided influence upon Hans, and all his doubts and misgivings were swept away by the convincing fact that even a layman, as well as the learned, has his place and special task to perform in God's kingdom.

A new light came to Hans as he felt that God had answered his prayers in a way different from his own views. With doubts gone his faith was strengthened. He felt assured that God had wanted him to continue as he had begun, and his confidence in his mission gave him courage to resume his extended journeys.

CHAPTER XXVI

Arrested in Fredrikstad

The year 1797 drew to a close. The Christmas festivities and visiting continued, and the Hauge family exchanged courtesies with their neighbors. Everything had changed so that drinking, dancing, and carousing was a thing of the past.

The young people of the invited guests amused the older ones with song and recitations and perhaps some old-fashioned Y u l e s p i l (play) while they all partook of coffee and Y u l e-k a k e (cake) with S u k k e r t o p (rock candy) and other good things.

The chief entertainment, however, was the ancient custom of story-telling—narrating the well-known tales of the Vikings and the valor of those ancient heroes.

Hans could well remember these harrassing tales from his boyhood days, and how some people were bent on having a fight to make it a celebration worthy of their ancestors, bracing their courage with strong liquor until they were quite drunk.

Even in church the Viking spirit had prevailed in bygone days, as Hans' father had seen when a boy. During a long sermon men often went to sleep. Once a man began to snore and his neighbor gave him a dig with his elbow to wake him up. The sleepy man woke up with a growl, and forgetting where he was, he challenged the other in a loud voice to come outside and he would show him who was the best man.

They both went out, and the congregation followed to "see fair play," forgetting all about the pastor who had reached his "secondly" and was not half through his sermon.

Hans, tired of these old stories, wanted to change this age-old custom; so he began to tell stories from the Bible—about Adam and Eve and their two sons —the proud and haughty Cain, and the meek and humble shepherd Abel—how the unreasonable jealousy of Cain made him murder his brother.

Hans had a special gift of conversation, and it was interesting to listen when he told stories and talked of God's wisdom. His way of explaining the Word of God was simply marvelous, so no one wondered why people came again and again to hear his talk.

* * *

After the visiting in the home neighborhood Hauge journeyed over to his relatives near Fredrikstad to visit. Here many neighbors gathered to hear Hauge speak, as he had done on several occasions before.

The weather was fine and the sleighing was good, so many people had come even from the city. The host offered Hans some refreshments, but Hans declined with thanks, as he knew many had come long ways and it was better to begin early while they could have daylight.

A hundred voices joined in and sang with heart and tongue the well-known Christmas hymn of Luther:

From heaven above to earth I come
To bear good news to every home;
Glad tidings of great joy I bring,
Whereof I now will gladly sing.

After singing a few verses, Hans opened up his Bible and read a part of the Y u l e E v a n g e l, and then spoke of the great love of God who gave His only begotten Son, that whosoever believed on Him should not perish but have everlasting life.

Hans waxed eloquent as he pictured heaven's glory and great joy when the host of angels came to earth testifying to the birth of Christ and sang of peace and good will. The eyes of those present shone with ecstasy.

Hans repeated again the angel's message: "Peace on earth and good will—"

There was a commotion outside, and Hans stopped. The people moved and yielded to admit the pastor, Rev. Urban Gottlieb Feierman, with a lieutenant and three soldiers fully armed, even to bayonets on their rifles. They squeezed up to the middle of the room and "presented arms."

Pastor Feierman was angry and red in the face as he turned to Hans and asked in a harsh voice, "What are you doing here?"

Hans fearlessly and with steady eye looked directly into the pastor's eyes and said, "We have sung, and I have read the Christmas Evangel."

"And what else?" the pastor demanded.

"I have made a few remarks," said Hans, "about the joy in heaven when Christ came to earth to save sinners. The angels brought the message to us on earth that we also should rejoice."

"Who gave you permission to speak in public?" the pastor abruptly demanded in a thundering voice.

"That was given by yourself, worthy pastor, when I was in Fredrikstad, your home parish, speaking in the house of Nils Barsø," said Hans in a most respectful manner.

"I want none of your talk," said the now furious pastor. "I gave you permission once because I believed it to be innocent; but now I see what this movement means, and this time you go with me."

The assembled people began to protest rather loudly about the unwelcome intrusion; but Hans turned to them and said in a quiet way, "No, do not interfere; the authorities must be obeyed."

Turning to the pastor he said: "I am ready to go with you," then to his brother Ole: "Give my love to father, mother and all at home, and do not grieve. God will sustain me in my trials. Good-bye!"

Hans followed the pastor and was placed between the two soldiers in the sleigh while the third was on guard behind the prisoner.

The assembled farmers of the neighborhood were so entirely taken by surprise that they simply stared with blanched faces into the dark, where their beloved Hans had disappeared.

"Peace and good will"—what a farce — —

* * *

In the evening they arrived at the Fredrikstad garrison, and Hans was turned over to the guard of the military prison. As the pastor bid them "Good night" he added, "and watch the prisoner close, that he does not get away."

Hans was placed in the guard-house with some soldiers under arrest. Someone had smuggled a bottle of rum into the room, and the prisoners were celebrating Christmas in a hilarious manner, singing lewd songs and swapping stories.

Hans found a wooden bench (wide enough to sleep on) with a blanket, and he sat down. He knew that it was useless to talk to these drunken revelers, so he lay down and rested, and in his heart communed with his heavenly Father.

Soon the heads of the carousers became heavy and they sank to the floor and slept.

When everything became quiet, Hans dozed off and slept peacefully during the rest of the night.

The next day some of the prisoners were taken out and others were brought in. Hans had seen many evil and wicked people, but none as bad and dissolute as these. They cursed and swore and amused themselves with vile and atrocious stories until the room rang with laughter.

One tried to make himself conspicuous by singing lewd songs. Hans found his way over to him, and in his quiet manner said: "That is a fine song, is it not?"

"Oh, I should say, the finest ever for a hole like this."

"Such a fine song. I suppose you learned it of your mother?" continued Hans in his gentle manner.

The young man glared at Hans and stormed: "That is none of your business; you cut that out and leave her alone."

The others suddenly became quiet and began to listen, possibly a fight was at hand—that would be great fun.

Hans was calm and ventured: "Perhaps your mother is dead?"

The soldier sobered, looked at the floor and at Hans and said somewhat tamely: "That's my affair, not yours."

"No, no!" said Hans, "I just happened to think that if she were alive now she would perhaps not be so happy."

The soldier looked at the floor but did not say anything.

"It is perhaps some time since she died," said Hans.

"No, it is not," said the soldier, "and none of your concern."

"Not exactly," said Hans; "it concerns you more than me, but anyway you have my full sympathy."

The soldier was lost in deep thought and did not look up.

"You have a good voice," continued Hans as he saw the soldier weaken; "it could be put to better use than singing ribald songs."

The soldier remained silent; but the others laughed uproariously, and one of them said to Hans, "You are a fine fellow!"

"Yes," said Hans, "that's why I do not sing such songs."

"But why are you here?" said one; "have you stolen something?"

"No," said Hans, "I sang and read God's Word, and asked people to refrain from doing things that make their mothers cry; that's why they sent me here, and—perhaps that is why you are here also."

They all became very quiet.

Then the jailer came and called them for dinner, and they filed out past the ever watchful prison guard. Hans came next to the singing soldier and said to him: "I hope you bear me no ill will?"

"No, I have no reason to," he answered with a sigh.

Hans smiled in his winning way and said: "It seems to me that you should become a child of God."

"No, no!" the young man said, "I could never be that," and he burst into tears.

Hans threw his arm around his shoulder and whispered: "Now I am sure you will be a child of God."

The young man answered, "My mother died last spring."

"But God is not dead," said Hans.

"Oh, but I feel so miserable," said the young man, "because I was disobedient to my mother."

"Yes, yes, I understand," said Hans.

"And I was mean to her, and said things I should not have said, and then ran away. Now she is dead and—and—you must help me in this—won't you?" the young man pleaded.

"Oh, yes, I will—and God will!" said Hans as they sat down to eat.

CHAPTER XXVII
Alone Near Death

In the afternoon Hans tried to speak to his fellow-prisoners about salvation of their souls. The new arrivals were angry because this and that officer had caught them. Hans' talk was spurned and cursed and drowned by raucous laughter and shouts of ridicule.

In the evening Hans drew forth his beloved testament (that the guard had overlooked) and read a chapter loud enough for all to hear; then he prayed for himself and for the rest of them and sang a well known evening-hymn. The singing so irritated them that some began to yell and shout: H o l d k j e f t! (Shut up!)

The guard came in and several pointed at Hans, that he was causing the trouble. Hans stood up. The guard looked hard at him a while and sneered: "Aha! You are taking certain liberties!"

Hans answered in his quiet way, "Yes, I took the liberty to read a chapter from the Testament and pray and sing the evening hymn, but I did not know it was wrong."

"Wrong! Of course it was wrong!" said the guard, "We have a chaplain to do that; but if you want to sing we can accommodate you."

The guard turned and went out; but soon he returned with two soldiers who took Hans between them and marched out.

They led him into the north wing where there was an empty cell called the "cage", and shoved him in with an oath, as the guard said: "Here you can sing without disturbing anybody."

The cell was cold. The little window on the

north wall had a broken pane, and the cold draft filled the room; but the soldiers cared not. They slammed the door and locked it and went into the guard-room to continue their card-game.

The midnight hour struck. Hans began to pace back and forth across the cell to keep from freezing. Oh! How bitterly cold it was. He called for help, but no one heard. He felt numb and dizzy and tired.

The clock in the tower struck one. One hour! He must keep on walking—walk all night and not go to sleep, or it would be his last.

He walked and walked; yet, as he moved about in the cell, he felt a strange gladness in suffering for the cause of God's kingdom. His soul was filled with joy and peace.

The clock in the tower struck two—three—and he was still pacing the floor; but he felt so queer and numb, and his feet wobbled. He sank to his knees by a wooden bench and poured out the anguish of suffering in prayer to God, that He would sustain him in his trial.

At last, overcome with fatigue, he huddled upon the wooden cot. He tried to rise, but his feet refused to support him and he sank back. He sensed a white calm that carried him off to regions white and flooded with light.

Christmas! Peace on earth! White and pure the snow covered the ground. White were the wings of the angels that proclaimed peace. Everything was white; even the gates of heaven shone white.

The dream picture drew his soul heavenward. Maybe he would see his Master face to face, and the angels would bring the white garments that he must wear in the heavenly mansions.

Hans sank deeper and deeper into dreamland. The cold—the freezing temperature he felt no more. His soul was soaring high above the white clouds towards the borderland of heaven.

The stars shone as millions of snow crystals in a brilliant light, and the white curtains of dreamland swathed his soul in ecstasies as he beheld the beautiful world beyond.

* * *

"Hans! Hans!" Someone shook him—shook him hard—shook him again. He tried to wake up, but he couldn't. Again he was shaken roughly, and someone shouted: "Get up, will you!"

Then a voice full of sympathy commanded, "Have a care! The man is nearly dead! Try and help him to his feet." But it took several efforts to get him up and out of the cell.

They carried him into the guardroom, where it was warm, and Hans sensed the change. He began to shudder, and every muscle felt shooting pains, but his limbs refused to function. He tried to rise, but his head swam and he sank back in a heap. They laid him on a couch.

"Here you! Drink this brandy." They made Hans swallow a big dose. Then they made him drink again. Hans revived and mumbled something with a wry face. He opened his eyes and looked about rather bewildered.

"Do you feel any better?" the corporal asked with sympathy.

"Yes," answered Hans rather feebly, "I am warming up inside."

"That's good; now you will soon be all right," said the corporal; "but it was a close call. The guards were drunk and forgot you."

As his reason cleared, Hans murmured, "Yes, it was a Godsend that you came."

The corporal smiled but said no more. He pondered on the report he had to make in the morning.

* * *

An orderly brought in a message to the captain of the guard.

It was an order to bring the prisoner, Hauge, before the king's marshal, Hr. Radich.

Hans was escorted between two soldiers into an open sleigh with armed guards to prevent him from running away. The jailer handed the order to the corporal and said, "Watch him closely!"

Hr. J. Radich resided at the manor about 10 miles from Fredrikstad, and on a cold day it was a chilly drive; but Hans was robust and strong. When they arrived at the manor about noon, Hans had a square meal.

The hearing at the Radich office was without results. After a series of perfunctory questions, Hans was requested to desist from speaking in public because it led people astray.

Hans answered that he could not see it that way. He had read God's Word to the people. He had urged them to live as true Christians and good citizens. He could not see how this was leading people astray.

The marshal had no answer to this, so he ordered Hans to the city jail at Fredrikstad to be tried before the district judge, Sievers.

On their return to Fredrikstad, the young corporal, John Blegen, wondered if Hans really was in his right mind, to refuse such an opportunity to free himself and asked, "Why didn't you promise to quit preaching when you had the chance to go free?"

Hans smiled and said, "You would do the same if you knew God."

The corporal pondered on this, and the guards were unusually quiet. What kind of a man was this, who would rather stay in jail than disobey God? This was different from anything they had heard or seen before.

Hans did not say any more, but prayed from his soul for the salvation of these men, and somehow he felt that God would answer him.

At the city jail they parted with a handshake as Hans said, "I do wish to thank you, corporal, for what you have done for me, and I wish you happiness in the days to come, but God alone can give it."

* * *

Then came the day set for Hans' trial. There was a mob of curious people at the city hall.

Pastor Feierman's attorney had subpoenaed a number of witnesses, and people wondered what they had to say. The many wild rumors and conjectures that were heard kept the mob guessing.

Reports had it that Hans was a sorcerer and that he had bewitched many good people in Thune parish.

"Hush! Here comes the judge."

The honorable Hr. Sievers ascended the steps of the court house, and guards made way for him into the courtrooms.

When he had rapped the desk for order, Hans was brought in and put on the witness stand. After the preliminaries, Hans was asked:

"Did you, contrary to repeated warnings from Pastor Feierman, conduct public services at the Eivindrude farmstead in Glemminge parish on the 27th of last December?"

Hans straightened as he answered quietly, "No, I did not."

The judge was surprised, and asked, "Did you not conduct services?"

"Oh, yes," said Hans in his cool way, "but it was not contrary to Pastor Feierman's orders."

"How is that?" asked the judge.

"I had on a previous occasion received Pastor Feierman's permission."

"Where was that?" the judge asked.

"Here in Fredrikstad, at the residence of Nils Barso, and Nils Stillougsen was with me at the time," Hans answered.

"Are they here?" continued the judge.

The judge arose and called: "Nils Barso! Nils Stillougsen!"

They both stood up.

"Are you witness to this?"

Both answered, "Yes."

"That is good!" said the judge. "You will be called later."

Then the judge turned to Hans and said, "You have not received any order of restraint forbidding such services?"

"No," said Hans, "I have not."

"Can you prove it?" asked the judge.

"I deny Pastor Feierman's assertion," said Hans, "and he must prove his claim."

The judge smiled indulgently and said, "So he must. But did you receive no order countermanding his given permission?"

"None whatever!" answered Hans. "I had not seen or heard from Pastor Feierman since he gave me the permit at Nils Barso's here in Fredrikstad, until he came with soldiers to Eivindrude and violently carried me to the military prison at the fort without law or warrant. Is this right before God and the king's law?"

The judge cut in, "The court will decide what is right or not."

Hans was sent back to jail while the hearing of the many witnesses continued. Two weeks more he remained in jail, until the authorities found that Pastor Feierman had erred and exceeded his authority—reading only paragraphs 14 and 15 of the Conventicle Act, and omitting to read the paragraphs 8, 12, and 17 of the same act.

Hans was released from prison, January 29, 1798.

CHAPTER XXVIII
Hauge Vindicated

The young man, Hans Nielsen Hauge, came brilliantly through the fiery ordeal of his first arrest and trial, and was fully vindicated through the many testimonials at the trial.

The judge sent a note of reprimand to Rev. U. G. Feierman for being over-zealous and guilty of exceeding his authority. This made Pastor Feierman very angry, and when Hauge went out of prison and out of reach of his vengeance, he became furious. Hence he began to persecute the friends that had testified rather favorably for Hauge at the trial, for in his estimate they were apostate members of the church.

One Sunday several of these friends came to church to partake of communion and went into the sacristy to register. As soon as the worthy pastor recognized them, he began to abuse and scold them most terribly. Then he grasped a rawhide whip, hanging handy on the wall, and lashed them right and left, shouting in stentorian tones: "Out with you! Get out of there! Out of God's house! Get out, all of you sanctimonious hypocrites! You spawn of the serpent!"

These high-handed acts of brutality engendered among the lay people a deep and lasting hatred of the ever dominant clergy.

A few weeks later a new complaint against Hauge and his friends was filed in the district court, but Judge Hofgard sent it to the state authorities with a personal letter of comment that ended as follows:

"This new complaint is somewhat peculiar, inasmuch as I, in my frequent travels through this district, have not heard any complaints whatever. On the contrary, this man, Hans Hauge, is spoken of by his neighbors as respectable, industrious, and well-liked; and they consider his spiritual talks as beneficial and uplifting. He does not advocate loafing or idleness of any kind, or waste of time and money.

"The evenings spent with him have changed the sentiment of the people so they turn away from drinking and carousing and instead gather peacefully to seek betterment and higher ideals.

"Many of the farmers and other prominent people testify to the fact that many of the social evils have been curbed and reduced since Hans Hauge began his spiritual talks."

This comment from Judge Hofgaard caused the complaint against Hauge to be quashed, and Hauge was left in peace for some time.

As the records of the trial were not made public, Hauge wrote an answer to Pastor Feierman's charges in pamphlet form, but the print shops in Oslo refused to print it.

The title of this little book was S a n d h e d e n s   E r k j e n d e l s e (The Acknowledgment of Truth). The closing chapter had the following challenge to the rationalistic pastors of the state church: "Were ye called of God, then ye would do God's work, esteem His Word holy and in high honor, preach it in season and out of season, reprove, rebuke and exhort with all longsuffering in love and pity those who live a wretched and miserable life.

"But ye are hirelings that preach for pay. Your own conscience will show you that ye seek selfglorification instead of seeking salvation for men and giving glory to God. Even if ye rightly preach God's Word, the truth is as Christ says: They bind heavy burdens and grievous to be borne, and lay them on men's shoulders; but they themselves will not move with their finger (Matt. 23:4).

"After your preaching year in and year out, the

evil increases. What are ye but blind leaders, hireling shepherds, careless watchmen heavy with sleep? Therefore, ye need be converted."

This and some more of the same order ended the last chapter of the book, and no wonder the printers in Oslo were afraid of it. But Hauge fortunately had made the acquaintance of a book agent, Dyrendahl, who helped him to get the book printed in Copenhagen, Denmark, and afterwards disposed of the book through his subagents.

Hauge meanwhile visited the parishes north and east of Oslo in the districts of Ullensaker, Ness, Odalen, Tangen, Loiten and Elverum.

Hauge won many friends wherever he went to preach, and his books, World's Follies and God's Wisdom, sold readily. His challenge to the clerical order was such a bold venture that it stirred everybody.

As he traveled up the Østerdalen, he came to Grundset at the opening of market week. Grundset was an ancient farmstead on the road from Trondheim to Oslo, with a ferry across the Glommen river.

There was a large hostelry and numerous smaller buildings with housing for strangers. It was an ideal mart for trading horses, cattle, goats, sheep or anything salable—knives, scythes, axes, saws, woodenware, etc.

Early in the spring there was a market week when the traders met and bartered for the things they wanted to buy or sell.

Some rented shacks and others built booths to display their wares. Everybody carried a pocket flask to "prime" backward customers or to speed up trade. Hucksters and peddlers and sjaker-judar were present with knick-knacks, tambak watches, rings and cheap jewelry.

Horse-trading, however, was the principal business, and many sharp deals were made. Some even gave their worn-out nags plenty of beer to make them look spirited to purchasers.

Hauge did not venture to speak in public, but walked around and talked with people in private about the betterment of their lives.

He tried hard to convince the people that the pocket flask was not an asset in trade, but a liability. What gained for him many friends was his winning smile, inoffensive manners and tact.

His stock of books was quickly disposed of, and his friends arranged several meetings for him before he left. That last evening the Spirit was upon him, and he spoke with unusual eloquence so that many believed. When he left the next morning, many asked him to return and have some more meetings.

CHAPTER XXIX

Again in the Capital

Spring work had just begun when Hans returned home, so he donned his work clothes and helped until seeding was over.

About this time Kristian Barso, a son of Nils Barso in Fredrikstad, came to visit the Hauge family. He was very much interested in the work that Hauge was doing, and offered to go with him to Oslo to get a supply of books and help to distribute them.

Hauge was very thankful for this, but he warned the young man that it might have serious consequences. The young man, however, was not greatly impressed by the warning, so the two started for Oslo early the following week.

Late in the afternoon of the third day the two came to Grønland, a suburb of the capital east of the Aker river, where Hauge was acquainted with a wheelwright, Ole Meyer.

Here they were well received, and a meeting was arranged for Hauge the same evening in the big shop near the river. A large number of people gathered—many friends and many from curiosity.

Later he was invited to speak at Sagene (manufacturing district) by a lumberman, Anders Kristofer Grøndahl, who arranged seating in a large drying-shed to accommodate the people.

Here, moved by the Spirit, Hauge preached both at noon and in the evening to a full house the remaining days of the week, and his urgent appeal found its way to many a heart.

On Pentecost Sunday they all went to church—Hauge always attended church when there was service—and he refrained from having any meetings or gatherings of his own.

Monday, the Second Day of Pentecost, was also a holiday, and Hauge attended the forenoon service in the Old Market church. After service, he was invited to lunch by a friend in Lakkegaden (street), who had also arranged for a meeting immediately afterwards, as the people wanted to hear Hauge talk.

As they were making preparations to seat the people, Captain Knoph and several policemen came and asked for Hauge.

Hauge immediately stepped forth and said, "At your service!"

"Is this Hans Nielsen Hauge from Thune parish?" roared the captain to impress upon them his authority.

"Yes," answered Hauge, calm and serene as usual.

"Is it a fact," growled the captain, "that you will hold public meeting here this afternoon?"

"Yes," answered Hauge very gently, "it is a fact."

"But I will stop it," roared the captain, "and I herewith arrest you in the name of the law."

"Yes, yes," answered Hauge in his gentle way, "you have the power of the law, but it is not God's law nor in God's name."

"Never mind!" ranted the captain. "Now you follow me."

Hauge's friends started to interfere, and Kristian Barso spoke up, "This is an outrage, to arrest a man before he has done wrong!"

The captain sneered, "Perhaps you are his partner?"

"Yes, we came together from the Thune parish," answered Barso.

"Aha!" blustered the captain. "Then you come along too. Consider yourself under arrest with your partner."

"Certainly I will," answered the youthful Barso patronizingly.

"Yes, you will!" grumbled the captain and marched them to the city jail, where the desk sergeant took their names and locked the men up.

Captain Knoph reported to the chief of police that he had arrested two vagrants. The next day the two were called for a private hearing, and the three policemen escorted them to the chief's office.

The chief looked at them long and searchingly. As customary he looked for signs of guilt, but the two prisoners had a clear conscience and stood calm and expectant.

Suddenly the chief said to the taller man, "So you are Hans Nielsen Hauge from Thune parish?"

"Yes, that is my name," said Hauge.

The chief spoke again slowly and with weight. "You are accused of vagrancy and unlawful conduct in this municipality of Oslo. It is a shame that you, the son of a respectable farmer, will conduct yourself in this manner and shirk honest work for a living. The result of such vagrancy will be that some day you will land in the penitentiary."

Hauge remained calm and dignified while the chief spoke. He took a step forward and said firmly, "The chief says I am accused of vagrancy and unlawful conduct; but this accusation is not true, nor that I am afraid of work."

The chief interrupted him sternly, "The captain made those charges in his official report, and it must be so."

"No, it is not so!" answered Hauge boldly, as he drew a document from his pocket and presented it to the chief. "Here is my legal passport from the bailiff in Thune," said Hauge, "and as to occupation —I have worked on my father's farm all spring, plowing and seeding. That can be proven by our neighbors."

The chief took the passport, read it carefully, and mumbled as to himself, "Yes, this seems to be in order."

"As regards the teaching and talks at public gatherings, I have strictly held to God's Word and the doctrine of Luther's Catechism—to keep God's Ten Commandments, serve God in faith and in truth, and help my neighbor to prosper."

"Yes, yes, this is well and good," said the chief reluctantly, "but it is not mentioned in the complaint. I cannot take it into consideration. The district judge, Hagerup, will be here tomorrow to investigate the statements made."

He nodded to the jailer, who took them back to jail.

The next day Hauge and Barso were taken to the courthouse.

Court was convened; Hauge was called. After the preliminaries, Hauge was asked, "What is your occupation?"

"Manual labor and general work on my father's

farm, your honor," said Hauge in his quiet, unassuming way.

"What errand have you here in Oslo?" was the next question.

"I have some manuscripts to be printed," said Hauge, candidly.

"Are they of a religious nature?"

"Yes, Sir," said Hauge cheerfully, "I have spoken

"Have you made any speeches since you came here?"

"Yes, sir," said Hauge cheerfully, "I have spoken to some people about our Christian duties."

The judge nodded and remarked s o t t o v o c e, "That would not be out of the way in some places."

"What is your doctrine?" asked the prosecuting attorney.

"Just what we have in Luther's Catechism and the Bible," was Hauge's ready answer.

"And you have not taught anything else?"

"No, nothing else!" said Hauge, and his honest eyes testified to the truth of his statement.

The judge turned to the "Aktor" and the clerk and said to them in an undertone, "I see nothing wrong in this." Then, turning to Hauge, he said, "My good man, I believe you are innocent."

Hauge's face lighted up with a smile when he replied, "And your honor is a righteous judge!"

"Oh, well, that is what we should be," answered the judge.

Hauge noticed a friendly look on the judge's face that gave him courage to ask, "Pardon me, your honor. Will you permit me a question?"

The judge nodded and said, "Most certainly! What is the question?"

Hauge stood up and in his slow and impressive way said, "Then I wish to ask if it is Christian that they who drink and fight shall have their freedom when I, a regular church-goer, because I some evening may entertain my neighbors with song and talk in true accordance with our state religion, am jailed and threatened with the penitentiary?"

The judge smiled and said, "No, that could not be called Christian, and it is not the intention of the law that it should be called so."

The court took a recess. The judge shook hands with Hauge and said, "It is really absurd that you should stay in prison. I will confer with the chief of police."

Hauge and Barso were again escorted to the city jail.

The next morning Judge Hagerup came to the jail and ordered the prisoners, Hauge and Barso, brought to the sergeant's office.

When they came in, the judge turned to them with a cheerful smile and said, "I have good news for you. The chief is now of the same opinion as I, and you may leave the prison today. But be careful," the judge added, "you must avoid collision with the authorities."

"That I cannot promise," said Hauge with a smile, "unless they be like you—fair and just."

The judge had to smile, as he said, "Oh well, you may meet with some that are worse; therefore it is wise to play safe."

Hauge, on the point of leaving, respectfully asked the judge for an "attest" (certified statement) of his release.

"That I will gladly give," said the judge, and wrote as follows:

"Hans Nielsen Hauge and Kristian Barso have been arrested, but they were found innocent, and moreover, honest and highly respectable, well versed in God's Word. As to knowledge of the salvation of souls they are well-informed. Therefore they were released from prison, and to all concerned well recommended. Oslo, April 20, 1798. Hagerup, Judge."

"I think this will be sufficient," said the judge as he handed the document to Hauge with a smile.

"Thank you! Thank you very much!" said Hauge as he clasped the hand of the judge. "For this God shall reward you in time."

The eyes of Hauge shone very brightly as he bid the judge farewell and left the prison a free man.

CHAPTER XXX

Arrested and Transported

Hauge had intended to return to his home in Thune, but his friends up at Sagene prevailed upon him to stay and have some more meetings in Kr. Grøndahl's lumbershed.

Hauge stayed, and the interest was so great that he preached every day during the noon hour and in the evening. These gatherings soon showed some results. Quite a number became converted and began to show improvement in their daily lives.

On the other hand, many took offense at these gatherings, especially the patrons of a K n e i p e (alehouse) nearby. Every time they went to hear Hauge, their conscience was smitten, and they returned to find balm in a "stein of beer."

This went on several evenings until they were all agreed that the Hauge meetings were a great nuisance, and ought to be stopped.

One evening the barkeeper had secured some unusually good beer (doctored) that they sampled and then went to the lumbershed.

The gathering was so large that the doors were blocked and many people stood outside. When the drunken rowdies started to sing they were hushed by those listening at the openings in the wall; and when they refused to be quiet some husky men hustled them to the K n e i p e.

The barkeeper evidently did not like this so he kept on "stirring up the animal" in those that came to sample his new beer, and they were very busy spreading stories about the "jail-bird" Hauge.

Then Hauge's enemies started another fake story, that he was preaching sedition and insurrection against law and authority. Nobody believed it; but it caused more trouble, and the police became worried.

Finally Captain Knoph decided to seize Hauge and have him taken away. After only eight days of freedom Hauge was again arrested and escorted by deputies to the sheriff in the next district. It happened that many of the sheriffs knew Hauge to be an honest man, so they let him go without escort when they had signed an affidavit that he had reported to them and was on his way home.

The second evening of his journey he found lodging with strangers. Later in the evening the local schoolmaster came in. He had heard that Hauge had been arrested in Fredrikstad and in Oslo and it would be dangerous to have such a bad man.

In a fit of anger the schoolmaster began to abuse Hauge in every conceivable manner, cursing and swearing at him.

Hauge refrained from answering until the schoolmaster was out of wind. Then he tried to show from the Bible that it was not Christ-like to let the passions rule or to behave badly.

"Behave badly!" shouted the schoolmaster; "and do you say that to me? You! You!" and Hauge received a smashing blow on his cheek.

Hauge jumped to his feet and towered like a giant over the little, red-headed schoolmaster. Hot blood coursed through his veins, his face was red with anger, and his grayish-blue eyes were black and burning.

Soon, however, Hauge was able to overcome his

anger, and in his quiet, gentle way said, "You should not have done this; at least"—looking at the scared women—"not in the presence of ladies."

The schoolmaster found new courage in Hauge's quietude, and ordered Hauge out of the house.

Hauge looked at him and said, "Are you the master here?"

"Well, I am that much of a master that I will have you out."

"Well, here you see my fist," said Hauge, holding out his clenched hand, "but I never use it to strike my brother."

"Out! Out with you!" screamed the frenzied schoolmaster, holding the door open, letting in the cold night air.

"Yes, yes!" said Hauge, "but wait until I have settled with the lady for the lodging." Hauge handed her the money, but she refused it, so he laid it on the table and found his coat and hat. He turned to Kristian, who was getting into his overcoat, and said, "Come, let us go!"

As Hauge buttoned his overcoat, he turned to the schoolmaster and said, "It is well to have warm clothes on a cold night, and still better to have the love of Christ in your heart, so that you can pray for those who despitefully use you and persecute you. Good night!"

The schoolmaster stood dumb. This was entirely beyond him. "What kind of man was this?" When they left he burst into tears.

Suddenly he ran out in the dark and called, "Hauge! Come back!"

"Yes!" came a voice from the dark.

"Hauge! Oh, Hauge! Where are you?"

"Here!" the voice answered.

"Hauge! Won't you come back?"

"It is getting late," the voice said.

The schoolmaster again cried, "Oh, Hauge! Can you forgive me?"

"Yes, certainly I will!"

The schoolmaster caught up with Hauge and pleaded, "But my sin is so great. Is there really any forgiveness for me?"

"Yes, God's grace is unlimited; He will forgive," said Hauge.

"Oh, help me, God, to believe that!"

Hans turned and walked to the road where Kristian was waiting.

"No, no! Don't go! Come back!" the schoolmaster cried.

"Oh, we have to go," Hauge answered.

"Where will you go?" the schoolmaster called after him.

"Where God willeth!" answered Hauge. "He will lead us by the hand and guide our feet in the dark. May God's grace and peace come to you. Farewell!"

Hauge and Barso disappeared in the darkness of the night.

* * *

Immediately after his return home, Hauge reported to Herr Radich and gave him the order from the chief in Oslo. Herr Radich smiled indulgently as he took the order and said, "But where is your escort?"

"Escort?" questioned Hauge. "I did not need any to find my way home, and the bailiffs knew that they could trust me."

"Yes, yes," said Radich, "that is well, and now we want you to be good and stay home."

"That I cannot promise," said Hauge. "With the freedom of the press to print whatever I want, I also have the right to sell the books I have printed, not only in my home district, but any place where people will buy my books, just as Kristen Gleng is peddling his goods."

"That is right," said Radich, "so far you are within the confines of the law, but we want no more preaching."

"That I cannot promise either," said Hauge. "When people ask me to sing and talk, it would be rather rude to refuse; and moreover, you never gave an order like this either to Kristen Gleng or to Tresko Ingebrit, when they were preaching."

"Oh, but that is different," said Herr Radich; "they did not amount to anything."

"Well! Is this to be considered a compliment?" asked Hauge smiling. "Then I must thank you and consider it a friendly hint that my intention and labors have not been in vain."

"Excuse me, but I am busy," said Herr Radich abruptly. "Good afternoon."

"Good afternoon," said Hauge, and went home.

CHAPTER XXXI

A Trip to Bergen

Hauge's stay at home to rest was of short duration. He says in his autobiography: "Within me there was an intense desire to commune and converse with my fellowmen about salvation; and, believing according to the Bible that it was my duty to do my share, I was not able to remain quiet for any length of time.

"The authorities varied in their opinions; some were for and some were against me. The Conventicle Act of 1741 was interpreted in different ways, even so as to cast me into prison. Yet, I could not forego my ardent longing to testify to the glory of my Lord and Master, Jesus Christ, and to urge my fellowmen to seek salvation through repentance and conversion."

Hardly a month had passed before he started out again.

He journeyed across to Drammen, where he had many friends. Through a wholesale merchant, M. Moeller, he became acquainted with the master of a merchant vessel from Bergen, who was getting ready for his return voyage.

Hauge immediately secured passage and went to see the city mayor, Strom, who knew him well, to get a passport for the trip. Everything went well, and Hauge felt so happy that he was singing all the day. The skipper said, "You may well be happy, for we are not going to arrest you or molest you— no, not in Bergen!"

Yes, Hauge was happy. When they sailed across the blue waters of Skagerak with a fair wind, the undulating motion of the vessel made him feel a little queer at first, but soon the indisposition left him.

After passing Listerland they turned more to the north, and the south wind gave them smooth sailing along the coast.

Hauge would stand enraptured, watching the ever-changing panorama to the east, or the vast expanse of the North Sea.

They had sailed and sailed, and Bergen was yet far away. When they came as far as Korsfjord the wind went down, and the sails hung limp.

Hauge went up to the skipper and asked, "When do we get to Bergen?"

"Not today, nor tomorrow," the skipper answered. "There is not any wind today, and tomorrow there may be a northwest wind, dead against us."

"Is there some other way of reaching Bergen?" quiried Hauge.

"Perhaps, if we found some fisherman heading that way," answered the skipper. "If I see one, I will hail him."

"Thank you," said Hauge, and he went into the cabin to arrange his things and make ready for a transfer.

Later the skipper came into the cabin smiling and said, "You are in luck. I hailed a rowboat with two men, and they are willing to take you." A hasty hand shake, and Hauge departed.

The next day Hauge landed in Bergen and immediately went to the chief of police to have his pass from Mayor Strom in Drammen viséed.

Hauge had no friends or personal acquaintances in Bergen, so it took him a day to find suitable lodgings. Soon, however, he became acquainted and found people that shared his interest in spiritual work.

One day he came to the shop of Erik Svarstol, a gunsmith, who had formerly been a member of the Hernbutt Brethren. The movement had died, and he was languishing in doubt and loneliness.

Becoming interested in Hauge, he invited him to come and have a meeting in a shed back of his shop, and himself began to send word around.

People came that afternoon in great numbers; especially from the market place where fishermen and gardeners had sold their stock and were ready to sail for home; but the June days were long, so they were in no hurry. Rude seats had been provided, and the room was filled.

After singing a hymn, Hauge read a Scripture lesson and began to talk. He was a little diffident at first, but as he warmed up on the subject his tongue loosened, his voice strengthened, and his delivery became more sweeping. Those inclined to be skeptic began to sit up and listen earnestly.

Everybody listened—it warmed their hearts. The message of God's Word brought home to them the one important question: "How is it with me? Am I right with God?" They were anxious to hear every word.

The preaching was the volcanic thunder of God's Law from Mount Sinai that had reverberated down through the ages to convict men of their sins. And because of these sins, incarcerated in death's prison with Satan as the jailer, no one can ever get out before the last farthing of the debt is paid in full.

Satan knows that, and we ought to know, but we do not until God's Law opens our eyes. Then we begin to see our lost condition—then we begin to see that we need one who can pay our ransom and liberate us from the horrible prison. We have One who has done this; and He will open the prison door for you, for me, for anyone who will accept Christ Jesus as a Savior.

Hauge closed rather abruptly with a short prayer and a closing hymn from the authorized psalmbook. Many came to shake hands with Hauge and express their wishes to hear him again.

When about all had left, a white-haired old lady, still in her chair, hailed Hauge and said: "Will you come over here?" and he stepped over.

Then she continued: "Your name is Hans Hauge, and mine is Maren Roes. I am happy to be acquainted with you! I'm getting old and weak—difficult for me to get anywhere; but I am not sorry for coming down here today." She grasped his hand and continued: "I wish to thank you so very much for that sermon. It was good; it made me young again—it reminded me of my girlhood days when I was converted by the old bishop, Erik Pontoppidan. It was springtime for me then, and the seed of God's Word, lavishly broadcasted, had a vigorous growth.

"Again I thank you, and may God's blessing rest with you and the work you have undertaken to do. Don't forget to look me up some day that I may have another chance to talk of these things."

She hobbled over to the waiting cab and was

helped in. "Farewell, all of you, and do not wait too long before you come and see me."

Meanwhile Erik Svartstol and Samson Traae had found time to debate the ideas of Hauge and his new movement, and the possibilities of success.

They not only endorsed Hauge's endeavors but decided to support him. Here they saw a man especially gifted, a man who was able to open the eyes of people to real Christianity. He would be a blessing to the community. Hence they helped to arrange meetings at which Hauge preached unmolested for over a month.

CHAPTER XXXII

Hauge Finds Protection

Then his enemies began to make trouble, and Hauge was summoned by the police captain to bring his books and give an account of himself.

He did so. After a preliminary examination he was commanded to give up his meetings and public devotions, or go to jail. Hauge would rather go to jail than promise that, but he was not arrested.

The next day Hauge was summoned to appear before the chief of police, and he went cheerfully. The chief asked some questions regarding the books and the doctrines that he advocated.

Hauge answered in his quiet way and quoted the Bible in support. He gave a brief sketch of his life and ended with the following words: "There is no harm in having people gather to sing and pray and upbuild themselves in the fear of the Lord, nor in turning away from vice and crime to live as real Christians should."

"No, I must agree with you," said the chief, "and if you are able to accomplish something in this respect you are more efficient than I am."

Hans smiled as he continued, "The authorities bear not the sword in vain. It is their affair to punish the evil and reward the good."

The chief laughed. "The evil we a r e able to punish; but to e l i m i n a t e it is not so easy."

"Oh, but it can be done," said Hauge, confident and undaunted. "At any rate if the authorities really protect the good work it can be done."

The chief laughed again as he said, "Yes, my dear Mr. Hauge; you mean through yourself; but the Conventicle Act of 1741 prohibits lay people from preaching. We have to uphold the law."

"Yes," answered Hauge, "it is even so; but there is also another ordinance, or law paragraph that says, 'Whoever is found cursing or swearing or blaspheming God's Word shall be put in the pillory.' How about upholding that law?"

The chief had no answer to this. "You ought to take a law course and become an attorney." Then he arose and added: "I will see the district judge, perhaps tomorrow, and present your case. You will have a final decision soon."

"I hope sincerely that the judge is fair and upright as our chief-of-police," said Hauge as he shook his hand and bid him farewell.

Shortly after this the chief went out for lunch. Near the Old Market he met a tall and stately figure that everyone in Bergen knew—a man broad-shouldered, heavy-built, with a high forehead, prominent nose, and bushy eyebrows that shaded a pair of brown eyes which were deep and commanding.

It was the well known Bishop Johan Nordahl Brun, provost and pastor of Korskirken in Bergen.

The chief hailed him and shook hands. "Pardon me, Right Reverend Sir; have you received anything from our magistrate Hauch, regarding a certain traveling layman from eastern Norway, Hans Nielsen Hauge of Thune parish?"

The bishop threw back his head, and with a pleasant voice answered, "Yes, I have, Herr P o l i t i m e s t e r (chief), and I have already given him my definite answer."

The P o l i t i m e s t e r never flinched, but looked deeply into the strong, brown eyes. "Oh, yes, I see; you want him to go free," said the chief, and smiled broadly at the authorative but kindly prelate.

The bishop's bushy eyebrows were raised as he said, "Yes, my God and Creator knows that it is my fervent wish. If half-baked people have the freedom of the press, according to the new law, to write and print criticism on God's Word for the many thousands; then why should not an uneducated man who loves the Word of God have the freedom to speak in a private house to a handful of people willing to listen?"

"But what of his writings, your Reverence?" ventured the chief.

"His writings, did you say? What of his writings?" and the bishop smiled patronizingly, "What did you expect of an untutored son of a farmer from the backwoods of eastern Norway? His writings are poorly constructed and poorly arranged in presentation; but there is nothing conflicting with the Word of God. Hence he is innocent. It is true that there are many inconsistencies, but anyone may make them, even our learned Confessionarius Bastholm." They both laughed very heartily.

Then the bishop quite earnestly said, "Herr Politimester," I want you to do what you can for this honest young man, and keep the street rabble from annoying him or his meetings. Such innocent devotions in all chastity and honor are by far to be preferred to the orgies with drinking-bouts and debaucheries that are spreading defiance of the law and ordinances and the excellent and efficient police force of the city of Bergen."

The chief smiled as he answered, "Yes, yes! We are fully agreed on this, and we may obtain some results—some betterment."

They shook hands and parted.

* * *

The next day Hauge was called to police headquarters and informed of the favors extended by the bishop and the magistrate. The dominant bishop, Johan Nordahl Brun, had spoken, and that was sufficient guarantee for Hauge to continue his work unmolested.

The following weeks and months were glorious days for Hauge. His books were printed, bound and sold; he preached almost every evening, and many were won for Christ, while the earlier converts distinguished themselves by exemplary lives.

Bergen had extensive connections with foreign countries. Hence it had been exposed to foreign influences, even in religion; but the eminently earnest Christian leaders, bishops Erik Pontoppidan and later Johan Nordahl Brun had held them in check.

One of the religious groups that Hauge had not met with before was a mystic cult which based its beliefs on Jacob Böhme's writings. Some of them wanted to argue, but they soon yielded to Hauge.

Then there was another cult, fathered by a Peter Farver whose ancestors came from Holland. In their worship Farver's followers trembled violently when possessed by the spirit. They jumped about trying to speak in tongues, as the "Holy Jumpers" in England were accustomed to do. The men were not permitted to cut their beards or shave; they must not wear boots, but laced shoes. They had fasting days and prohibited certain kinds of food.

Hauge tried to show them that these external observances had very little bearing upon salvation —that it is not "what goes into the mouth," but "what cometh out of the mouth" that makes man unclean. He told them that it was not the cleansing of hands, but the cleansing of hearts that God wanted.

Only a few yielded to Hauge's way of thinking; but many came to his meetings to pick flaws or get an argument with him. They had the idea that an ignorant farmer boy could easily be beaten in an argument; but they soon found it so difficult that they let him alone.

Meanwhile Hauge received letters almost daily from his eastern relatives and friends who wondered why he tarried in Bergen. They needed him badly there, and everywhere. There were complaints of slackers and converts, of backsliding or erring in various ways. Many hours were spent in answering letters alone.

Early in October he preached his farewell sermon in Erik Svartstol's shed. As Hauge shook hands with them at parting, there was a unanimous request that he must promise to come back again.

The next day was stormy and no ships went out. But Hauge found some fishermen from Lervik who were going home, and he obtained passage in an open boat to their home village.

Here he had to stay over on account of storms which raged fiercely for several days. Then he went in an open boat to Haugesund and from there to Stavanger. In all he had traveled in open boats 160 kilometers, or about 110 miles.

The weather continued stormy and cold, so Hauge decided to travel on foot to Egersund, then to Vanse. Here he rested for a few days and made the acquaintance of Rev. P. O. Bugge, who received him very kindly and helped to arrange meetings for him. Hauge next continued on to Kristiansand where he visited with friends.

He went on foot to Arendal and then on to Kragerø, and further on to Skien and Tunsberg, finally reaching Drammen two days before Christmas. He had traveled about 840 kilometers, or over 500 miles —perhaps 600 miles, as he did not always take the "short cuts."

By this time Hauge had sold all his books and had preached nearly 100 sermons at more than 50 places along his route, so his friend Moeller, the merchant prince of Drammen, urged him to stay and "take a good, long rest," as he put it.

On Christmas Day, Hauge went to church as usual. Afterwards he had many requests to come and give talks at various places. They were so persistent that he had to promise, and his "long rest" was cut short.

CHAPTER XXXIII

Happenings at Eker

The calendar had reached the twenty-seventh of December, and the year 1798 was drawing to a close. At the Hoen farm near Eker, about twelve miles west of Drammen, the people were preparing for New Year. The farmer Kristofer Hoen was standing at the gate smoking a pipe.

At the roadside a tall and heavily built man sat in his sleigh, holding back a nervous and restless horse. In his shaggy, wolfskin coat he looked a veritable giant, and the heavy, blond beard on his square-jawed face gave him the look of a fierce Viking. His dark blue eyes were cold as steel. It was the well known sheriff, Jens Gram of the Eker district. He had swapped horses with a neighbor and wanted Hoen's opinion of the deal.

Kristofer Hoen drew a few puffs from his pipe, looked at the horse critically and very deliberately, then spat—and said, "That is too weak a horse for you, Herr Sheriff."

The sheriff smiled, "Oh, but I think he will do."

Hoen spat again and said, "Well! You have one consolation; if the horse gives up you can pull him through, but there will be little speed."

The sheriff laughed, but there was a certain coldness in his laughter as he said, "There need not be such haste."

Hoen joined in the laugh too and added, "Oh, no, not haste; y o u are mostly well-timed when coming."

Sheriff Gram did not like farmer Hoen's rather taunting remarks, so he said curtly as he made ready to go, "Perhaps, it happens."

"By the way," said farmer Hoen as he took the pipe from his mouth, "do you know that Hans Nielsen Hauge has come?"

The sheriff jerked his head around as if stung, "What!—when did he come," he cried.

"He came last night," answered farmer Hoen.

The eyes of the sheriff darkened. "Where does he stay?" he asked.

"He stays with me," Hoen said.

Sheriff Gram's face reddened and he swore, "The devil, you say!"

"No, I did not say that." And the eyes of the farmer shone darkly.

Gram smiled derisively but he said no more.

"Yes," said Hoen, "there will be a gathering here New Year's Eve. You are welcome, too."

Gram smiled again as he answered, "Thank you! Perhaps I w i l l come."

"Yes, I wish you would. I have invited the pastor also; then we can see if there is anything wrong in hearing the Word of God."

In a somewhat sinister way the sheriff nodded assent. "Yes, we shall see," he said, and he turned the horse to the road and drove off.

* * *

On New Year's afternoon there was an extremely large gathering at the Hoen farmstead. Most of the influential farmers in the district were present and filled up the spacious rooms.

The pastor, Rev. Fr. Schmidt, had arrived, and with him came Sheriff Jens Gram. It was safer to have the sheriff along.

Kristofer Hoen went out to receive them in his cordial way, and when the sheriff's face darkened at the sight of the "mob" the farmer explained, "Yes, we have a respectable gathering here this afternoon. I hope you have not come to arrest the whole community."

"Oh, no," answered the sheriff, "I will be satisfied with less."

"Well, come right in," Hoen said, "the house is full, but we'll find a place. It may be narrow though, for a giant of your size."

Hauge arose and gave the number of the hymn to be sung. Then Pastor Schmidt stood up and, with a dignified wave of his hand to the audience, stated with authority, "My dear parishioners! Before going further I will read to you the Conventicle Act of January 13, 1741. Then perhaps to continue will be superfluous."

He coughed and cleared his throat as he opened the document, then read it aloud, the audience remaining profoundly silent.

As he finished reading he looked around and then explained, "From this you will understand that such devotional assemblies are unlawful, and such roving lay preachers are guilty of a misdemeanor and have incurred a penalty according to law. Therefore you must separate and go back to your homes quietly. I presume that until now you have in ignorance been offenders against law and good order."

Hauge had sat quietly while the pastor read the ordinance; but now he stood up and with a firm but gentle tone said, "This is not through ignorance as your worthy Reverence has presumed. I am quite well acquainted with this Conventicle Act, and it does not say that lay people are forbidden to read God's Word together. If it were so that a Christian community had such an unchristian law, then would I call the attention of your worthy Reverence to a higher ordinance that reads, 'We must obey God rather than men.'"

There was a satisfied murmur running through the audience, and the worthy pastor turned red with anger. He jumped up and shouted, "This assembly must disperse immediately. In the name of the law I demand obedience to the government and its magistrates."

The sheriff now arose, tall and commanding, to give weight to the pastor's fierce demands.

Farmer Hoen had been standing ominously quiet. Now he spoke with dignity and a determined ring, "Stop, worthy pastor. You may sit down, Sheriff Gram. Neither of you is in command here. This is my house. My neighbors here are my guests and I do not want them insulted. The only person you have a right to demand is Hans Hauge, but you have to prove him guilty of false doctrine before you arrest him. We want to hear him preach."

The farmers arose in a body to support Mr. Hoen and repeated his demand, "We want to hear him preach; that's what we came here for. And you shall stay and hear him too, worthy pastor."

Pastor Schmidt, seeing the many angry faces around him, found it advisable to sit down, and so did the sheriff.

Hauge read a few verses from Revelation about the vices of the harlot and the wanton frivolities of the world. He made a burning appeal to turn away from the wicked world and seek God's kingdom in the time of grace. In closing Hauge showed them the beauty of a Christian life and the blessing of right living, working together in peace and harmony, strengthening one another, and doing good to one and all.

Hauge sat down. His talk was brief but telling. Wrinkles of disdain and scorn were plainly visible on the pastor's face, and the eyes of the sheriff blazed with hatred at Hauge.

Pastor Schmidt arose and said, "According to what I now have heard, I find that Hauge's conduct is both illegal and irregular. His talk with its many quotations from the Bible shows ignorance and poor understanding. It is poorly constructed, ill-advised, and improperly applied. It is evident that he needs to learn rather than to teach others.

"Furthermore, Hauge has preached out of the book of Revelation. This alone shows how immature he is. My sainted father, who was a very learned man, never ventured to expound Revelation, for it is a closed book."

Hauge, standing near, patted the pastor on the shoulder and with a smile said, "Revelation is not a closed book, for then it would not be called Revelation. We read every book in the Bible and talk as God gives us grace and wisdom. Of ourselves we are nothing; that you know as well as I. But to God nothing is impossible. The Spirit of God may dwell in the illiterate as well as in the very learned scholars."

The pastor sat down. Nothing could be said to this; but then something came to his mind. He was an officer of the king and of God.

Again he arose with all the dignity and prestige he could command and said, "As rational remonstrance is of no avail, we are wasting time, and I am compelled to call upon the sheriff to execute the will of the government according to law. Do thy duty, Sheriff!"

The sheriff went forward to Hauge and took him by the arm saying, "You have to come with me!"

Hauge, turning around quickly, wrenched himself free. "There is no need of violence, Herr Sheriff. I am a law-abiding citizen and will go with you in peace."

The farmers began to stir and murmured, "It is wicked and outrageous to use violence on a peaceful man."

"The law will have its course, so do not interfere," said Hauge to those standing near him, as he shook hands with them and bade them farewell.

The pastor, the sheriff and the prisoner forced their way out.

"Come here, Hauge!" the sheriff shouted.

"No," said Kristofer Hoen, "it is not proper for either pastor or sheriff to sit in the sleigh with Hans Nielsen Hauge. I am a simple farmer as he is, and I will serve as the sheriff's assistant today."

"You sit here, Hauge," Hoen called and turned up the heavy robe.

The sheriff did not like this arrangement, but seeing the threatening looks of the crowd, he simply said, "All right, Hoen! You may convey the prisoner. I don't object."

"Yes," answered farmer Hoen, "drive ahead, Hr. Sheriff!"

As they started, Hoen nodded to the bystanders. They all noticed that he was driving his best race horse, and they hurried into their sleighs to see the race. The sleigh bells jingled lustily, but there was no race.

When they came to the Eker church, the pastor turned in, waving his hand in farewell. The others turned in on the side roads to their respective homes, somewhat disappointed that there was no race.

At last only the two rigs remained, and the

sheriff breathed more easily for he had feared trouble from the farmers.

They were jogging along easily until Hoen happened to touch the racer "Borken" with his whip, and like a flash he passed the sheriff and raced up the road as on a race course.

When Hoen neared the sheriff's residence, the sheriff was almost half a mile behind; but Hoen did not stop. He went on to the Drammen river and turned east on the old race course, where Borken, his horse, had won many victories.

When the sheriff reached the home hill, he could see the Hoen rig as a dark speck moving more than a mile away.

The sheriff was boiling within, cursing his foolishness in letting that foxy farmer make sport of him. But he was not in the humor to yield, so he started in pursuit. He might yet get Hauge.

After driving several miles on the Drammen river he turned up on the highway to Roeken. At the first farmhouse he stopped and inquired if they had seen Kristofer Hoen pass along that way.

"Yes, he went by a while ago."

"Which way did he go?"

"Evidently heading for Roeken."

"Did he drive fast?"

"I should say! He drove Borken."

Sheriff Gram drove on. He stopped at several places and inquired. The same answers were given even at the last farm in his district.

He knew he was beaten, but he wanted to find out for sure; so he went on a few miles and came to a farmstead where a relative of Hoen resided. Here he turned in and saw Hoen's racer hitched to a post.

He tied his horse and went in.

"Good evening, Gram! Welcome!" said Hoen, who was sitting with Hauge at the table drinking coffee.

Sheriff Gram did not deign to answer. His face blazed with anger. He came over to Hoen and pounded his fist so hard on the table that the teacups jumped and jingled.

"I will get you for this, Hr. Kristofer Hoen," he shouted.

"Get me? For what?" said Hoen innocently. "Didn't I follow the given order to the letter to bring the prisoner out of the Eker district and into the next on his way home?"

The sheriff knew this to be correct, but Hoen was not a sworn deputy, so the sheriff simply ignored him.

He turned abruptly to Hauge and said with intense bitterness, "Now, you have to come with me, and no fooling this time."

Hauge deliberately poured some coffee on the saucer, balanced it on his fingers and cooled it before he drank it. Then he said, "No, Hr. Sheriff, I shall not need your escort on my way home. I have traveled alone before and I can do so now. Moreover, you are outside of your district, and you have no authority here. You have not even a warrant for me. I was deputy sheriff in my home district," continued Hauge, "and I may as well remind you that it is best for both you and me to stay within the limits of the law."

Of course the sheriff knew this, but it added fuel to his anger, and he turned abruptly to Hoen, struck the table again with his heavy fist and roared, "This shall be costly fun for you, Mr. Kristofer Hoen!"

Mr. Hoen rose from his chair, took a step nearer the sheriff, looked him squarely in the eye, and advised, "Now listen to me, Hr. Sheriff. Hans Hauge gave you good advice, but you are still blustering. If you persist in this manner, I may have to serve as flunky again, but then it will be y o u receiving free conveyance out of the district. For the good name of Eker L e h n (county) cannot afford to have a sheriff that spitefully seeks to molest innocent people and put them in jail."

Hoen, who was filling his pipe, turned to the fireplace to light it.

The sheriff, grumbling something about rustic impudence, turned and left, slamming the door.

The visitors and the family could not help having a good laugh. Even Hauge smiled as he said to Hoen, "This was not according to my good will and intention."

"No, but it was according to mine—and that of Borken," said Hoen. "I wanted the sheriff to know that he had bought a poor horse."

CHAPTER XXXIV

Second Trip to Bergen

Hauge continued eastward, but the sheriffs of the eastern counties gave no trouble. He sold his books and preached from place to place, even to the boundary of Sweden. He did not reach home until the first of April, 1799.

As usual, he helped with the spring work. Every mail brought him letters from his many friends, requesting him to come and help them. The most persistent came from Bergen, where his friends were not molested by the authorities, but were living in peace. This was perhaps the safest place for Hauge himself in all Norway at this time.

Thus, like Putnam, he left the plow and started for the field of action. He went to Drammen where his good friend Jens Strom, the city mayor, again furnished him with a passport to Bergen.

Then he continued his journey to Eker, to visit Kr. Hoen who had helped him the winter before. Sheriff Gram had spotted him and arrested the lone traveler on the highway where no one interfered. Out of spite he had kept him in jail several days without warrant or hearing. Hauge's friends, however, were busy, and the sheriff hurried Hauge over to Kongsberg where Judge Jonas Collett gave him a hearing. Here the district council set him free, to the great disappointment of the sheriff.

Hauge stayed at Kongsberg for some time and preached to the men working in the mines. A spiritual awakening resulted. Later Hauge extended his mission into Nummedal and up the valley into Norre and Opdal, then across the mountains into Hardanger and on to Bergen.

His friends in Bergen were glad when he came. They offered him inducements if he would settle there and make his home with them. The wealthy old lady, Maren Boes, was perhaps the most insistent, and she invited Hauge to her home.

He accepted this invitation and a very handsome lady met him at the door. She showed him into a room where Madam Boes sat dressed for company.

The young lady took a long look at Hauge and stepped aside. She evidently thought him a fine young man.

Madam Boes asked him to be seated and began, "Yes, I sent for you, because your sermons spoke to my soul in a way I never experienced since our venerable Bishop Pontoppidan died; it made me feel young again. But my body is old and weak, and soon I must leave. Yes, I thank God who sent you here to warm my heart and edify my soul when I had become cold and callous in my advanced years. I appreciate it more than you think or understand; and therefore, I want to do something handsome for you. I have here a valuable estate and no heirs, so I have thought that when I have to depart in the near future you shall have what is left after me—if you will locate here."

She looked at him with a warm and genial smile on her face.

"Well, what do you say to that?"

Hans Nielsen Hauge had had many surprises in his day; but this was a novel experience. He could hardly believe his ears. His face paled and his eyes stared in bewilderment.

Visions of a nice, elegant home and a beautiful wife, a tempting glimpse of paradise on earth, flitted through his mind.

His eyes shone, but became cloudy as he was reminded by the inner man that earthly pleasures are but vanity, quickly passing. The struggle was hard, but did not last long. He shook his head.

Madam Boes in turn became surprised. Was it diffidence, or what? She stared and wondered.

Hans, regaining his mental balance, stood up and grasped her hand. Then, in a voice weak from emotion, he said, "I want to thank you a thousand times for your kindness and love and your good intentions towards me, and the cause of God's kingdom; but it is not for me—I cannot accept."

"Not accept! And why not?" It was Madam Boes who now stared in bewilderment.

"No, I cannot accept," continued Hauge, "because of God's kingdom. For me it would be very pleasant to stay here in Bergen among these many good friends. I could wish for nothing better here in this world. But think of all the spiritually starved souls throughout the land. They sit in darkness—waiting for someone to start the fires. It would be a mortal sin against these people if I stayed here in peace while they suffered."

Madam Boes had listened in silence, but now she stood up, grasped his other hand, and, with eyes brimful, spoke, "Hans! You are a wonderful man of sterling worth. I never dreamt of meeting one like you. But I feel that you are right. The gifts and talents God gave you must not be buried but spread far and wide, that the harvest may be so much greater."

"Now, you go where God directs you. I will not tempt you away from such a blessed undertaking. God bless you and be with you."

"Farewell!" said Hans, "and God bless you for your goodness." His voice was husky from restrained emotion.

In the entry he again met the young lady who had opened the door for him. She held out her hand, and, preoccupied in mind though he was, it dawned upon him that he had seen the girl before.

"God's peace and blessing!" she said, a warm color on her face.

"Thanks! And peace to you," he replied. "But you have changed," he added with warmth. "I did not recognize you. How did you happen to come to Bergen?"

"I have relatives here," she answered.

He hesitated a little, and then, "Have you found salvation?" he asked.

"Yes," she answered, "and, thanks to you, I have found peace; and I thank you evermore for what you told me that evening in Fredrikstad."

His eyes grew big with wonder.

"I remember only that it was the most shameful evening of my life," he put in, with downcast face.

"Yes, I know," she hastened to add; "but I knew you were good, and you tried to make me good, even though bad men came and forced you to drink to make you as bad as they were. But that opened my eyes as nothing else could have done. I did not believe it when you said that God-fearing people were happy; but afterwards I felt that I would rather by far be unhappy as you were, than be happy as they were that evening. When I heard that you had left I left for home too. I wanted to know more about what you told me, and I had an aunt who was a "lesar" (a Bible reader), who could help me. She was glad when I came, and more so when she heard what I wanted. Last year I came to visit my relatives here and became acquainted with Madam Boes, who engaged me to be with her in her advanced years."

"God be praised!" Hans said devoutly; "now I can see God's finger where all was darkness before. How wonderful it was that God found you in such a manner!"

"Yes, wasn't it!" she exclaimed, "and—I believed once that a child of God could never be happy. How dark is our reason, how foolish are the worldly people. Only yesterday I had run errands until I was very tired, and when I came home to rest, Madam had another hamper full of eatables to take out to a sick widow with several children. My mind rebelled, my limbs and muscles and everything within me rebelled; but I went. When I came to the place the door stood ajar and I heard a tiny voice praying, 'Give us this day our daily bread' and I waited outside until they were through praying. When I came in and saw the happy, expectant faces of the starved children I forgot all about being tired. I forgot everything except being glad with them."

She held out her hand—"I want to thank you again for the wonderful words that you gave me to open my eyes."

"We will thank God," he answered, "and may God's grace and peace remain with you in the days to come. God has been kind to you, and you will appreciate it more and more in the service of Madam Boes who is such an earnest and devout Christian."

"And—I am so glad I have met you again," she said, "you preached a valuable sermon for me today when talking to Madam Boes. I shall not soon forget. God bless you—"

Their hands met in a firm clasp. There was a lingering look as he bid her farewell and wished her God's blessing.

"May God keep you and protect you!" she answered. "Farewell!"

Hauge walked down the street as in a dream. He felt that his resolution to remain firm to his calling was tumbling. Human nature within him was very strong, now that it was aroused.

Thoughts on this subject occupied his mind until he reached "Fiskebryggen" wharf. Then, seeing the great number of boats at the landing, he decided to leave. His friends protested, but he was firm and told them that other places needed him far more than Bergen.

* * *

He traveled north and visited the parishes in Søndfjord, Nordfjord, Sunmør, Surendalen and Rindalen and landed in Trondheim the first week in August, 1799. The journey had taken two months, but he felt that the time was well spent. He had found many willing to turn to the Lord.

CHAPTER XXXV

At Trondheim

Of the various newspapers in Norway at this time the Intelligents-Sedlerne in Oslo had perhaps the largest circulation. It was radically conservative and of course made sport of the "Laymen's movement." Other papers followed in its wake and quoted Intelligents-Sedlerne as an authority, especially in criticism.

The leading paper in Trondheim was Trondhjemske Tidende. In its issue dated August ninth, 1799, an editorial thundered loudly against laymen. Translated, part of it read as follows:

"One of the peasant preachers, Niels Iversen Riis, nineteen years old, who, according to I n t e l-l i g e n t s-S e d l e r n e, has infested the southern part of Norway with this lay preaching, has of late strayed into these parts. This frantic freak is ranting against sin and the lust of the flesh, valiantly defending his claim to preach the true Word of God. According to reports he was recently arrested in Molde and tried, but appealing to a higher tribunal, he was brought here and lodged in jail.

"It seems that too much reading in the Bible and too much prayer and devotion has caused derangement of his brain and unbalanced his mind. He claims that the Holy Ghost has injected this drollery into his head.

"Sound reasoning is of no avail, and he refuses to be convinced. With quotations from the Bible he refutes anyone trying to gainsay him.

"Against the wicked ways of the world and the lust of the flesh he is especially enraged. Jail does not depress but rather uplifts him, making him think he is worthy of a martyr's crown."

Further on the editorial continued:

"The notorious Hans Nielsen Hauge, the high-priest and chief of this holy gang which has been roving about the country, has also arrived; but so far he has not been arrested. These vagrants may become dangerous to public safety if revolutionary ideas enter their heads.

"These crippled souls are most dangerous enemies of progress and civilization. Multitudes gape in wonder at this exotic display, raising bulwarks against honest efforts of public teachers to dispel the darkness of ignorance and want of knowledge.

"It is therefore to be hoped that these religious vagabonds be subjected to drastic measures, apprehended for actual vagrancy and taken to the house of correction."

* * *

A layman, Lars Olsen Hemstad, from Stange parish, had traveled and held meetings all the way north into the Trondheim diocese without being arrested. However, at Inderøen he was apprehended, to be transported to Trondheim for trial. The bailiff knew him to be honest and permitted him to go alone.

Arriving at Trondheim, Hemstad reported immediately to the district judge, Count Moltke, who, upon reading the documents, asked a few questions and then dismissed him.

He went to the newspaper office and got a copy of the last issue of the paper. Upon reading the above quoted editorial he was glad to find that H. N. Hauge had arrived. Shortly after this he met Hauge at a printing shop where he was making arrangements to get his books printed. The two men went to a lodging house, and Hemstad handed Hauge the paper, showing him the article he had just read.

Hauge, too, read the editorial, then looked at Hemstad and shook his head. "So great then is their wickedness," he exclaimed.

"Yes," answered Hemstad, "and we cannot expect anything else from worldly-minded people. They look upon us as visionary fanatics."

Hemstad next related what had happened along the way from Hedemarken to Levanger, and how he had been arrested when he came to Inderøen, thirty miles northeast of Trondheim.

Hauge smiled when Hemstad related how the bailiff let him go alone to the judge to present himself for trial.

"That's right," Hauge said, "Let them understand that we are honest and law-abiding citizens, and that we aim at the welfare of the land. But what about Riis? Is he still in jail?"

"No," said Hemstad, "they let him out, and he returned to Meldalen to continue preaching. They tried to arrest him again, but the farmers went to the pastor and demanded his freedom. Their demand was immediately granted, as the pastor did not like the threatening looks of the crowd."

Hauge nodded as he said, "It is too bad that injustice can stir people to use force. It is apt to bring evil results which will be grave hindrances to our cause."

* * *

When Hauge brought his passport to chief of police Klingenberg, it was viséed without any questions. Shortly afterwards a policeman ordered Hauge back to headquarters.

The chief of police asked him, "Are you the notorious lay preacher, Hans Nielsen Hauge?"

"Yes, Hans Nielsen Hauge is my name, but I claim no notoriety."

"Well, you will come with me to the district judge, Count Moltke, under guard of police," said the chief.

When they arrived at the tribunal, the chief of police presented complaint against Hauge and demanded that he be adjudged a vagrant and transported to his home parish.

Hauge protested against this. Handing the judge his passport he declared, "The chief of police has endorsed it, and I have freedom to come and go and carry on my business wherever I please."

The chief turned red with anger. His bluff had miscarried. The peasant boy had more "spunk" than he had thought. So he said, "That is your privilege, but as a vagrant you are still a lawbreaker."

"I am no vagrant," answered Hauge. "I came

here to have my books printed, and I should be permitted to do that here in Trondheim as well as at any other place in the land."

"Where will you have the books printed?" asked the judge.

"At Stefansen's job printing shop," Hauge replied.

"The books will be sealed and sent back," said the chief.

"Is that the law?" Hauge asked. "And is the press so hampered?"

The judge arose and began to pace the floor. After a while he said, "The law may perhaps be so construed."

"You may do as you think best and warrantable," answered Hauge.

Finally the judge turned to Hauge, saying, "You may go!"

"Thank you," said Hauge. "But what about the books?"

"You may print them," responded the judge. Hauge bowed to the two in authority and left.

"A remarkable man," exclaimed Count Moltke when the door closed.

"A dangerous man," amended Chief Klingenberg.

"No, I do not think so," said the judge. "Do you remember Gamaliel?"

"Yes, but anyway he is a most dangerous man when he can win even such men as you," said the chief.

CHAPTER XXXVI

Interviewed by Authorities

Hauge was a busy man now. The old adage, "Make hay while the sun shines," became truly his motto. He wanted his books off the press while the authorities were friendly.

One day one of his friends, Ole Roersveen, came all the way from Bergen to visit him. It was a surprise to Hauge, but he was glad to have fresh news from his many friends. "Yes, they send you their greetings, especially Samson Traae and Madam Boes, who think you should come back to Bergen and settle down," said Roersveen. "In fact we all think you should settle in Bergen as a resident citizen and engage in trade, to destroy the idea of vagrancy. In short, we want to make this lay movement permanent, with headquarters at Bergen and you as our leader."

Hauge sat quiet, in deep thought. A warm, gentle smile illumined his face; the light of an awakening passion shone from his eyes.

Roersveen looked at him, wondering what Hauge had on his mind. Hauge saw and understood; so he said, "I had the same vision when I was in Bergen and Madam Boes made that wonderful offer—I saw myself just as you pictured it. But I do not think God wants it that way. The apostle Peter said, 'We must obey God rather than men.'"

Roersveen sat spellbound. How could a man be so devoid of selfishness that he would sacrifice everything for God's kingdom? No, this was beyond him.

* * *

Hauge was busy with his books, and Hemstad and Roersveen were busy talking with people about their spiritual welfare.

A week later Hauge came to the office of the judge, Count Moltke, to report as ordered. The judge received him very kindly, invited him to be seated, and said, "I want to have a good long talk. First I want you to explain about your home life and how it came about that you have taken up this activity of preaching without being a minister."

Hauge felt elated at this show of friendliness. He narrated freely the outstanding features of his life, and without reserve.

The judge listened understandingly, with an occasional nod.

When Hauge had finished the judge remarked, "I cannot say otherwise than that the work, as you have explained it, has a very commendable object and must be good."

"Yes," answered Hauge, "God's Word is true and good, and it has been the guide of my doings as it is of yours and of other good people's."

The judge did not answer this, but continued in his own train of thought, "Persuading people to abstain from swearing and drinking, from immorality and vice cannot be evil, or I am no judge. I just wish we had more men like you to combat the evils of today."

Hauge arose and said, "God will surely raise up more men, especially if the authorities will help them on."

"I shall certainly put no hindrance in the way of the good cause," promised the judge, "if everything is conducted with decorum and within the confines of the law."

"Assuredly I will do that," said Hauge, "provided that temporal law does not conflict with the Word of God."

The judge smiled. "We assume that they do not conflict."

Hauge sobered as he said, "Yes, we assume that

our laws conform to God's Word, but man-made laws are not infallible. They change with time according to circumstances. Your Honor, with your authority and influence, you would be the first one to change what is unjust or in conflict with God's Word."

"You refer to the Conventicle Ordinance of January 13, 1741, forbidding lay preaching?" queried the judge.

"I dare say I do," answered Hauge.

The judge nodded. "That ordinance may be rather antiquated now that we have freedom of the press. But that law can be interpreted to adapt itself to local circumstances."

"I understand," said Hauge. "It is a good ordinance, where we have a good Christian government, but bad where authorities are contrary."

The judge was silent for some time before he said, "We shall hope that it may not happen very often." Count Moltke arose then and patted his visitor on the shoulder as he said, "Whatever then the consequence may be, you will continue to do what is right and what is good, and in these efforts no one shall hinder you. Farewell, my friend!"

"Farewell," said Hauge as their hands clasped firmly. "Farewell! May peace remain with you. God will reward you for this."

*　*　*

As the judge went out to lunch a little later, he met the Rt. Reverend Bishop Schonheyder on the street.

"Today I have talked with a most remarkable man," said Count Moltke to the bishop.

"With whom, my dear Count?" he asked.

Count Moltke smiled and said, "With one of your clan!"

The bishop registered some deep thought. "No,

this is beyond my ability to conjecture," he said, with a wondering look.

"I have talked with that extraordinary lay preacher, Hans Nielsen Hauge," ventured the count.

The bishop took a hasty step backward and looked at the count with staring eyes and coloring face, as he exclaimed, "What! Is he here? He shall be arrested!"

"No, absolutely not! The man is not only remarkable, but eminently useful."

"Ah!" said the bishop with head thrown back and eyes wide, as if greatly shocked. "Do we understand that he is under protection?"

The count nodded as he replied, "No, your Reverence, I desire not so much to protect him as to render him justice. Examine him yourself. He is a very remarkable man. Adieu, your Excellency."

They shook hands and set out in opposite directions.

* * *

The next day Hauge received orders to appear before Bishop Schonheyder to give an account of himself. He came to the bishop's study at the appointed hour. As Hauge came inside the bishop leaned back in his easy chair. He sat as in a trance. Was this an apparition? At last he managed to say, "You are Hans Nielsen Hauge!"

"Yes," answered Hauge in his quiet manner, "that is my name."

The bishop took another long look, then said, "Oh, indeed!" Then he took off his spectacles, apparently awakened from his trance, and sat up in his chair, continuing, "Judge Count Moltke tells me that you have come up here to preach the gospel and convert people."

"Yes, to show people what is good and to teach them to abstain from what is bad, as drinking, gambling and swearing," added Hauge.

The bishop's eyes opened wide as he looked more carefully at this unusual man. Then he said, "That is p e r s e commendable, but have you a call for this?"

"Yes," said Hauge, "every Christian has a calling—yea, a duty—to lead his brethren to what is good."

"In a way, yes, that is true; but this traveling around the country, devoting yourself to the work of converting people, necessitates a special call."

The bishop stared fixedly at Hauge and then said, "And you have this special call, have you?"

"I have," answered Hauge. "Through struggle and suffering the call has been made clear to me."

The bishop looked at Hauge as if he had made up his mind and said, "You should become a schoolmaster; for whoever wishes to become a teacher in a Christian land must have a certain assigned service officially recognized by the government; otherwise it is an offense against the Conventicle Act of 1741."

"Thank you, but I could not do that, your Excellency," said Hauge. "To become a schoolmaster takes many years. This work that I have cannot be postponed. Wherever you go you meet people cursing and swearing, addicted to drunkenness, vices and unlawful doings. All such wickedness must be fought against with might and main if the whole people shall not perish."

The bishop's brow wrinkled as he reluctantly said, "Well, yes. If you understand the art of curing people addicted to strong drink, no one will forbid you this activity; but converting people from vice is difficult."

He arose from his chair, as Hauge answered, "I have had some experience in the short time that I have traveled. Unfortunately, however, not all will be converted; but I have by the help of God turned many away from their evil ways into a Christian life. That gives me cause to continue, even if many remain in their sins. Your Excellency continues to preach, too, although so few, as you say, turn away from vice."

The bishop reddened at the bold words and said, "Indeed I will continue, and you may do the same, provided law and order is observed. And now farewell!" He held out his hand and Hauge shook it heartily.

As Hauge walked down the street the bishop observed, "A remarkable man! Hm—a most remarkable man; but he is also a dangerous man." Then he took a pinch of snuff.

CHAPTER XXXVII

Leinstrand and Melhus

Hauge had been very busy during these weeks, getting his books off the press; yet he had managed to have meetings in the various parts of Trondheim. Especially was he successful in the Baklandet suburb, where quite a number were converted.

Fortunately, the judge, Count Gerhardt Moltke, was able to protect Hauge, so he held meetings unmolested. He also traveled and held meetings in ever-widening circles around Trondheim.

The leading man in Melhus, Mikkel Grendahl, was won by Hauge, and he became a staunch friend. Years later, when Grendahl was elected member of the Storthing (Parliament), he worked hard to awaken sentiment for a repeal of the Conventicle Act. But he failed in every attempt. It took forty years before the sentiment changed enough to have the law repealed.

From Melhus, Hauge came to Leinstranden. Here he won the sheriff and preached at his house. Many that formerly were addicted to drink and accompanying vices were converted. Drinking bouts began falling off, and on Sunday evenings the neighbors gathered to sing and read and pray—even singing on their way home when the weather permitted.

Perhaps one of the happiest was the sheriff, Iver Monsen, who stoutly defended Hauge when he saw the good results of his preaching; he freely admitted that the Word of God had proved itself stronger than the arm of the law.

On the other hand the seventy-seven year old pastor of Melhus, Hans Eriksen Steenbuch, who came down to the Leinstranden annex to preach once a month, did not like this s v e r m e r i (swarming like bees) as he called it. He was an out-and-out rationalist who wanted to do all the preaching himself. From the pulpit he thundered against l æ s e r i e t (reading the Bible) and threatened the l æ s e r e with prison and penitentiary.

Pastor Steenbuch ordered Iver Monsen to arrest Hauge, but the sheriff refused and sent a remonstrance to the pastor.

But the old rationalist wanted revenge and sent word to Bishop Schonheyder in Trondheim, who came on the ninth of December, 1799. He ordered those who had conducted meetings within the parish to appear before His Reverence, Bishop Schonheyder, in Melhus parsonage.

Hauge and Hemstad came and were admitted to the presence of the prelates. Schonheyder shook hands with them. The hand-shakes angered Steenbuch, whose face was scarlet beneath his halo of white hair.

The bishop spoke, "And you have begun in this neighborhood?"

"Yes," answered Hauge, "and it was with your permission."

Pastor Steenbuch, who was rather deaf, raised

his hand to his ear to catch the words. "Permission! Did you say permission?" he shouted.

"That I never gave!" shouted the bishop in a loud voice for the benefit of Pastor Steenbuch.

This surprised Hauge, and he said, "When last we met, there was nothing in the way." He stood straight and quiet.

Pastor Steenbuch again shouted, "What was in the way?"

Hauge went over and shouted into his ear, "Nothing!"

The pastor jerked his chair aside to prevent a contact with this vulgar brute, and looked at the bishop.

The bishop spoke in a loud voice, "You have grossly misunderstood me." Then, turning to the pastor, "He has misunderstood me."

Steenbuch nodded eagerly and said, "Of course, of course! Such men willfully misunderstand everything."

Hauge's face turned red at this insult, but he overcame his anger and said in his firm and quiet manner, "Your Excellency said, however, very plainly, that you had nothing against my activities. As to that there can never be any misunderstanding."

"That I never said," shouted the bishop. "Only when law and ordinances are observed have you my sanction, otherwise not—of course."

"Then," answered Hauge, "I know that I am not guilty of having disturbed law and order or the public peace, but rather have I helped to uphold and maintain the law."

The bishop was impressed at Hauge's strong answers, and said, "All this is quite possible. I do not doubt your good intentions—" The bishop pondered awhile, then continued, "Do you know the ordinance of 1741,—the so-called Conventicle Act?"

"Yes, I do," answered Hauge. "It is an antiquated act that should be repealed, as it is against the Word of God."

"Against the Word of God!" shouted the bishop.

"Against the Word of God!" echoed the pastor.

"Yes," answered Hauge. "God's Word commands all Christians to make all mankind partakers of the truth, and to proclaim God's Word to everybody; but the ordinance of January 13, 1741, will punish with prison and penitentiary anyone who obeys this command."

The bishop turned away from Hauge, looked at the pastor for an inspiration, scratched his head, and turned again, saying, "Evidently you have not read what Paul says (1 Cor. 7:20), 'Let each man abide in that calling wherein he was called.'"

"Yes," said Hauge, "I have read that, and also the words in the next verse: 'But if thou canst become free, use it rather.' God hath delivered me from the bondage of sin, and I cannot continue to see my neighbor remain in the chains of sin and be silent."

The bishop cleared his throat with a rasping sound before he spoke. "That is another question, my good man. If you had remained at home and talked with your neighbors—the real neighbors—all would have been well. But to roam about the land is against the Conventicle Act, as well as against law and order in any well-organized community."

A faint trace of a smile flitted across Hauge's serene face as he heard this. He answered calmly, "I never thought that my neighbors were limited to a small circle around my home. When God commands: 'Love thy neighbor as thyself' He has not set any limitations. He does not say, 'Love thy neighbors in Thune parish and hate the people in Melhus,' and I do not think your Excellency sees it that way."

The bishop turned to Hauge and said, "You do not understand this, but you will soon understand. I demand obedience to the King's law. If it is not given, severe punishment will immediately follow, 'for he beareth not the sword in vain'" (Rom. 13:4).

Hauge calmly put in, "In this you have the privilege of doing as you please, and you can defend yourself before God and man."

The choleric pastor grew more angry as he shouted, "You are attacking us most viciously. You are charging us with every imaginable vice—you—you—you!"

The aged man's wrath deprived him of voice and words.

Hauge walked close up to him, looking him straight in the eye. "Your Reverence is mistaken," he said. "I have never mentioned your name, nor did I know you at the time I wrote the words you refer to, neither you nor His Excellency, the Bishop. The intention never was to hurt either of you."

The pastor looked sadly at the bishop as he said, "No, no. But—hm—err—" He tried to clear his throat.

The bishop interrupted him, "Yes, but that is not the question at hand. The question is," addressing Hauge, "Will you stop conducting religious meetings, or will you not?"

Hauge thought a while, then shook his head and said, "I dare not promise that. One must obey God rather than men!"

"That's good!" answered the bishop. "Then you will be arrested."

Hauge had expected this, so he stood resigned and calm as if nothing had happened, and only repeated, "That is y o u r idea of what is right and good."

CHAPTER XXXVIII

Hauge in Prison

The sheriff of Melhus soon arrested Hauge and Hemstad and the next morning transported them to Leinstranden. There he turned them over to the sheriff of that district, who should transport them to the next, and so on until they reached Trondheim.

Sheriff Iver Monsen of Leinstranden read the warrant handed to him. He shook his head and said to the sheriff of Melhus, "I refuse such dirty work. To arrest our best citizens on such flimsy charges is an outrage that I will not countenance; nor will I lend a hand in their transportation."

"Well, that is your affair," said the sheriff from Melhus. "I have brought them here, and all I want is your receipt."

"That you will never get," answered Monsen. "I will resign first."

"Then I call upon you all as witnesses that I left the prisoners, H. N. Hauge and L. O. Hemstad, in Monsen's custody. Farewell!"

And the sheriff from Melhus left in a hurry, because he did not like the threatening attitude of the people.

Sheriff Monsen shook hands with the prisoners and said, "Pastor Steenbuch could not stay his hand, even against better advice." (Monsen had sent promemoria to Pastor Steenbuch, giving a full account of the good work that these men had done and urging that he must not hinder them.)

"No," answered Hauge, "he did not stay his hand; nor did the bishop, although he had promised me he would."

"They charge you with sv er me r i and fanaticism," said the sheriff. "I'd like to know who are the real fanatics. As for you, Hauge and Hemstad,

I will not send you away. There will be a new sheriff first."

Hauge took a step forward and grasped the sheriff's hand, saying, "I want to thank you for this. It was fine, but you must not sacrifice your office in our behalf."

"What do I care about the office?" said Monsen. "We are brothers in the work and will make sacrifices for one another."

Hauge's face shone with love as he said, "I know, I know. But—is it right in a case like this one?"

"Well, I shall resign," said Monsen. "I am not going to be a party to such dastardly proceedings."

Hauge had to smile at this rather vehement outbreak. But his voice was earnest, "You are a royal good fellow, Monsen. I wish they were all like you. However, we will do what is right, and, to save you, Hemstad, I will go to Trondheim to report."

Sheriff Monsen remonstrated, but it was of no avail. Hauge and Hemstad were firm in their decision.

The sheriff yielded and bade them farewell.

* * *

The next evening they arrived in Trondheim and in the morning they reported to the magistrate.

Count Moltke was absent on a journey to Copenhagen so they were conducted to the chief of police, who asked them to come back the next day.

When they came the following day, instead of giving them the usual hearing, the temporary Judge, Angell, ordered them to jail. He thought that such dangerous criminals should not be left at large.

The jailer took the two men into custody the eleventh day of December, 1799.

Two weeks later court was held in Leinstranden, and the two prisoners, charged with vagrancy and violation of the Conventicle Act, were sent there for trial. A number of persons had been subpoenaed to give evidence.

Of the thirty-six witnesses examined, not one had anything but good to say about Hauge and Hemstad, and the various offenses charged against them were shown to have had no foundation whatever. The only blame that could be fixed upon them was that they had preached God's Word.

After the court session the two were transported back to Trondheim and lodged in jail where they stayed five weeks before the judge sentenced them. Hauge's sentence was imprisonment of one month; and Hemstad, being a soldier, was given one month of hard labor at the Castle.

Hauge accepted the sentence cheerfully, "This is the sixth time I go to prison for preaching the Word of God," said he. Now he would have a chance to write a new book, and some letters to his friends.

Bishop Schonheyder, in his rounds of visiting prisoners, often called on Hauge to show him that he was mistaken about his calling, and to remind him of the folly of butting against the law.

One day the bishop was so provoking that Hauge lost patience. "Your Excellency," he burst out, "far rather will I stay here in prison and chains than wear sacerdotal robes and persecute the least in God's kingdom."

* * *

At the end of Hauge's prison term he was turned over to the sheriff to be transported south to his home in Thune parish.

This passing from one sheriff to the next in the districts along the route was rather tedious, and the sheriffs, knowing Hauge, handed him the order to escort himself to the given destination.

Hauge left the prison in Trondheim on the sixth of March—exactly three months after his arrest in Melhus—but he was not treated as an ex-convict, rather as a hero. He declined, however, the many invitations to preach in Trondheim, and started afoot on the 800 mile trip to his home in Thune parish.

But Hauge was happy. He tramped all day, and preached in the evening wherever he stopped. People flocked to hear him preach. And by the time he reached Roeros, near the headwaters of the Glommen River, his stock of books was exhausted.

Fortunately for him the superintendent of the copper mines, who upon order from Pastor Kragh had confiscated a consignment of Hauge's books to local distributors, had not destroyed them. Together with a sack of pamphlets they were found intact in his office.

After some palavering Hauge obtained possession of his books and pamphlets. He rejoiced. God had let his enemies help him in a wonderful way. Now he had a supply that would last him for weeks.

Hauge went on preaching, both day and evening, when his friends had so arranged for him. The seed was not broadcasted in vain. The number of converts increased daily.

The trip south through Østerdalen, from Roeros to Grundset, was a continuous triumph for the Lord.

Hauge was not molested. The authorities let him go in peace. On Sundays he did not travel but went to church with the people where he stayed, and afterwards he talked with people. The journey proved to be one of the most successful he ever had.

In the Elverum district the roads were tangled, so he often lost his way and was delayed. Thus he preached in many places far away from his regular route. One day he went in at a farmstead to ask about the way. Only two young girls were home, but they went with him to a ridge and pointed to the way he should go.

Hauge thanked them and as usual took the opportunity to speak to them, "You have showed me the earthly way. I wish to show you the heavenly way. God has revealed the way to us in His Word, the Bible. It happens every day that we go wrong; but when we use His guide-book we shall find the right way and be happy. Will you do that?"

There came a timid—"Yes,—yes—." Soon Hauge left them.

The older girl succeeded so well in after years that she became a leader in church and religious activities. Her name was Martha Govik. She was famous in charity work. But she never tired of telling about her first meeting with Hauge.

About two weeks later Hauge arrived in Oslo. From his friend Grøndahl he received the sad news that his brother, Mikkel, and his friend, Torkel O. Gabestad, were still in prison, because they would not promise to quit preaching.

He was also informed that his sister Anna had been sick all winter. She was becoming weaker and weaker and could not live long, he learned.

Upon hearing this he left immediately for home, arriving at the Hauge farm on an April evening in 1800.

He had been away a whole year.

CHAPTER XXXIX

Anna's Death

Hauge was thinking of his sister as he walked up to the house, "She was the first one to understand me and my perplexities in my young days, and when I surrendered to the Lord she did also. She was my confidante in everything; she helped and comforted me in my spiritual afflictions and rejoiced with me when peace was found.

"Now she is dying. Soon the gates of heaven

will open and reveal the wonders of the mansions prepared for her. Would that I also could leave all strife and suffering behind to be with her in glory; but—he thought of his mission—God's will be done."

Now he was at the gatepost. For a minute he leaned there; then he dried his tears and went in.

A genial warmth emanated from the fire-place where a dry log was lazily burning. An open Bible lay on the table.

The door behind him opened and his father came in and grasped his hand fervently, but emotion paralyzed his tongue. Then slowly came the words, "God be praised! I have you home again."

"Yes, father," Hans answered, "God be praised, now and forevermore."

They continued to stand there, clasping hands, as if afraid of losing one another. Then the father said, "I am so glad you have come. She yearns for you."

"How is she?" Hans questioned.

"Just now she is more quiet," answered the father, "but she has had some trying times. Doubt has assailed her time and again, so severely that we feared for her reason."

After a moment of silence Hans ventured to ask, "Is it true that soon she will be leaving us?"

Emotion nearly overcame the father. "Yes, the time is short; the doctor says that nothing can be done," he managed to say.

Hans bowed his head in deep thought. "God's will be done," he whispered.

The door to the alcove opened and his mother, her eyes brimming with tears, came into the room. But a smile broke through the tears when she saw Hans, big and strong as he was.

"I am so glad to see you home again," she said, embracing him. "But—I am worried about Anna.

Come!" and she led him into the sickroom where Anna lay, pale and thin and wasted. She smiled as she saw him and held out her hand.

"Welcome home," she said, "it makes me happy to have you here."

"Yes," answered Hans, "God is good. His mercy endureth, and through His grace we have met once more."

"Yes," she whispered, "He carried me through when I was lost."

"So I have heard," said Hans.

"And, God be praised," she continued, "He found me and comforted me when I had given up."

She closed her eyes. Tired but contented she continued to hold his hand.

Hauge sat down. Tears came to his eyes when he saw how frail she was. How thin her hand was! He stroked it gently. Then she opened her eyes and smiled.

"And you are not afraid of death, of the grave?" asked Hans.

"No, not now," she whispered, "I am not afraid now! The Lord shall be my stay and gain my victory."

She closed her eyes again, as a tired child, and dozed.

Hans sat very quiet so as not to disturb her.

After a while she opened her eyes again and stared as if she were thinking of something. Then she whispered, "Hans, will you do something for me?"

"Yes," he answered; "what is it?"

"Promise to hold my hand when I die."

"I will," said Hans, and he wept.

* * *

Three days later death hovered above the sickbed. Anna was saying farewell to her relatives and friends.

"There is one missing," she whispered; "where is Mikkel?"

"He still remains in the Oslo prison for preaching God's Word," Hans responded.

"God bless him for that," she murmured.

A little later she whispered, "I want to thank you for leading me to God."

"No, it was you who helped me," Hans answered.

She whispered something again, inaudible to the group gathered round the bed.

Hans bent his ear to her lips.

"Where is mother?" she murmured.

Hans beckoned to his mother, who bent down and kissed her daughter on the forehead.

"Thank you, mother," she said, as her breath came slower and slower.

"Hans, it's getting dark," she breathed.

"The light of God is near," he answered.

"Did father come?" she whispered.

"Yes, he is here." Hans nodded to his father.

The aged man kneeled on the other side of the bed and took her hand. Fresh tears welled up in his eyes.

"Thank you, father," she murmured.

She closed her eyes and the minutes dragged along slowly. A spasm of coughing shook the slight body. Then she whispered, "I hear the bells ringing. No, they are singing." She opened her eyes. Then, barely audible, came the request, "Pray for me."

Hans answered, "Can you hear me?"

She nodded her head.

The three kneeling by her bed united in the Lord's Prayer, and her lips too moved a little. She was trying to follow, but no sound came.

Slowly the pallor of death came stealing over her face.

Hans bent lower to listen.

"I believe in God the Father, and in the Son, my Redeemer, and in the Holy Spirit—" came faintly. There was a gurgle and a spasm, then another spasm. She struggled to say something.

"Yes," faintly, "sing—."

Hans understood, and with a strong, vibrant voice he sang:

Jesus, I long for Thy blessed communion,
  Yearning for Thee fills my heart and my mind;
Draw me from all that would hinder our union,
  May I to Thee, my beginning, be joined;
Show me more clearly my hopeless condition;
So that my nature may die in contrition,
  And that my spirit may live unto Thee!

Hans felt a faint pressure from the hand he was holding.

Mightily strengthen my spirit within me,
  That I may learn what Thy Spirit can do;
O take Thou captive each passion and win me,
  Lead Thou and guide me my whole journey through!
All that I am and possess I surrender,
  If Thou alone in my spirit mayst dwell,
Everything yield Thee, O Savior most tender,
  Thou, only Thou, canst my sadness dispel.

Hans looked at the ashen face. A faint trace of a smile seemed to linger there. He sang again:

Jesus, Oh, shall I find rest in the haven?
  Heavy the burden, remove it from me!
Lord, shall I see Thee, my Savior in heaven?
  Rise, Lord, and quiet the wild troubled sea!
O loving Jesus, show mercy most speedy;
  Hide not Thy countenance, Lord, now from me.
Thou, purest wealth of all inwardly needy;
  Fill Thou my heart, precious Savior, with Thee!

As Hans was singing the last verse her head

---

* German, 1712; tr. Danish P. J. Hygom, 1740, (English) G. T. Rygh, 1908.

sank lower, her eyes closed, and she went to sleep with a lingering smile on her face.

Hans folded her hands.

"Rest thou in peace, dear sister!" Then he quoted:

> *O death, where is thy sting?*
> *O grave, where is thy victory?*
> *But thanks be to God!*
> *Which giveth us the victory,*
> *Through our Lord, Jesus Christ.*

"Her victory is won," he mused, "and she is waiting for us."

A burst of weeping from the next room interrupted the silence of the death-chamber.

According to the church records Anna Hauge was buried on the eighteenth day of April, 1800.

There was an unusually large funeral. Anna had been a favorite with everybody, good-natured, kind and cheerful, ready to help wherever needed, and smiling wherever she went. Now they all mourned for her; but no one felt the loss so keenly and deeply as did Hans.

In his letter to Grøndahl in Oslo announcing the death, he said, "The brightest light here has left us. She grew up as a flower in the light of God's grace. Existence has lost its charm for me since she died. Never have I been tempted so to give up my calling as just now; but God is gracious and will give me strength to continue."

CHAPTER VL

Journey to Copenhagen

After the funeral Hauge stayed at home for some time, having meetings in his home parish, or making short trips to nearby places.

Late in May he made a trip to Fredrikstad to visit his relatives and friends, and to inquire into the spiritual growth of the converts. The "Seeberg Movement" was dying out, and other converts were not very active.

This fired Hauge's spirit. He held a number of ringing revival meetings that stirred the community from Fredrikstad to Fredrikshald. Many new converts were made.

At a meeting in Strand, a suburb of Fredrikshald, a well-known fiddler and dancing-master, Jon Hansen Sorbroden, tried to get into an argument with Hauge to "show him up" before the people. He waited until after the sermon, however, but then he had so many points to argue that he did not know where to begin. He pondered all evening and most of the night, and somehow came to the conviction that Hauge was right.

Early the next morning he came to Hauge for a confidential talk—and the heart-to-heart talk continued until Sorbroden was won for Christ. He was well-educated, a fluent talker, and in time became the leader of the laymen's movement in the Fredrikstad district.

* * *

Hauge returned to Fredrikstad to meet Peter Meier, a son of his old friend, Ole Meier, in Oslo. The young man had been converted and wanted to consult Hauge. Hauge had decided to go to Denmark, so he invited Peter to go along. They obtained passports from the city mayor in Fredrikstad and sailed for Copenhagen, May 30, 1800.

Hauge's object in going to Copenhagen was to discover the sentiment of the king and his cabinet regarding the laymen's movement.

He also wanted to print new editions of his books, former editions having been completely sold out.

As usual he went to the chief of police to get his passport viséed. There was no "hitch," he was welcome to have his books printed. He immediately went to various printing offices to make contracts for printing, and to start work.

In those days there were no swift linotype machines nor speedy rotary presses. The hand composing-sticks and Franklin presses had a "big job" when 5,000 copies were ordered.

5,000 copies of the World's Follies were printed in A. S. Thiele's shop, but he could not print the other books in the short time asked for by Hauge.

In P. H. Hoeker's print-shop Hauge contracted for 5,000 copies of God's Wisdom, at C. T. Holm's shop for 5,000 copies of the Confession of Truth, and at the shop of H. S. L. Winding, 5,000 copies of Miscellaneous Writings, which he had written in the prison at Trondheim.

Hauge was a very busy man. According to his diary he was up at three o'clock in the morning and worked until ten at night preparing corrected manuscripts, reading proof in the evenings, and so on.

His young friend, Peter Meier, helped in the book-bindery. He packed and shipped the books as soon as they were ready.

A copy of each book was presented to the chief of police.

Everything went smoothly. In about ten weeks Hauge had sent 20,000 books to his friends scattered all over Norway, many of whom had sent money in advance.

How the people valued Hauge's efforts to revive and awaken them into spiritual activity is best shown by the contributions to the "bookfund." A rich farmer, Guttorm Kolbjornsen Haftun in Hallingdal, had sent fifty dollars to Hauge in Copenhagen for books. Upon receiving the books he was so well pleased that he sent one hundred dollars more as a personal gift to Hauge.

As to the intention of K a n c e l l i e t (the king's cabinet), Hauge remained ignorant. Copies of his books had been sent them, but no comments were made, and no action was taken.

Hauge thus took it for granted that they were favorably disposed towards his mission.

However, as a matter of fact, Kancelliet had not given any attention to him. His books were given to Prof. Nyerop at the university, who gave his verdict in L æ r d e Ef t e r r e t n i n g e r (Learned Review), that the books were a "harmless jumble of pietistic nonsense, mentioned as a curiosity that will not be believed in our enlightened age."

During these months, Hauge had found time to write two new books, R u l e of C h r i s t i a n Life, and Fundamental Doctrine of Christianity. It took about six weeks to get these books off the press and bound. Then he packed up and sailed back to Fredrikstad in October. Many of his friends came to meet and consult him. Fortunately the new books answered most of their inquiries.

He went home to visit his parents and rest a while but he remained only a few days. So many invitations came that he found no rest staying at home. So he started out on the road again, arranging his route so as to make a continuous journey. Hauge visited his old friends, Grøndahl and Meier in Oslo, too, and, hearing of the trouble in Hedemarken, started north.

Arriving at Romedal, where the trouble began, he held a series of meetings, showing the people their errors in explaining the Bible in a physical sense: "Salvation in fear and trembling" could not possibly mean going through life shaking the body to gain salvation. (Evidently these people had heard of the Shakers or Quakers in England, and in their crude way of thinking tried to imitate them.) After

Hauge's visit the excitement soon died out, and the laymen's movement in that vicinity was brought back to normalcy.

At Lillehammer Hauge met many of his friends and had several well attended meetings, yielding many converts.

Hauge then continued to Faaberg, where his oldtime friend, Lieutenant John T. Blegen from Fredrikstad who had tired of military life, had bought a farm and settled down as a farmer. He was a warm Christian, and his home was a center for the laymen in that district.

Hauge spent several days at his home, meeting the many friends. Then he continued west through Gausdal and south to Biri, having meetings two and three times a day. The day after his arrival at Biri he was arrested by a deputy and sent to prison at Swennes, but Hauge's friends persuaded the deputy to let him go.

Hauge continued westward through Snertingdalen, then across to Thorpe, and south to Randsfjord. He continued south along Randsfjord to Gran and Jevnaker, stopping where his friends had arranged meetings.

In Lunner, annex to Jevnaker, a spiritual awakening took place. He left his friend, John Hoidale, an intelligent worker, in charge, to help those in need of spiritual advice.

The local pastor, Rev. U. Lange, was a rabid rationalist, who thundered against this s v e r m e r i. Later he caused a poor farmer, Hans Dalen, to be arrested for holding meetings in his own house.

The farmer was fined thirteen dollars, but he had no money. So the sheriff took the only cow he had, but Dalen's friends bought another cow for him.

Hauge continued west and south to Hønefoss, Tyristrand, Vikersund, Modum, Aamot and Bakke.

He traveled and preached, and preached and traveled, his energy, endurance, and fortitude being really marvelous.

CHAPTER XLI

Building a Paper-Mill

In the second week in December Hauge came to Eker and found his friend Kristofer Hoen, in ill-humor, but he smiled when he shook hands with Hauge.

"It is a good thing that you have come," said Hoen; "everything is going wrong, and no one can set it aright."

"How so?" questioned Hauge.

"Well, some are back-sliding or misguided, so they fall away from God's Word and the truth," said Hoen.

"In what way?" asked Hauge, and told of the trouble in Romedal.

"In many ways," answered Hoen. "Peder Roer has yielded. He was let out of prison when he promised never to preach God's Word again."

Hauge's face blanched. "Can this really be true?" he asked.

"Unfortunately it is," Hoen answered, "and it may be contagious and lead others to do the same thing."

"A merciful God will judge," Hauge sighed; "what do we know?"

"And," continued Hoen, "there is a man from Bergen who claims to possess prophetic gifts. He predicted the end of the world on October fourth, but now he has changed it to New Year's Day. People believe him and have quit work."

Hauge began pacing the floor, then asked: "Has he been arrested?"

"No," said Hoen, "he has not, because he is not considered dangerous. "They will believe a lie but reject the truth."

"No, they do not believe!" said Hauge, "God is plowing the ground and sowing the good seed, but Satan plants the weeds, and unbelief chokes faith. But I shall put a stop to this doctrinal travesty."

Hoen looked at him and wondered.

"I will go directly and show these people that work is their greatest blessing, but idleness is the mother of all wicked deeds."

"Not so fast, my friend," said Hoen; "we need you here a while."

"I will be back very soon," said Hauge, smiling. "I have in my mind some special work to do here in Eker."

"What will Sheriff Gram say to that?" Hoen asked.

"I am going to get people to work," answered Hauge, "and the sheriff cannot arrest me for that."

"Work," said Hoen, "are we not working?"

"Well," said Hauge; "I have something different on my mind; I am going to start a paper-mill, manufacturing paper."

"Here, right among your enemies?" said Hoen.

"Yes, right here," answered Hauge; "in the enemy's stronghold. We must invade the enemy's territory."

"And what next?" said Hoen.

"We have to show our worthy authorities," said Hauge, "that we are not vagrants, as they are pleased to say, but useful citizens. Then perhaps Sheriff Gram and Pastor Schmidt will have their eyes opened."

"This staggers me," said Hoen, "but where will you get the money?"

"I have the money already," replied Hauge. "We

are six in a partnership; my brother, Mikkel, and Torkel Gabestad are two of them."

"But they are in prison," argued Hoen.

"Yes, but their money is not," said Hauge. "Then we have your neighbors, Ole Foss and Nils Braaten, and Soren Stormoen from Nummedal and Kristen Solseth from Gausdal."

"And you and I," interrupted Hoen; "that makes eight."

"No, no," said Hauge, "not for me. I want to be a free man—to come and go as I please."

"Yes, I know," said Hoen, "you are a hard man to hold."

"Well, I have the Lord's blessed unrest in my body, and anxiety in my soul to see that God's work is not neglected," explained Hauge.

The following weeks Hauge made his rounds in the neighborhood parishes and then came back.

* * *

Hauge was busy as ever. He had studied the manufacturing of paper while in Copenhagen and was familiar with the machinery. He had the plans drafted and local carpenters started building immediately after New Year, 1801.

While they were building, Hauge left for Hallingdal. In the Ness parish he was arrested as a dangerous vagrant, but was released for lack of evidence. A man selling his books is no more a vagrant than a man selling a horse or a cow.

Afterwards he visited the Goel parish and Hemsedal. From Hemsedal he traveled on skis across the mountains to Hoel and to Aal, where he had several meetings.

While Hauge was preaching one Saturday afternoon, the sheriff of the Aal district and his deputy came to arrest him. The farmers did not like that. They crowded around Hauge, and a prominent farmer spoke up, "You just leave him alone, Herr Sheriff!"

"Leave him alone! Leave him alone!" cried several others.

But the sheriff, armed with the law, was not to be bluffed. He pressed on. Then an elderly farmer, a veritable giant, arose and grabbed the sheriff by the arm and held him as in a vise, while he said, "You stay out of this! All the godless people can do all kinds of wickedness in peace, but this man who is warning us against sin and vice, and advising us to do what is good and what is right is threatened with arrest. It shows clearly that you tolerate the wicked rather than the God-fearing. Now you behave yourself, or I will chuck you into a snowdrift where you can cool off."

"Out with him! Out with him!" cried several voices.

"Wait!" Hauge stood on a chair and in a powerful voice called, "Wait, my friends! We must not use force to defend ourselves, but in patience and resignation to God yield to the authorities. It is my duty to go with the sheriff if he has a warrant."

The din subsided immediately. As Hauge stepped down and followed the sheriff not a hand was raised to stop them. Next day (Sunday) his friends came to visit Hauge in prison, but they were not permitted to see him.

A rabble of loafers hung around the prison to get a good look at Hauge whenever the guard opened the door. They laughed and joked and swapped salacious stories to irritate the man inside.

The sheriff came, and when he saw the rabble, a broad grin spread over his face.

"Now we shall have a dance," he said as he came up.

"Then Hauge will be the fiddler," said one.

A chorus of raucous laughter followed.

"No, he is no fiddler, but we will make him dance."

Another braying chorus came from the crowd.

The sheriff spoke to a deputy, and he left immediately.

A sporty girl stood jesting with the men, and the sheriff, seeing her, went over and asked her if she would go inside to Hauge and get him warmed up for a dance.

The girl laughed and said, "Do you believe I can?"

The sheriff took her arm and swore a red-hot oath that she could, and she need not be bashful about it.

Laughingly the girl answered, "Perhaps—I can try."

The sheriff took her in and shoved her into the seat next to Hauge, who sat writing some letters.

"Here is one that wants to be converted," said the sheriff.

The girl laughed merrily. This was to be real sport, and she moved up closer to Hauge.

Hauge moved aside and took a long look at her. He sighed and spoke in a soft, melancholy way, "Is there something you wanted?"

The girl did not answer but continued laughing.

Hauge asked again, "Is there something?"

"You are without a girl tonight, the sheriff told me," she said.

Hauge turned scarlet, then went pale again. "And you offer yourself?" he said.

Her laugh came forcedly, but she did not say anything.

Hauge gathered up his papers, looked at her long and seriously. "No, I have no girl; but are you a real girl?" he asked.

"Well, ain't I?" she demanded.

"No," said Hauge with some force, "you have lost the finest thing a girl should have."

The girl jerked away, turned scarlet, and trembled. "What?"

"You, who should be a pure child of God, ought not to live in sin," and with tears in his eyes he added, "Oh, and such sin!"

The girl stared at the floor. Her fingers plucked at her apron. She dared not lift her head.

Suddenly she jumped up and went over to the fire-place as if she were cold and said, "It was the sheriff that made me do it."

Hauge came and took her hand, patted it, and with deep feeling said, "You go home to your mother—and pray God to forgive your sins. Then you will be glad—happier than you have been for a long time."

He dropped her hand as she burst into tears, and then she ran out. The rabble outside crowded around to hear the fun, but she broke away through the crowd and screamed at them, "Don't talk to me!" She ran down the road towards her home weeping.

Just then the deputy returned with a fiddler, followed by a rabble of youngsters, boys and girls, who laughed and jested.

The sheriff opened the door and invited them to come inside.

Then turning to Hauge he shouted, "Here comes the parson and his flock"—and in tumbled the boisterous crowd after the sheriff and his corpulent wife.

The fiddler had tuned his violin and cut in with a "Halling" air, wild and weird as a ghost dance.

"Now we shall dance!" called the sheriff to Hauge, as he took his wife by the hand and spun her around like a top. Then he crouched low, dancing on his haunches and his heels,—made a spring, and turned a somersault, kicking the crossbeams above his head.

"Hurrah!" they roared in chorus, "that is a real Hallingkast."

"Now it is your turn," said the sheriff's wife to Hauge, holding out her hand. Hauge took it, saying, "All right, if the fiddler will play the tune I want."

"Which one?" asked the fiddler.

"This one," said Hauge, and he sang with his powerful voice:

> *Now ought no sin o'ercome us*
> *Or rule with might and main;*
> *When we may cast it from us*
> *And flee it with disdain.*
> *For—we are baptized, and*
> *In God's grace well accepted*
> *And in His Word instructed*
> *To Satan's wiles withstand.*
>
> *And as regenerated*
> *In Christ unto His death;*
> *If we thus consecrated,*
> *Will sin again—forthwith.*
> *Why not shun wickedness*
> *And sin in every manner?*
> *While at the Savior's banner*
> *Our sins can find redress.*
>
> *What comfort will it give you*
> *That Christ from death arose,*
> *If you in sin continue*
> *And rush to endless woes,*
> *All steeped in filth and sin,*
> *In wicked, crafty highways,*
> *In lewd and wanton byways*
> *With morals mired within.*
>
> *No, no! Let sin not master*
> *Our daily life and deeds;*
> *Pray, save us from disaster*
> *Thou knowest, Lord, our needs.*
> *That daily we may rise*
> *From sin and worldly actions,*
> *From vile and base attractions*
> *In Jesus' name arise!**

---

* Thomas Kingo's *Sjungekor* 1689. Tr. (Eng.) A. M. A. 1931.

As the hymn rose strong and gripping in the prison-hall, the sheriff's wife jerked her hand away and stood aside, while the sheriff—eyes cast down—stood as if stricken with palsy.

Hauge sang the four verses with a fervor and a vehemence that struck home. A clap of thunder could not have paralyzed the crowd more effectively. He looked around at his audience before he spoke, "Today is Sunday—His day who died for you. From Him I bring a message to you. I stand here today jailed as a criminal, scorned and sneered at because I wanted to serve Him and advocate His cause; and yet I am freer than you are. You are chained in the fetters of sin, but I have been liberated in Christ, thanks be to God.

"It is the Lord's Day, and God's grace is yet open to you; but there will be another Lord's Day when He comes, not as a Savior but as a Judge, and you will be compelled to give an account of yourself. On Judgment Day you must account for every sinful thought, every angry word, every evil desire, every wicked deed. The churches will then be closed. There will be no more confessions; the days of grace will be ended forever.

"You want to dance, but you cannot dance away from the living God, or the Day of Judgment. You m a y some day dance to the fiddler with a cloven hoof, and dance to a death not to your liking.

"Or, do you believe that dancing on Sundays will cancel the sins of the week? That revels and frolics and levity on Sunday evenings can mend the weekly evil, sorrow and burning conscience?

"No, no! You cannot quench a glowing coal by blowing on it, nor in ribaldry laugh yourself into God's kingdom.

"Christ had to die for your sins—think of that seriously and you will not care so much for dancing on Sunday. Now you may go home and pray to the Almighty God to have compassion and be merciful unto you, and to make you better men and women."

There was a dismal silence.

Those nearest the door began to sneak out, and soon the others followed, even the sheriff and his wife.

Outside, the young men looked glum, and some women were weeping.

Everybody hurried to get away.

An old man spoke to the sheriff, "A great sin it is to commit this man to jail. You had better let him go, Herr Sheriff."

The words of Hauge had burned into the very soul of the sheriff. He found no peace. Taciturn and morose he pondered until late in the night, when he ordered the guards to take Hauge to Ringerike —nearly thirty miles away—to get a hearing before Judge Hørby.

Hauge arrived at Ringerike the next day. The judge read the complaint and asked about it.

"Have you held meetings in this district?" the judge asked.

"Yes, I have," Hauge answered, "and the last one was held in the jail at Sundre yesterday."

"How did the people get into the jail?" the judge asked.

"The sheriff invited them," said Hauge.

"You are accused of having caused a woman to commit suicide," said the judge. Did you know her?"

"I never heard of her until now," Hauge replied.

"Did she attend your meeting?" asked the judge.

"I cannot say, because I do not know the woman," said Hauge, "but perhaps the guards can tell."

The judge turned to the guards and asked if she had been there.

They both shook their heads, and one of them

said he was positive she was not, because the woman committed suicide before Hauge came.

"Your Excellency," said Hauge, "they accuse me, without reason, of many things. Even if I had known the woman and she had attended my meetings I could not have been more guilty of her deed than was Christ when Judas committed suicide."

"That stands to reason," said the judge, "and, as for preaching in the jail there is no law forbidding it."

The judge dismissed the case, and when the guards left, Hauge asked him for a passport. This the judge readily gave, and handing it to Hauge said, "I have heard of you from far and wide but have not observed any evil results. On the contrary, much good has been done."

"I thank you," said Hauge, rather embarrassed by the kind words; "you are an upright judge."

"That is what I hope to be," he replied. "And now farewell and a successful journey." They shook hands and Hauge left.

* * *

Hauge traveled north through Aadalen, Hedalen, Reinli, Bjorgo, and Aurdal. Meetings were held everywhere, and people flocked to hear the famous man. He was not molested in any manner.

From Aurdal he traveled north to Slidre, then westward to Hurum and Vang, spending several days at each place. Crowds gathered to hear him and good results were apparent. His enemies made no trouble in these districts, either.

By this time Ole Roersveen had joined him; and the two traveled now on skis across Filefjeld to Hegg and Borgun, Indre Sogn and Lerdal, where they had a number of meetings and some good results were seen, especially at Husum in Lerdal.

As they now had reached the sea, they left by boat for Gudvangen, then on foot to Vossestrand.

Afterwards they visited Vinge, Tvinde, Vossevangen, Evanger, Dale, Bruvik, Haus, and Arnevaag.

The pastors of the churches of the Voss district started to make trouble, but Bishop Brun in Bergen held them in check.

CHAPTER XLII

Citizenship in Bergen

When Hauge arrived in Bergen there was great rejoicing among his friends. The two merchants, Samson Traa and J. N. Loose, together with Madam Boes, urged him vigorously to settle in Bergen and showed him the many advantages and the protection he would have.

Hauge considered the matter from different viewpoints and finally decided to settle in Bergen, at least for awhile. But he would never give up his deep concern for the many outside Bergen who were waiting to hear him.

About the middle of June Hauge left for Stavanger. At Renneso he met a young man, John Haugvaldstad, who had been concerned spiritually but who was assailed by doubt. After a few days with Hauge his mind cleared, and a new light and a real insight into the way of salvation gradually came. Afterwards John Haugvaldstad became the leader of the laymen's movement in the Stavanger districts.

A letter from Hauge, posted from Haaland (near Stavanger), June 26, 1801, tells of the success of this journey, and the willingness of the people to listen to the Word of God. The letter has an admonition to the believers that they must "let their lights shine in temporal things as well as in spiritual things."

When he returned to Bergen he found letters

with calls from various localities to come to visit them. His business was to preach God's Word in such a way as to awaken dormant souls to a spiritual life. Hauge neglected temporal business for the spiritual.

Shortly after we find him in Sondfjord, preaching and selling his books. Later we hear of him in Daviken, Gloppen, Horningdal, and Sunnelven in Nordfjord. Still later he is preaching in Surendalen where the sheriff invited him to preach in his house.

When the local pastor, Rev. Finkenhagen, heard of this, he hurried over to get Hauge arrested. After the meeting they had a lively debate, and Finkenhagen was surprised to find Hauge better posted in doctrine and Biblical knowledge than he himself was.

Pastor Finkenhagen then offered to help Hauge to become a minister, but Hauge declined with thanks. He was a citizen of Bergen, excepting a "trades commission," and had the freedom to look up trade anywhere.

Then Pastor Finkenhagen became angry and ordered the sheriff to transport Hauge out of his parish. This was done, but at Aune, where they had to rest, the friends who followed requested Hauge to preach once more before he left them. He did this willingly.

Hauge continued up the valley to Haandstad and Rindalen, where he had several meetings. But he was not arrested. Then he crossed the mountain to Garberg in Meldalen, where he had a series of meetings with many good results. From there he traveled down the Orkla valley to Skogn and across to Buviken and Leinstranden. All welcomed him.

He arrived in Trondheim early in January, 1802. His stay was rather short. Evidently he was busy looking up avenues of trade, and, as he held no meetings, the authorities had no cause for arresting him. A week later he was having meetings in Leinsvik, forty miles west of Trondheim; and when the authorities commenced to make trouble, he crossed the mountains to Snildalen.

Here he attended services in the church and afterwards gave a talk outside. Then he went on to Hevne and south across the Romsdal district.

* * *

When Hauge obtained resident citizenship of Bergen with "trades commission" as a merchant, Madam Boes and a number of other friends loaned him money with which he bought a small freighting vessel. Through his friends at Eker, Oslo and other places, he bought grain from the southern farm districts and freighted it to Bergen, and afterwards to Trondheim.

His friends in the Trondheim districts who had suffered from frosts the previous year hailed him as a godsend for he brought good grain for seed as well as for bread.

His enemy, Pastor Hagerup, writing in F a l l e n s e n's M o n t h l y (July, 1802) said that "he (Hauge) was a dangerous proselyter; that in this year of crop failure he brought grain to sell with his books and preaching, a tempting bait indeed."

Hauge had traveled overland, ahead of the freighter. When he came to the districts where crops had failed he let farmers have grain on contract, provided they took it off the ship at the various landings.

This they gladly did because they obtained the grain so much cheaper. By the time his freighter reached Trondheim all the grain was sold.

Instead of going back immediately for another cargo he headed north to Gaslingerne (Gosling Islands), where he could buy fish to take with him on the return trip.

Contrary storms sent him to Valdersund Harbor, however. Here a person claiming to be an officer came and asked to see Hauge's passport.

Instead of examining the passport, he ran away with it.

A few hours later he came back with some drunken rowdies, and when they did not find Hauge, who had gone to another place to preach, they went on board the freighter and committed various outrages before they left.

Hauge sailed on to Gaslingerne, and while his men were buying fish and loading the vessel he visited the neighboring districts and preached wherever opportunity offered an opening.

One day as Hauge was helping load the freighter a deputy sheriff came on board to arrest Hauge and seize the freighter. He had believed the rumors that Hauge was an impostor. Hauge had full clearance from the custom-house in Bergen, however, and proved by witnesses that he was a citizen of Bergen with a trades commission.

Still the deputy held him until he had furnished bail.

When the freighter was loaded, Hauge sailed south to Beian to cure and prepare the fish for market.

While the crew was doing this Hauge went in a small boat to Trondheim to arrange some commercial affairs. This done, he started overland for Leinstranden. On the way he was held up by three men who conducted him to Sheriff Wolfe of Bynesset.

Under heavy escort Hauge was then transported to Strinden. The justice was "busy", reading papers, and kept Hauge standing outside for several hours where the rabble of the neighborhood had assembled to "have some fun with Hauge."

At length he was called in and given a "curtain

lecture" by his Excellency, Justice Berg, on coming back to forbidden territory. Then Hauge was ordered transported to Trondheim to be tried by Count Moltke. The judge, Count Moltke, was not in his usual good humor that day; so he too gave Hauge a reprimand. But then he dismissed the case.

Hauge was, however, ordered to be transported back to Bergen. Sheriff Wolfe brought him as far as Leinstranden, and after that Hauge traveled alone. On the way Hauge preached as usual—two, perhaps three times a day at places where he was well acquainted.

In Surendalen he caught up with his friend Mikkel Grendahl. They traveled together for some time, and Grendahl learned some valuable lessons from Hauge.

At Sunnelven they parted, Grendahl going east to Geiranger, Breidal and Skiaker, Hauge going west to Wolden and Vanelven, then south to Daviken, Gloppen and other places in Nordfjord. At Gloppen, where he had a host of friends, he remained for four days' preaching.

Of his further traveling through the districts of Sønfjord, Sogn and Voss, the records are silent, although he had many friends there.

Hauge arrived in Bergen June 26, 1802, after being away about nine months. It took weeks to straighten out his business affairs so he could not preach for some time.

CHAPTER XLII

Recrossing the Country

Early in August Hauge was ready for his next journey. He followed the highway to Dale, then traveled up the valley to Voss where he remained a whole week, preaching at a number of homes. From

Voss he journeyed to Aurland in Sogn, where he spent a few days.

Then he went north to Hafslo, where he spent several days preaching in the open, as there were no houses big enough to accomodate the great number of people who gathered to hear him preach.

At Venjum, near Hafslo, a somewhat educated farmer tried to force Hauge into a debate on predestination. Hauge referred him to Rom. 8:28-30, Eph. 1:5, and a number of parallel places in the Bible.

Afterward Hauge preached on the subject, and the sheriff and the two schoolmasters present changed their minds about Hauge. In fact they came and thanked him for the clear solution of this perplexing problem. It is not what God knoweth, but what man willeth, that decides predestination. God willeth, that a l l men should be saved; but so many reject God's will!

Hauge knew that arguments never brought anyone to Christ; hence he avoided discussions and kept on preaching from place to place. The sheriffs and schoolmasters in the various districts were among the many converts that remained his best friends.

He crossed the fjord to Lyster, and hosts of people assembled. More eloquent than ever, Hauge won many for Christ.

At Dalsøren he preached at the military barracks to thousands of people; and at Lerum he preached in the public hall at the sheriff's residence. There were so many people that he had to preach again outside.

The provost, Quale, in his reports said that all the sheriffs and all the schoolmasters in the Indre Sogn communities were zealous admirers of Hauge. They helped him to hold meetings.

Hauge continued up the valley to Fortun, preaching wherever there was a gathering of people. Returning to Lyster, he continued south to Lerdal and up the valley to Borgund. Here he had to cross the mountains to Hemsedal, where his many friends gave him a hearty welcome.

He preached and visited on his way south to Goel, Hoel and Gjeilo; and then traveled across to Dagali and Opdal. Hauge continued down the valley to Nore and Rollag, where he had many blessed meetings.

* * *

August had passed, and it was far into September when he reached Eker, where his papermill was still standing unfinished. At Eker a number of his friends had gathered to welcome Hauge. His brother Mikkel, who had served two years and five months in prison in Oslo for preaching the Gospel, was now a free man.

He had taken up his residence at the mill, and now, when Hans came, they started to raise the money to complete the mill.

The many friends present were helping them to raise funds. Among these was T. O. Bache from Opdal, who was advised by Hauge to settle in Drammen as a merchant and buy grain from the farmers in the southern districts.

Bache found this to be good advice. He went home and resigned as sheriff, moved his family to Drammen, and settled there as a merchant.

Meanwhile Hauge had arranged the affairs at Eker; and the work of completing the paper mill was in full swing. Hauge left sooner than he intended, however, because of summons from the bishop in Oslo, the Rt. Reverend Chr. Schmidt, to appear before him immediately. When Hauge and his two friends came to the bishop he gave them a "curtain lecture" because they had interfered with his son, who was pastor at Eker.

Hauge tried to defend himself, but the bishop

called in a policeman who arrested Hauge and his two friends. They were held only until next day, however, as there were no specific charges against them.

Hauge left for Thune. He had not been home since his sister had died. This time he found his mother was ill, so he remained at home a few days.

Afterwards he went to Glemminge and Fredrikstad to visit his relatives and friends there. Then he continued south to the Berg parish, where his friend John Sorbroden, had invited him to preach. When the local pastor heard of it, he ordered the sheriff, Jacob Svane, to arrest them in case of any "irregularity."

The sheriff came at the beginning of the meeting. His report to the pastor shows "that there were many people; that Hauge's passport was in order; that he had had a call from God to preach; and that he (the sheriff) had examined Hauge in many ways but had found nothing at variance with the state religion. Hauge preached with an accuracy that was amazing."

The sheriff did not arrest Hauge but sent his report to the pastor for further consideration. Hauge did not wait for this, but went across Kristiania Fjord to the Vallo Saltworks, and then on to Skien, where his friends had arranged meetings for him. Then he continued his journey up the valley.

The pastor, Rev. Bramer, a rabid rationalist and a bitter enemy of Hauge, came to a meeting at the Tvedt farmstead. He listened quietly throughout, but by the time the sermon ended he was red in the face from anger. "Twee! What rotten parrot-talk!" he shouted, and then spat in Hauge's face.

Hauge—hymnbook in hand and ready to announce the closing hymn—wiped his face with a handkerchief and said, "Let's sing: 'Depart thou unclean spirit.'" The audience sang lustily while His Reverance rushed to the door, swearing vengeance upon Hauge.

Hauge continued his meetings the following days at the farmsteads of Simon Klovdal, Thor Ytterbo, Sten Tufte, and Johan Heisholt. After the meeting at Heisholt's house, warning came that Rev. Mr. Bramer was bringing the sheriff. They all knew what that meant. "Come," said Heisholt to Hauge, "we will not wait for them;" and they went to the stables and climbed into a hayloft where they hid in the hay.

Pastor and sheriff came and asked for Hauge.

The people outside, getting ready to go, shook their heads—no one seemed to know. The meeting was over, and Hauge was gone.

"We shall search the house," said the pastor, but they searched in vain. Then they went outside and looked around.

"Where is Heisholt?" shouted the pastor; but the people outside looked at each other and shook their heads.

"Where is Heisholt?" demanded the sheriff.

Then several spoke up and said, "Presumably he went with Hauge."

"I'll make them pay for this," growled the pastor, as he climbed into the Kariol. The sheriff also climbed in, and together they drove off at breakneck speed, evidently thinking that they could catch the fugitives.

The pastor was brutally vindictive. He made so many charges against these farmers that the courts later fined them fifteen dollars each and costs.

The sheriff, after leaving the pastor at the parsonage, took the road to Skien, while Hauge went north to Boe in Telemark. Here he held a few meetings, and then went on to Seljord where he had some more meetings. Hauge then turned northeast to Gran.

When Hauge met someone and inquired about the way, they in turn wanted to know who he was. When informed of this, they would perhaps say, "Not the Hauge who wrote R e l i g i o u s S e n s a-t i o n s?" It was so extraordinary to meet a man who had written books.

Hauge was a sensation wherever he went. For had he not written whole books? Such men were not met at e v e r y cross-roads, so he was welcome everywhere. If it was near the noon hour he would be invited for dinner or lunch or coffee, so that they could talk with the great man. Others would drop in and fill up the rooms, and then they would ask Hauge to preach.

From Tin, Hauge traveled westward to Rjukan where he spent an hour at the waterfalls, noting the great power available there.

Then he visited Kvanbek and Moe, and had a number of meetings with "blessed results." From Moe he evidently traveled up the valley to Vinje, as a little later he crossed the mountain wilderness from Haukeli to Røldal. Here he had several meetings. Then his journey took him down the valley to Nesflaten and Roalkvam.

Hauge kept on down the valley to Suldal and Sand and Ryfylke. He also visited Jelse, Nerstrand, Tysver, Avaldsness, Torvestad, and Haugesund. As it was nearing Christmas he sailed directly from Haugesund to Bergen without stopping on the way.

In the coast towns many of the pastors were friendly to Hauge. Rev. Sverdrup, pastor at Avaldsness, tells how he let Hauge preach in the roomy parsonage while he was hearing confession in the sacristy.

CHAPTER XLIV

From Bergen to Lofoten

In Bergen Hauge was received by a circle of friends who congratulated him upon the success of his journey, and that he had returned a free man. For the attitude of the rationalistic prelates and clergy was becoming more threatening every day. Only Bishop Brun in Bergen stood firm in defense of Hauge and his friends.

Many of Hauge's friends had held revivals in the diocese of Bergen, and Bishop Brun allowed no one to interfere with their gatherings. Now they had returned to Bergen, rejoicing, to celebrate Christmas; and a real merry Christmas it was.

One of the ablest of Hauge's assistants was Samson Traa. When the freighters were on long trips, he, like Hauge, used the time to hold revival meetings. Now he was back from an extended journey through the Hardanger parishes where he had had some good results.

At Vikør, one of the largest parishes, many were converted, among them the schoolmaster, O. Bjotvedt. This so irritated the local pastor, Rev. Rasmus Tonning, that he, with the provost's sanction, suspended the schoolmaster.

This was reported to Bishop Brun, who wanted definite charges against Bjotvedt. There came some flimsy charges, signed by thirteen men. Then came a remonstrance demanding that Bjotvedt be re-instated, signed by 52 men.

Bishop Brun ordered Pastor Tonning to re-instate Bjotvedt as schoolmaster. Tonning refused and went to the magistrate; but, getting little satisfaction from that quarter, he wrote to Bishop Brun that he would agree to re-instate Bjotvedt, provided he would apologize.

Bishop Brun's answer was sardonic: "Apologize for what?"

Bjotvedt was installed without apologies.

In revenge Tonning sent a "Jeremiad" to the K a n c e l l i (king's council) in Copenhagen, accusing Bishop Brun of protecting "these illiterate s v e r m e r e and brainless tramps, who are a public nuisance."

Thus the rationalistic war upon the "laymen's movement" became more and more bitter. At the beginning of the year 1803, it was estimated that several thousand, mostly young men and women, were preaching the Gospel throughout Norway.

* * *

Hauge's two freighting vessels—one from Drammen and one from Oslo—had returned to Bergen, loaded with grain.

During Christmas, Hauge had bought two more freighting vessels, and immediately after New Year, 1803, he left Bergen with his little fleet of four freighters, two sailing direct to the fishing villages in the Namsen district, while the two laden with grain sailed to Trondheim.

Hauge disposed of the grain in the same manner as the previous year. In Trondheim he called on Bishop Schoenheyder. Here he was received in a very kindly manner. "You are far more welcome now that you have brought us seed grain than when you brought us religious talk," said the bishop.

Hauge answered, " 'But seek ye first the kingdom of God and His righteousness, and all these things shall be added unto you.' The Word of God is of far greater value than grain, but the two go well together. It is God's almighty Word that preserves everything and regenerates souls. By the Word everybody shall be judged on the last day, and I shall be cleared of jail-sentences and vagrancy."

* * *

Hauge left with his freighters for the Gaslingerne islands where the fishing of cod was good. The first freighter was soon loaded, but the second, unfortunately, was lost in a storm.

During the loading Hauge made a journey north to Bindalen, where Sheriff Gaupen, a real Christian, arranged several meetings. Then Hauge crossed the bay and came to Vik, where he called on Sheriff Stene, who also was a converted Christian.

Hauge was well received, and the sheriff arranged a number of meetings. On Sunday he talked at the church after service; but there came so many people that he had to preach from the cemetery wall.

The next day he went on to Velfjord, and later to Brønø, where he preached at several places. On the next Sunday afternoon people came from neighboring parishes in numbers so great that Hauge had to preach from a barnloft bridge, in order to be heard by all.

From Brønø he crossed the fjord to Vega, and went then north to Alstadhaug and Dønna, having meetings at each place.

From Dønna he sailed in through the Ranfjord to Hemnes, where he had a number of successful meetings. From there he went up the Ross valley to Korgen, preaching at several places.

An influential man in the Hemnes district, Erick Ottesen, became a devoted friend of Hauge and continued to be a leader among the converted people in Ranen district as long as he lived.

From Hemnes Hauge sailed on to Moe, where he had a few meetings; then he traveled up the Ranen valley to Dunderland and Bellaanes, and had frequent meetings.

He continued up the Bellaa valley to Gilaa, where he hired a guide to take him across the mountains to Saltdalen. They were caught in a snowstorm the second day and lost the trail. The guide was so bewildered that he turned south instead of east to Lonsdal.

Hauge sensed that either they or the wind had turned, so he found his pocket compass and proved to the guide that they must turn to the left. Evening came. They had no food, and there was no house within twenty miles. They tried to sleep in the snow behind some rocks, but it was too cold, and hunger prevented sleep.

They continued eastward, and late in the evening reached the Lona river where traveling became easier. Some time after midnight they reached the uppermost house in the valley. Here they ate "bark-bread" and salt herring—and they ate it with relish, as they were quite starved.

They slept on the bare floor with comfort for two hours, but it was Sunday morning, and there were 28 miles to church. So Hauge arose and with his friends set off. They did not stop for breakfast but sandwiched some salt herring between slices of "bark-bread", and ate it on the way.

After the regular service Hauge was invited to the Sundby farmstead where he had his first good meal in four days. In the afternoon many people gathered, and he preached to them in the open. He also gave a talk at the Sundby farm in the evening.

As he found fishermen going north next morning he continued his journey with them as far as Lovo island in the Steingen district. Here he stayed for a few days and had meetings with good results.

Afterwards he found that the island was for sale, and he induced his friend Kristofer Brateng from Biri in the Mjøsen district, to buy it and start a fish mart. This was done, and soon Lovo island became the center for Hauge followers in the north.

The local pastor, Rev. Simon Kildal, testified

some years later that these "Haugians" were quiet, industrious and model citizens.

Hauge's pet idea was not only to broadcast the seed of God's Word throughout the land; but also to plant God's loyal citizens here and there throughout Norway, that they could show by example how to live a Christian life, and also build up strong, Christian communities.

This has often been overlooked, but it remains a fact that this was the secret of Hauge's success in making his revivals really permanent. Hauge had a number of friends "located" in this manner already, and more found places later on.

The planting bore fruit, and more fruit—fruit that lasted for generations and still is very much in evidence.

CHAPTER XLV
North to Finmark

Hauge now crossed the Vestfjord, to Lofoten, but the fishing season was over and the people had sailed for home. Nothing daunted, he continued north to Ibbestad, then on to Salangen, conducting meetings in each place.

Then he traveled inland to Bardo valley where people from the south had bought land and cleared it to raise barley and potatoes.

Some were spiritually wide-awake, being familiar with the laymen's movement; they were glad to have a visit from Hauge. They arranged a number of meetings for him in the Bardo valley.

At Finseth several successful meetings were held.

Hauge continued down the valley to Fagerli. As he heard the roar of the waterfalls nearby, he went over to estimate its power.

Towards evening people assembled to hear the renowned man preach; but when they found that he was at the waterfalls they began to suspect the man of worldliness because of his interest in temporal matters.

Soon, however, Hauge came, shook hands with the people, and without any preparation started a well-known hymn. Then he preached on John 3:8: "That the wind bloweth . . . thou hearest the sound . . . so is everyone that is born of the Spirit."

"You wonder why I looked at the waterfalls this afternoon; but it inspired me with the wisdom of God's handiwork and the power of God's Spirit brought into action.

"'Oh,' you say; 'water falling over a wall of rocks is merely obedient to nature's law independent of anybody's will.'

"Yes! But who made the laws of nature?

"Was it not He who created nature for the preservation, use, and benefit of man, who made these laws?

"And here are these waterfalls with the power of 200 horses, running idly and of no use to anybody because man will not use it.

"Christ was not sitting by a waterfall when Nicodemus came, or He might have used it as an illustration; but He sat in a place where the nightwind was sighing plaintive airs through open windows.

"But even the nightwind could be used as an illustration of the new birth. Christ did not explain the laws of nature to Nicodemus; but He showed him how they are allied to the spiritual laws as closely as the soul is allied to the body. The laws of nature harmonize with the spiritual laws, else we could not understand them.

"On Sunday morning you go to church and hear a good sermon from a spiritually gifted pastor. A volume of God's Word and the force of the Spirit are there. But your hearts! How did your hearts respond? Were your souls attuned to receive the message as spiritual food?

"Some people have poor digestion, and the richest food pains them. How is your spiritual digestion? Does God's Word give you pain?

"Or maybe your hearts are callous, like the rocks at the bottom of the falls. The flow of eloquence striking your hearts is dashed into a misty spray that befogs your soul and clouds your vision.

"The volume and force of God's Word is wasted like the falling waters, and the efforts of God's Spirit are lost on you.

"God revealed Himself to us in His Word—the highest wisdom ever attained on earth! But have you attained any of it, or are you still groping about in the dark abyss of ignorance?

"Christ tried to make Nicodemus understand the ways of God—tried to show him how 'he must be born anew'—be born of the Spirit of God to a new spiritual life.

"And what Christ taught Nicodemus, He tries to teach you.

"In the falls over yonder there is power to grind thousands and millions of tons of fertilizers from the 'waste' of fish in the neighboring fish-dressing stations.

"In God's Word there is more than sufficient power to Christianize the whole world, but nothing is accomplished when there is no man willing to go to every corner of the earth to do His work. God wants men—real men! He wants men with red blood and the courage to stand up for Christ—to work for His kingdom, and to work for the betterment of this world, not only in things pertaining to spiritual life, but also in our temporal affairs.

"Thanks be to God that there are some willing

workers, but God wants more—He wants you all!"*
Then they sang:

> *Awake, awake! O worldly dreamer!*
> *O lukewarm Christian, come, awake!*
> *Come, hear the cry of thy Redeemer:*
> *Awake and watch, life is at stake!*
> *Awake from slumbers deep in sin!*
> *There yet is room for you within.*
>
> *Awake! from sin's dread night of terrors;*
> *The light is coming—night must flee.*
> *'Tis He who rectifies your errors,*
> *Forgives your sins and sets you free.*
> *If you refuse—think! what a shame!*
> *That you have borne a Christian name.*
>
> *Awake! may be your soul is willing,*
> *But flesh and blood is very weak.*
> *O come, accept the offered healing,*
> *A balm for ailing sinners meek.*
> *Come, use your sense; come now, today,*
> *To Him who gladly leads the way.*
>
> *Awake! To fear the serpent's cunning;*
> *His craft and wiles are everywhere;*
> *Your own conceit and wayward running*
> *Will surely lure into his snare.*
> *If you are wise, then turn away*
> *And seek the Savior—now, today!*
>
> *Awake! and listen, death is calling,*
> *While you are unprepared to go.*
> *The aged die—the weak are falling,*
> *The young and stronger die also.*
> *For no one knows death's hour or place!*
> *Then come and be prepared in grace.*
>
> *Awake, in haste the Lord is coming,*
> *To sit upon His judgment seat;*
> *And all the world in fear forthcoming,*
> *No place to hide in safe retreat.*
> *Come now, acknowledge your account,*
> *Ere He upon His throne shall mount.*
>
> *Awake, awake! the voice of thunder*
> *Is loudly roaring: Break away!*

---

* We are indebted to the son of Hr. Fagerli for this concept of Hauge's talk in a letter to Iver Moholt in Trondheim, 1803.

*From torpid slumbers fatal blunder!
And flee to Him to plead and pray:
To take away your sin, and shame,
Awake! awake in Jesus' name!**

From Fagerli Hauge went down the valley to Moen, Maalselven and Malangen; then across to Urfjord, Mostervik and Balsfjord. He gathered people around him wherever he went. In the Balsfjord district there were many K v æ n e r (Swedish Finlanders). When Hauge came and held meetings in their district, one of these Kvæner, Henrik Mattison, was constantly present and was converted.

He invited Hauge to his home, and the two became close friends. He was somewhat educated and became a leader of the converted people in the Balsfjord and Lyngen districts.

Afterwards Hauge came to Tromsø, which at that time was only a fishing village with perhaps 100 inhabitants of the roughest kind.

He turned south from Tromsø, and visited Finseth and Bardo to say farewell to his friends. Then he continued south to Senjen and later to Trangø. Here he sent a letter (dated July 11, 1803) to J. N. Lose in Bergen, telling of his journeys in the far north.

Very little is known of his journey further south through Lofoten, Salten and Helgeland to Brønø, except that he visited friends and had some meetings.

CHAPTER XLVI

A Long Journey

Hauge crossed to the mainland and traveled through Namdalen along the Namsfjord. At Sorvik there was a good harbor. Hauge saw the ad-

---

* L. A. Gotter, 1698; Tr. Danish, Brorson, 1742; Tr. English, A. M. A., 1918.

vantages of establishing a trading-post at this point, so he bought the place for a friend, Otto Bakkerud from Hedemarken, who shortly afterward took possession and built up an extensive trade.

The stay in Namsen was cut short by the new magistrate, Judge Angell in Trondheim, who sent orders to all the sheriffs in the Trondheim diocese to arrest Hauge. When Sheriff Plesner of Namsen received this order he went to Hauge privately and showed it to him.

Hauge understood his kindness and thanked him, saying, "If the thirty or more sheriffs in this diocese are out to arrest me I may as well leave and save them the trouble."

Hauge went directly to Trondheim and told his friends about the order. He expected to be arrested, but when the officials failed to do this he started south through Guldalen to Støren, and then up the Soknedal and across to Austberg in the Orkla valley. Then he crossed the Dovre mountains from Opdal to Lesje in Gudbrandsdalen.

Here he was outside the jurisdiction of the "fire-eating" Angell of Trondheim, and could more safely pursue his vocation to preach the Gospel to people willing to listen, as well as to sell his books.

From Lesje, Hauge continued south to Lom, where he found his old friend Erik Skamsol very sick. Erik had been of the earliest converts, and a leader among them, but now he was near the end and worried about his having done so little for God's kingdom.

Hauge was of great comfort to him, showing him how God knows far better than we do about our work and when it is finished. Hauge held several meetings in the neighborhood, remaining until Erik's death. Then he went east through Vaagaa and had many successful meetings, and finally north to Foldalen and east to Tønseth.

Here he learned that veins of copper had been discovered in the Vingelen district, about forty miles northwest of Tønseth. He urged that his friends, as many as possible, go there and locate claims. This was done, and Vingelen became a center of the laymen's movement and activities in the Tolgen district.

Hauge traveled south along the old highway in the Glommen valley, and stopped only where friends invited him to preach or visit the sick.

At Elverum he stopped a few days to renew old acquaintances.

Then he turned west to Romedal and Stange, and south to Eidsvold and Ness, where he preached at the ironworks to a large audience.

Hauge continued south to Bjerke, Nannestad, Holter, Skedsmo, Nittedal and Aker, having one or two meetings at each place, and sometimes three. In the Holter parish many were converted.

When Hauge came to Aker he rested a few days staying with the Grøndahl family. He continued to Drammen and up to Eker to see his brother Mikkel, and his beloved paper-mill.

Everything was in fine working order, and the output of the mill had exceeded their expectations. His stay was short. A few days later he was at Sande, ready to cross the fjord to Fredrikstad.

Hauge then visited his aged father and mother in Thune. It gladdened their hearts to see him safe and sound after being away over a year. Afterwards he visited Sorbroden and Berg and neighboring parishes.

He then sailed from Fredrikstad to Skien, where he journeyed up the valley to Ulefoss, Boe, Siljord, then across to Kirkeby, Laardal, Moe, Bandak, Kviteseid, Vraadal, Nissedal, Treungen and Aamli, having two or more meetings at each place.

He continued down the valley to Aardal, Valle,

and Evje, where he had great success, and found people more intelligent than farther up the valley.

Fennefoss, a waterfall in the Torris river between Valle and Evje, interested Hauge, and first consulting his friends, he bought the falls and a strip of land along the river, where they built a sawmill, a flour-mill, and a paper-mill, and founded a colony of friends.

Afterwards Hauge continued down the valley to Hegland and Overbo, where he had several successful meetings.

In January, 1804, Hauge came to Kristiansand and called on his friend from Hedemarken, H. T. Bakkerud, who with Hauge's help had bought a printing establishment and a local paper.

Hauge immediately began preparing for new editions of his books, which again had been sold out but still were in demand. Besides the former books, he also published two new books during the stay at Kristiansand. One was a collection of prayers and songs for morning, evening, and holiday devotion. Later he published a collection of his sermons, arranged according to the texts for the church year.

When everything was ready to go to the press, Hauge continued his journey westward to Mandal and Farsund, then on to Flekkefjord, Sogndal, and Ekersund, holding two and sometimes three meetings a day.

People were so interested in Hauge that they traveled as far as twenty or thirty miles from the inland for a chance to talk with him or hear him preach.

On the Eger island he had several large gatherings. It was evidently here that he first met Amund Helland who was then quite a young man.

Helland says in his Notes: "I will thank God as long as I live that I met this man Hauge."

At Ogne, then Annex to Ekersund, the whole

congregation turned out to give Hauge an ovation. The local pastor, Peder Lund, was angry, and reported to the bishop that "the people are crazy after Hauge, and the sheriff is smitten so hard that he refuses to arrest him."

Hauge never lost his head, however, but turned people's attention to the industrial advantages God had given them.

Between Ogne and Haa he tested the sea in several places to find the best location for saltworks. Some people began to doubt Hauge's sincerity as an honest Christian.

Hauge then preached to them a sermon similar to the one at Fagerli in northern Norway the year before. He held that their spiritual life was like the ebb and tide of the sea, up and down; but the movement kept the sea-water from stagnation and the salt kept it fresh. He quoted, "Ye are the salt of the earth; but if the salt have lost its savor, wherewith shall it then be salted" (Matt. 5:13).

Then he expounded, "God's Word is the salt, but ye must absorb it like the water in the sea before ye can become the salt of the earth. And yet, how easy it is to lose the savor; you cannot retain it by outward show and demonstrations, but by the use of God's Word.

"God salted the waters of the ocean, and that keeps them pure and clear, even with all the dirt and filth of the world going into them. Thus God wants His children to absorb the salt of God's Word to keep them pure and sweet in a filthy and decaying world.

"Just as much as you need salt in your food, and salt on your table every day of your life, so will you need the salt of God's Word every day of your spiritual life if you expect to live a pure life and improve your surroundings. As your body is dead without a soul, so is your faith dead without deeds or works pleasing unto God.

"If you are idle in the market place you will rust and soon become useless. God wants you to work in your calling very faithfully to prove your faith in God and show the world what faith means.

"Moreover, you must make use of the gifts and the advantages God has given you. Here you have millions of tons of salt right in front of your homes, but when your salt-cruses are empty you send to Denmark or Holland for more. Why not make the salt yourselves, here at home?

"So in spiritual matters—you should read your Bibles and train your minds for your own benefit and the edification of others; then you need not wait for me, or make any demonstration on my account. The Lord is the shepherd who cares for you."

Then they sang with Hauge:

May God our actions deign to bless,
And loose the bond of wickedness,
From sudden falls our feet defend,
And guide us safely to the end.

May faith, deep-rooted in the soul,
The flesh subdue, the mind control;
May guile depart and discord cease,
And all within be joy and peace.*

CHAPTER XLVII

From Bergen to Denmark

Hauge had to preach often because of the many people who came to see him. At Høiland, near Stavanger, so many came that they had the meeting in a large warehouse. The leaders sent word to the local pastor, Knute W. Brown, asking him to honor

---
* Ambrose of Milan, ca. 380. Brorson, 1745. Tr. F. E. Cox (English), 1841.

the meeting with his presence, and he answered that he would.

While they waited Hauge preached, and after talking an hour he rested. It behooved the pastor to let the people wait, it seemed, for when he finally did appear he was more than an hour late. Then he ordered Hauge to begin. Hauge felt no desire to preach, but, seeing the many eager faces waiting expectantly, he began again.

Hauge had this text: "For God hath not called us unto uncleanness, but unto holiness" (1 Thess. 4:7).

"He depicted a life in sin and its gruesome horrors so vividly and terrifying that it struck like forked lightening into their hearts," said Amund Helland, in his Notes.

Then he pictured a life in holiness with an enlightened reason, a God-devoted will, and a heavenly peace of conscience.

At the end the pastor stepped up to Hauge and thanked him for the sermon, remarking that he would be glad if his efforts could make people better.

* * *

Hauge's stay in Stavanger was very brief. He sailed with a fisherman to Kvittingsøi, and the next day to Karmø, where he visited Akre and Avaldsnes. Here the local pastor, Rev. Sverdrup, again made good use of him. From Haugesund Hauge sailed direct to Bergen, where he arrived on the last day of March, 1804. On his arrival in Bergen he found that he had been away nearly fifteen months. During this time he had traveled about 4,500 miles.

During his stay in Bergen, Hauge bought several properties for his friends in eastern Norway. First he took a trip to Søndfjord and bought the Svanø island for his friend Ole Torgerson from Hallingdal.

Next he bought Strudshavn near Bergen for his friend Ole S. Bergh from Hedemarken, and others.

Here they built three factories that furnished steady jobs for hundreds of friends.

In July he had his business affairs in Bergen in good shape so that he could leave, sailing south with his freighter to Kristiansand.

When Hauge arrived in Kristiansand he went to Bakkerud's office to find how his books were coming, but they were so far behind with the work that Hauge had to stay six weeks to help them get the books off the press and get them distributed.

About the middle of August he sailed for Denmark, arriving at Horsens; afterwards he visited the noted layman, Peder Laursen, at Veile.

He also visited Haastrop and Grundet, and afterwards the institutions at Kristiansfeld where the United Brethren had their headquarters. Here he stayed two weeks to examine their industries.

Some things he liked and other things he did not like, but he said very little about them, even after he came back to Norway.

From Kristiansfeld Hauge went to Kolding where he wrote a letter to his brother Mikkel, and his friends in Norway, but very little was said about Denmark.

From Kolding he visited Faaborg and Nyborg in Fyen, and then went to Copenhagen where he visited former acquaintances and the printing offices. There he found that some of his orders were still unfilled.

From Copenhagen he went to Helsingor and sailed across to Fredrikstad where he went to visit his old friend John Sorbroden.

John was not at home. His aged father Hans, lay sick abed, so Hauge stayed a few days to read and pray and bring words of comfort.

Then news came to Hauge that his sister Bertha (now Mrs. Saxgaard) was dying, and he hurried on to Thune. He found his sister very weak, but it was a great comfort to her to see him once more. The aged parents came to bid farewell to their daughter. The older brother Ole also came making it a sort of a family reunion. They sang and read and prayed.

A few days later Bertha died and Hauge was busy comforting his parents and helping at the funeral in various ways.

Afterwards his friends arranged meetings for him in the neighboring parishes of Raade, Moss, Soon, and Norstrand. He finally arrived in Oslo where he rested a week with his friends. Then he continued to Drammen, Haugesund, and Eker, visiting his brother Mikkel at the last named place.

CHAPTER XLVIII

Celebrating at Eker

It was a mild day in October, 1804, and the woods had changed their green summer dress for the brilliant colors of autumn. It was an ideal day to be out-of-doors.

At Eker there was a holiday. Rumor had it that Hauge had returned from Denmark. He had been expected daily at Eker to visit his friends and relatives before going back to Bergen.

Mikkel had just received a letter from him stating more precisely when he would come, and the working force at the Eker paper-mill was very busy preparing a reception for Hans. The neighboring friends were flocking in to bid him welcome. Men and women, dressed in their best, arrived on foot or in carriages to attend the celebration.

Near the door stood Mikkel Hauge, Torkel Gabestad, Torleif Bache, Ole Foss, Kristofer Hoen, Karl Gunderson and Niels Braaten. Braaten had just arrived and informed them that Hans had held a meeting at the home of Lars Brekke in Hougsund the day before.

Mikkel sobered as he heard this—he thought of the sheriff, Jens Gram, who still hated Hauge with intense bitterness. Aloud he said, "Maybe something happened," and he looked searchingly at Niels.

But Niels smiled and said, "I think not, or we should have heard of it long before this."

Time passed. Clouds rolled up and the sky became dim. There appeared a shadow in the road beyond the gate. Yes, it was a man, tall, broad-shouldered, strong and commanding in appearance; and they recognized Hans Hauge. As he approached the crowd he began to shake hands. A smile illumined his face when he noticed so many of his old-time friends present.

When he reached his brother Mikkel the handshake was firm and lasting as he said, "I thank God, brother Mikkel, that you remained firm while in prison, against all the horrible temptations. God will certainly reward you for that."

Mikkel was unable to say a word, but introduced his wife Inger. She immediately invited them all to the spacious dining hall in the mill, where tables were set in long rows ready for the guests.

When they had all been seated Mikkel led in devotion. Then they all sang loudly and cheerfully and in a spirit of festivity:

Our table now with food is spread;
O God, who giveth daily bread,
Bless these Thy gifts upon us so
That strength of body they bestow.

O feed the hungry, God of love,
Who sigh for bread to heav'n above;
Give to our land prosperity,
And bless the earth and sky and sea!

Defend and bless our government,
And give us all a mind content!

*O grant our souls the heav'nly food
Which Jesus purchased with His blood.**

Then the hungry guests "fell to with a right good will." Most of them had been in too great a hurry to have a mid-day meal. But hunger did not stop them from exchanging pleasantries and benign smiles, and many laughed out loud, although it was considered not in good taste.

Etiquette could not wholly subdue the festive spirit as conversation grew more spirited and laughter more frequent. They related their experiences from their travels, both the sad and the humorous. Those sitting nearest Hauge asked him to contribute some of his.

Hauge smiled, shook his head and said, "They are too numerous and too varied to be related here; but I will write them down in a book where you can read them."

As their appetites began to be appeased—Mor** Inger had seen to it that they had plenty—Mikkel arose and asked for a hearing.

The commotion subsided and he began: "Friends and neighbors! We have gathered here to welcome my brother, who has returned to us safe and sound after many hazardous and fatiguing journeys, and we all feel thankful to God. We are happy to have him with us and to give him a hearty welcome.

"We have no strong drinks and fancy dishes on our tables. Yet it has not caused any drawback in our rejoicing. It is the best evidence that God's children need no ardent spirits to animate them when they celebrate and sing God's praise and glory."

Then they sang one of their favorite songs:

*Sing praise to God who reigns above,
The God of all creation;*

---

* Th. Kingo, 1689. Tr. (Eng.) G. T. Rygh, 1909.
** Mor,—abbr. of mother.

*The God of pow'r, the God of love,
The God of our salvation.
With healing balm my soul He fills,
And every pain and sorrow stills;
To God all praise and glory!*

*The angel host, O King of Kings,
Thy praise forever telling;
In earth and sky all living things
Beneath Thy shadow dwelling.
Adore the wisdom which could span
And pow'r which formed creation's plan,
To God all praise be given.*

Mikkel interrupted the singing to call upon Niels Braaten for a toast.

Braaten responded by giving a brief sketch of the history of the paper-mill and what a blessing it was for them. Then they sang:

*What God's almighty pow'r hath made
His gracious mercy keepeth;
By morning glow or evening shade
His watchful eye ne'er sleepeth;
Within the kingdom of His might,
Lo! all is just, and all is right;
To God all praise and glory!*

*The Lord is never far away,
Forsakes His people never;
He is their refuge and their stay,
Their peace and trust forever;
And with a mother's watchful love
He guides them wheresoe'er they rove;
To God all praise and glory!*

Here Mikkel interrupted again and called on Kristofer Hoen.

Hoen responded by giving a brief sketch of the social progress and improvement which the laymen's movement had produced.

Again they sang:

*I cried to God in my distress,
His mercy heard me calling;
My Savior saw my helplessness
And kept my feet from falling;
For this, Lord, praise and thanks to Thee!
Praise God most high, praise God with me!
To God all praise and glory!*

*When every earthly hope hath flown
From sorrow's sons and daughters;
Our Father from His heav'nly throne
Beholds the troubled waters;
And at His Word the storm is stayed,
Which made His children's hearts afraid;
To God all praise and glory!*

Several began to call for Hauge.

Hauge responded by thanking them all for the spirit of good-will made manifest during the evening. They had done well in temporal improvements and—best of all—they had become God's children.

Now he wanted to leave with them a Bible verse found in Revelation 2:10: "Be faithful unto death, and I will give thee a crown of life." Then Hauge continued, "How sad it is to begin well and end poorly in temporal affairs; how much more sad would it not be for the soul to begin upon the way of life and afterwards become lost in the cares of this world; therefore be faithful in your calling both in temporal affairs and spiritual life; never yield, never turn away from what is right. 'Be thou faithful unto death, and I will give thee a crown of life.' "*

Hauge closed with a warm and fervent prayer, and then they sang:

*Thus all my pilgrimage along
I'll sing aloud Thy praises,
That man may hear the grateful song
My voice unweared raises.
Be joyful in the Lord, my heart!
Both soul and body, bear your part!
To God all praise and glory!*

*O ye who bear Christ's holy name,
Give God all praise and glory!
All ye who know His pow'r, proclaim
Aloud the wondrous story;
Cast each false idol from His throne,*

---
* T. O. Bache's memoirs.

The Lord is God, and He alone;
*To God all praise and glory!**

It was getting late so they all came up to bid Hauge good night. He had a warm smile and a good word for every one of them.

CHAPTER XLIX

Talking Improvements

When most of the guests had left, Hauge turned to Mikkel with a smile and said in a cheerful voice, "Now, brother Mikkel, you are glad, are you not?"

"Yes," answered Mikkel, "and mostly because you are here."

"No, no!" said Hans and shook his head, "that is of little consequence if I am here; but God helped, and that makes us glad."

Mikkel grasped his brother's hand, and with feeling said, "Without you it is a question if God would have been so near at hand to help us in the hour of darkness."

"Oh, do not say that, brother Mikkel," exclaimed Hans, "God can reach us in many ways, and without me, but I am glad and very thankful that I could be of service to further His kingdom."

A few remaining friends had listened, and suddenly Kristofer Hoen spoke up: "How many times have you been arrested, Hans?"

Hauge counted on his fingers the various places, then said, "In all, nine times; and brother Mikkel, two times; that is not so bad for a beginning of persecutions."

"You have had your freedom for some time now," inquired Braaten.

"Yes," said Hauge, "I have, but that is due to circumstances."

---

* J. J. Schulz, 1675. Tr. (Danish) Brorson, 1728. Tr. (Eng.) F. E. Cox, 1864.

"Well, God be praised!" said Mikkel; "and as to being arrested for vagrancy, you have been quite an active vagrant."

"Yes, his vagrancy ought to make quite a few miles," put in Hoen.

Hans sat in deep thought a while; then he raised his head and smiled approvingly as he said, "It has sometimes amused me to compute the miles I have traveled and to jot it down for reference. The total up to the present amounts to about twelve thousand miles."

They pondered on this, but no one ventured to say anything.

"But," said Hauge quietly, "now it will be drawing to a close. There is a vague premonition in my soul that soon I shall have a long rest. When God's Word begins to take root in the land they will find a way to arrest me."

There was a deep silence. His friends knew all too well that this was true.

"You go to Bergen without delay," said Niels Braaten; "here you can never be safe anywhere."

"That is my intention," Hauge answered, "as soon as I am ready."

His friends felt sad when they thought of the parting.

"It is good to know that this mill is running and a blessing to many," mused Hans.

"Yes, it is running," answered Mikkel, "and running well; soon it will be running so well that it will be known all over Norway."

Hans nodded in assent. "The Christian slogan is 'work and pray', and it should be the slogan of our people. Too many reject work when they are awakened, and busy themselves only with spiritual things. It is like placing an empty pot over the fire; it has plenty of heat but no food, and soon the pot is destroyed.

"God created us with soul and body, but the soul rules the body as a master rules his servant. It is a foolish master who neglects to feed his servant until he is useless and unfit for good work. God put Adam to work in the garden of Eden while he was yet an innocent man; and thus we conclude that work is not a punishment for our sins but a blessing to adjust the relations between body and soul.

"Idleness is the root of all evil, and idlers are sinning greatly against the ordinance of God: 'In the sweat of thy face shalt thou eat bread.' Thus shall the mill be a permanent warning to idlers that they are failing to get God's greatest blessing."

Then Hauge related how he had called the attention of people to the industrial possibilities in the various localities, how he had urged them to make use of them and in some places had bought real estate for his friends.

"Thus will I plant good industrial 'trees' all over the land, and in time they will bear fruit and seed that will spread beyond the boundaries of Norway to countries far beyond.

"We must teach them, show them, and prove to them that we are not vagrants or S v e r m e r e, but honest Christians that are willing workers, thanking God for our blessed privileges."

CHAPTER L

The Final Arrest

Hauge inspected the workings of the mill, suggesting improvements that he had seen in Denmark, and explained to his brother Mikkel how they would facilitate the work.

Yet he found time to talk with his many friends that came to visit him, and also to give them a word of cheer.

About noon of the fourth day after his arrival he was talking with Mikkel's wife, Mor Inger when Mikkel came rushing in. "Hans, you must try to get away; I see the sheriff coming, and you know he is after you again," he said excitedly.

Mor Inger turned to Hans. "Come this way, Hans! I'll let you out the back door through the wood-shed, and you can follow the path back of the warehouses into the woods."

"No, no! Mor Inger," said Hauge, and a fire of deep passion burned in his eyes; "I do not leave this place through any back door, not for Sheriff Gram or any one else. My conscience is clear and at peace, and I have nothing to hide."

Mikkel stared hard at him. "You are just as stubborn as ever, Hans. And," he added softly, "God be praised!"

"And you are my brother, Mikkel, who stayed in prison two years rather than deny God and your God-given right to proclaim His benevolence. Now go and receive the sheriff, I will soon be ready."

Mikkel went out without a word.

"And now we'll never see you again," cried Mor Inger.

"Oh, yes," said Hans, "there is no power on earth that can prevent God's children from seeing each other in heaven."

"I know," said Mor Inger, "but it is terrible that they will not let peaceful people live in peace."

Mikkel Hauge and the sheriff came in.

The sheriff shook hands with Mor Inger as she asked him to be seated.

"Thanks! But I cannot stay," said the sheriff, turning to Hauge. "My errand is concerning you."

Hans nodded and said, "Yes, yes. I understand."

Mor Inger placed herself squarely in front of the sheriff. Her face had a heightened color. Her eyes burned into his as she said, "See here, Sheriff Gram!

Don't you do anything wicked; it will be bad for you! To put a man in jail for being good to everybody is not going to bring you any good whatever, and some day you will regret it."

"No, no, Mor Inger!" interposed Hans, coming close, "the authorities will do only what is good; that is easily seen. There is no authority but of God, and Sheriff Gram is going God's errands."

The sheriff turned very red in the face and in his gruff way stammered: "No, thank you, I have nothing to do with God's errands; I am doing only what the law commands."

"And you do it gladly," added Hans. "Let's hear your errand."

Sheriff Gram put on his hat. "I have an order from Judge Collett, that he wants to have a talk with you," he said.

Hans put on his overcoat and hat and shook hands with Mikkel. "Farewell, brother, and thanks for the time we have been together."

Then, turning to Mor Inger, he took her hand and said, "Hold fast unto God and nothing can harm you. He shall reward His faithful servants. And now farewell, and thanks for the good things that you have done in this enterprise."

"God bless you both, and—keep the mill going!"

Together they went outside. The sheriff and Hans climbed into the K a r i o l. Mor Inger waved her hand and called: "May God's peace remain with you, and the Lord keep you from all harm."

The sheriff touched the horses with his whip, and off they went. Mikkel and Inger stood with tears in their eyes looking until the K a r i o l disappeared beyond a turn in the road.

After driving half an hour, they turned toward Hougsund.

Hans asked, "Where do we go?"

"To Hougsund," came the gruff answer.

"But Judge Collett is not in Hougsund."

"No, that was only a blind; you will go straight to jail."

"Without a warrant?" queried Hauge.

"We don't need a warrant for arresting vagrants and tramps."

"But you know that I am neither, and that I am here on legitimate business," retorted Hauge.

The sheriff said: "I know only this, that you go with me."

When they came to the jail Hauge held out his hand and said, "Well, I must thank you for a good ride, Herr Sheriff!"

"Hold on, Herr Hauge," warned the sheriff; "here is something more to be thankful for." And he put the handcuffs on. "And here is yet some more," he said, as he put fetters on Hauge's feet. He laughed loudly. "I'd like to see you run away in these," he added.

Hauge looked at him in sadness. "Well, I can carry these chains, but some time, Sheriff Gram, these chains will weigh heavier on your soul than on mine."

The sheriff went out hastily and slammed the door shut.

Hauge was arrested October 24, 1804, and remained in irons at Hougsund jail 29 days. Then he was transported to Oslo prison in extra chains with a guard to prevent him from running away.

The authorities wanted to impress upon the people that Hauge was the most dangerous criminal in Norway.

This hostile stand taken by the authorities is further evinced by the fact that Kristofer Hoen and a number of other wealthy friends of Hauge offered any amount of bail for his freedom until court was set, but all the offers were sternly refused. The only privilege granted by the Hougsund jailer was to allow Hauge to remove the handcuffs, so that he could have his hands free. He was also allowed to keep his Bible and writing materials, so that he could write to his friends.

A perfunctory hearing was held on the first of November, without results. Nothing was proved against Hauge except that he had preached. Then he was promised freedom if he would quit preaching. Hauge said he could not promise that, so he was remanded to jail in irons.

While in Hougsund jail Hauge wrote a small tract entitled, A Prayer for the Christian Church.

The authorities took offense at this, and after his transfer to Oslo prison he was not allowed any writing materials.

Hauge had written several letters to his friends while in Hougsund jail, stating that he would hold out as long as life would last and God gave him strength. He counselled them to live so that if he should not meet them again in this world they would meet in heaven.

* * *

In Oslo prison Hauge was relieved of his irons, as they had cut into the flesh and caused ugly wounds about his ankles, but his Bible and other books and writing materials were kept from him. Hauge, reputed to have been a rich man, was found to have but two dollars and forty-eights cents when he came to the Oslo prison. The authorities were nonplussed because there was not more.

His property in Bergen was confiscated by the authorities, also his freighters and everything else he had. The foreign authorities were bound to break him and make of him an example to terrorize his adherents.

Hauge languished in a "lone cell behind many locks" in the Oslo prison. Christmas came and passed, but he had no Bible from which to read the Christmas story; yet it was a comfort to him to rehearse Bible verses and chapters that he had committed to memory.

Solitary confinement too began telling on Hauge. There was no one to speak to, no books to read, no daily exercises in fresh air, no chance to write, not even a chance to jot down the thoughts that flitted through his mind.

Hauge complained of this to the jailer, and one day he brought Hauge a Danish translation of Voltaire's writings.

Hauge read and read, but this kind of reading irritated his soul. He could not understand why people, intelligent and learned, could be so blind as to reject God's Word without a thorough examination into the holy truth while they believed such crafty philosophy.

Sometimes he itched for writing materials to write a refutation of this false reasoning and to show up the fallacies of such ridiculous conclusions.

Hauge soon found that these volumes of Voltaire and other infidel books that they had brought him were seriously injurious to his peace of mind. He quit reading and began to look about for something else to make time pass without harrassing his mind.

One day he noticed that the jailer's mittens were worn so that they had big holes in them. This set him to thinking how in his boyhood days he had helped his mother knit socks and mittens.

Next day he asked the jailer to bring him yarn and knitting needles, so that he could knit him a pair of mittens. This the jailer did, and Hauge soon had a pair of mittens for him. The jailer was so well pleased that Hauge had to knit some more.

Then they agreed that the jailer should sell his goods on commission and both make a little money.

That kept Hauge so busy knitting socks and mittens that the rest of the winter passed quickly, and he had money to buy a few necessities.

When spring came and woolen goods were not in demand, Hauge changed to skeins of fine cotton and silk, supplying fastidious persons with gloves and scarfs that sold readily, because "Hauge made nice things."

Thus passed the first year of Hauge's incarceration. He had grown thin and hollow-eyed because of scant food and lack of fresh air.

He was not permitted to see his friends or to commune with anybody. He had no attorney, and his case was rested during the year 1805. It was a most miserable time for Hauge. He became despondent, gloomy and even resigned to his fate. There seemed to be no hope of getting a hearing for his case.

CHAPTER LI

Solitary Prison Life

Christmas Eve, 1805, found Hauge more despondent than ever. He was kneeling by his bed and praying for strength to be faithful to the end. "But Lord, how long must I wait?" came the cry from his heart. He remembered the angel's message: "On earth peace and good will." Peace!—good will—.

Outside people were hurrying home with their Christmas purchases, and many of them were carrying small Christmas trees. In Kirkegaten there was a traffic jam, and policemen were busy moving the crowd.

The chief of police, Jacob Wulfsberg, and Judge Peter Collett came walking down Raadhusgaten, but stopped at the crossing.

They talked about Hauge, and the merits of his case.

Chief of Police Wulfsberg had recently resigned from the commission of investigation of Hauge's case, and Judge Collett had just been appointed to take the chief's place, and was seeking information.

"It is an extremely difficult case, my dear judge," said the chief; "Hauge has traveled extensively over Norway, and it will take years to conduct hearings and collect evidence against him."

"With my duties here I could not handle the case with efficiency; and I am thankful to the K a n c e l l i that they found a man with your energy and ability to succeed me," continued the chief.

"Oh, no," said the judge, "that's flattering! No one could better handle the case than the chief of police. Of course, when it is so desired, I'll do the best I can."

"Well, then," said the chief of police; "the case is in good hands," and he started to cross the street.

Judge Collett stopped him, however, with the question, "Beg pardon! But what reason did the district judge, Jacob Aars, have for his resignation from this commission?"

"Probably the same reasons that I had," said the chief.

"Were there more reasons than the one given?"

"Yes, between us I must admit that I do not like the case. There is something peculiar about this man; he inspires confidence in a way unusual. One is forced, whether he will or not, to believe him innocent; and it is not agreeable to assume that he is not."

"I understand," said the judge, "that this Hauge is quite prepossessing and very persuasive; otherwise he could not have caused so much trouble and harm throughout the land."

"No, no! it is not that," said the chief of police; "I am not so easily duped! No! It is something else

—well, you can see for yourself—you have the chance from now on."

And the two walked together up the street to the court-house where the guards saluted them as they went in.

* * *

A key was inserted, and the door to the dark and gloomy cell of Hans Nielsen Hauge swung open. The jailer held out his lantern. It threw some light at least into the gloom.

"Come with me," he said to Hauge; "the chief of police wants you."

"Yes, yes," said Hauge, as he arose wearily and followed through a long corridor to the police court.

As he came into the well-lighted room his red and swollen eyelids glimmered in the strong light; his pale face had an ashen hue, and was furrowed deeply with wrinkles of worry and sorrow.

At the desk sat Chief Wulfsberg and Judge Collett.

The chief nodded to the jailer to remain outside. "I'll ring when you are wanted," he said.

The jailer saluted and left.

Then the chief turned to Hauge and said softly, "Come a little nearer."

Hauge walked up to the desk and "straightened up."

Judge Collett looked at him long—inspecting him closely as if adjusting the measure of the man. "So you are Hans Nielsen Hauge?" and his voice mellowed down to a degree of respect for the man bowed in grief and pain.

"Yes, I am," answered Hauge in a broken voice. After a little pause the chief of police turned to Hauge and said, "I have some news for you. Judge Collett here has been appointed a member of the commission to investigate your case."

Hauge looked searchingly at the new member.

"And that will hasten proceedings?" asked Hauge.

The chief of police smiled as he said, "Judge Collett is my successor; he will do it better than I."

Hauge did not smile. Collett was his sworn enemy.

"The chief of police, of course, has his hands full," said Hauge; "there are so many incarcerated here."

The chief of police looked at the judge.

"Your case is very far-reaching," said the judge; "it will assume a spacious and extensive magnitude."

"Yes," answered Hauge; "the case is great, and has a strong tendency to grow in magnitude and results."

The judge looked sharply at Hauge. "That is the very thing we fear," he said.

Hauge voluntarily took a step nearer. "That the Word of God has taken root in the minds of people is nothing to be afraid of," he said; "and if it had taken root all over Norway I would gladly let go my life here as I stand."

Hauge said this with force, yet with a dignified calm.

The officials exchanged glances. They felt a peculiar sensation; they felt the presence of a spirit stronger than theirs.

"I hear that you have faith in your cause," said the judge.

"Yes, I have," answered the prisoner.

"And are you not afraid of the results?"

Hauge was smiling now as he responded, "No! I have too good a defense—and Defender."

The judge looked at the chief of police.

"What defender?" he said, turning to Hauge.

Hauge's eyes shone with mild intensity. "Your Honor knows that."

Judge Collett wrinkled his brows and said somewhat sharply, "No, I do not know who will defend you."

Hauge looked at the judge more intensely.

"That is too bad," Hauge explained. "God is my defender and helper."

"Oh, well," said the judge, "everybody can say that."

"No!" answered Hauge, "everybody can n o t say that."

The judge was perplexed. He looked at the chief of police; but the chief was looking at the floor evidently lost in thought.

"You seem to think that too little progress is being made in your case," spoke the judge.

"Yes," Hauge answered. "Time drags, when we are idle and lonesome; and it is not easy for a man to carry the burdens of life with patience,"—his voice was sad—"but worse it is for all those throughout the land who are waiting for me. There are so many that need help."

Judge Collett's face turned red and sparks of anger flew from his eyes as he said, "You think, perhaps, that you are the only one that can preach the Word of God here in this land of Norway."

Hauge shook his head in sadness. "I am not so conceited as that; but it may be that I am one of the few that knows how to speak to the common people in a language they understand. I am but a common man and I understand them."

"You would perhaps do more good," said the judge, "if you held to your vocation as a farmer and left the preaching of God's Word to the examined and ordained ministers."

Hauge heaved a deep sigh and said, "Yes, that is the way it ought to be; but so many of the ministers preach nothing but dead knowledge. That is the reason there are so many empty churches, while the dance-halls are filled with our young people."

Judge Collett was silent.

Chief Wulfsberg then spoke up, "The ministers are working in their rightful calling, the same as you ought to do."

Hauge met his eye with a firm look. "The apostles of Christ were neither scribes nor learned men," Hauge said. "They were common fishermen, yet Christ called them to preach the Gospel."

Judge Collett's face reddened. "So you consider yourself equals of the apostles of Christ?" he demanded.

All were silent for a while.

The judge turned to Hans with an official air: "Tomorrow, according to the king's order," he said, "I enter upon the duties of this Commission of Inquiry that is appointed to try your case; and you may feel assured that the investigation will proceed to a speedy conclusion and settlement."

Hauge stepped up closer. "I want to thank you for this, your Honor. Time passes heavily when one sits idly waiting—and waiting—"

Judge Collett nodded assent.

"But you could busy yourself with something to pass the time," he added.

"That is difficult," answered Hauge, "when I have no writing materials, no books, no work, nothing left but to pray. Prayer without work is not according to God's command, your Honor, and idleness has always been a pest to me; all wicked thoughts are fostered in idleness."

Judge Collett looked at the chief of police.

Wulfsberg nodded and whispered softly, "Means of precaution necessarily used."

Judge Collett nodded.

Chief Fulfsberg rang the bell, and the jailer came in.

"Farewell, Judge Collett and Chief Wulfsberg,"

said Hauge, "and I wish you God's peace and a Merry Christmas!" Then he turned and left.

Outside they saw two men that Hauge knew. The prisoner stopped to speak to them. But the guard ordered "Forward, march!" and Hauge was escorted to his dark cell without speaking a word to his friends.

CHAPTER LII

Visitors Not Allowed

As the prisoner left the judge remarked, "Hauge looks so pale and emaciated; is he not taking care of himself?"

The chief of police shook his head.

"He is said to be a rich man," continued the judge, "and ought to provide for himself."

"No," said the chief of police, "he is not. When he came here, he had two dollars and forty-eight cents; and no money has come to him since."

Judge Collett stopped short; his eyes big with surprise. "That's queer," he said, "everybody talks of the 'Holy Treasury.'"

"That as well as a number of other stories about this man," said the chief, "is nothing but wild rumor which really has no foundation. You will have the opportunity now to investigate all such allegations."

As the two left the courtroom, they met two men in the entry.

The chief of police stopped to ask, "Was it something you wanted?"

"Yes," said the smaller of the two, whose name was Ole Roersveen; "we—could we have leave to talk with Hans Nielsen Hauge?"

The chief of police looked at them searchingly. Then he said, "No, it cannot be allowed."

"Only a few words," Roersveen pleaded.

"No, no! Not now," answered the chief, then, inquiringly, "Where do you come from?"

"We come from Bergen," Roersveen answered.

"Did you come by sea?"

"No," said Roersveen, "we traveled on foot across the mountains."

"And what is your errand?"

"We came to see our dear friend Hauge and talk with him in his distress. And now we are not allowed to see him."

"No," said the chief with some sympathy, "it is against the law."

The two officials turned and left.

The chief mused a little; then said, "It is so pathetic to see how these people are fascinated by this man, and—they are just as harmless as they are ignorant."

At Østregate they parted with a—

"Merry Christmas to you, Chief Wulfsberg!"

"Merry Christmas to you, Judge Collett!"

* * *

Hauge found his cell more gloomy than ever. The little candle had burned low. The charred end of the wick was blurring the light. The meager supper was on the table—a piece of salt herring on a slice of coarse brown bread—but Hauge had no appetite. He sat down on the wooden cot with his head resting on his hands, lost in sad musings on life's tragedies. This night, the Savior's night—the festival of mercy, the festival of love and peace and good-will—what a farce!

How bitter was this confinement within prison walls, while all the world was singing in happiness and joy because a Savior had been born this blessed Christmas night.

Even now he heard distant church-bells ringing forth the festive call. Then he remembered the two friends that evidently had walked across the mountains from Bergen to Oslo at this time of the year for a few words with him. But the prison door was shut. And he fell to musing: The many thousands who had longed to see him and to talk with him during these fourteen months in prison—how disappointed they must be! And possibly he would not be able to see them again.

Here he had to be idle in a prison cell, alone and in darkness—never to see the sun or feel the fresh air; never to see the happy faces of his friends— "O God, hast Thou forsaken me," he cried in grief. And the strong, valiant, kind, mild-mannered, God-fearing man broke down in despair.

Silence reigned in the lonely cell for a long time.

Hauge was kneeling by the wooden cot in silent prayer. He prayed in childish simplicity to the omnipotent Father who listens to all, even to the simplest of His children. Would He listen to this lonely prisoner praying for light in the darkness, for help in his suffering, remission of sin, saving grace, strength to resist temptation, for comfort, grace and peace in his agonized soul?

Something illuminated his mind, and a vista of heavenly visions appeared. He saw the white city of Bethlehem and the star that shone like a sun among the other stars. Out of this sun came an angel proclaiming the Savior's birth.

The star grew bigger, blazing into a host of shining angels who came sailing through the sky, singing louder and louder: "Glory to God in the highest; On earth peace; to men good will."

Hauge jumped up. It was the chimes of all the church-bells in the city that rang louder than ever; but Hauge was thankful for the vision just the same; this was God's way of answering his prayer.

And the angel had said: "Fear not!"

What had he to fear if God and a host of angels

were with him? He felt so cheered that he began to sing.

Jesus, I long for Thy blessed communion.

He sang the whole verse until the prisoners in the neighboring cells listened, and the guard in the corridor stopped to listen, and two men outside came around to listen.

They were Ole Roersveen and Samson Traa from Bergen.

Yes, they knew this voice among a thousand others; and it gladdened them now, as it had done so many a time before.

The men wanted to shout, but dared not for the guards. Then they remembered that it was Christmas night and that they would be allowed to sing the N o e l. So they sang:

*None shall ever be confounded
Who in God will freely trust;
Though they be by woes surrounded,
God's a rock to all the just;
Though you deem He hears you not,
Still your wants are ne'er forgot;
Cry to Him when storms assail you,
Let your courage never fail you.*

*Learn to mark God's wondrous dealing
With His people that He loves;
When His chastening hand they're feeling,
Then their faith the strongest proves.
God is nigh, and notes their tears.
Though He answers not, He hears;
Pray with faith, for though He try you,
No good thing can God deny you.**

Hauge turned to the window. He knew the melody. By straining his ears he caught the words. What faithful friends, he was not alone!

But it was so sad, after coming the long way, that they were not permitted to see him, and he was barred from everybody.

---

* J. Olearius, 1671; tr. Brorson (Dan.), 1728; F. E. Cox (Eng.), 1841.

He sat helpless; he could not give them a single word of comfort—was not allowed to send a word of cheer to the many thousands far west by the beautiful fjords, or north in the fishing districts, high up among the ice-covered mountains, or in the deep and fertile valleys, or to the thousands in the lowly cottages that were waiting for him, and where Christmas bells were ringing.

Hauge suddenly thought of a message he would send. He took the candle and stepped up and placed it in the window.

"Look! Look!" Ole Roersveen cried. He was getting excited.

"Yes, God be praised," said Samson Traa, "now we have seen his silent message: 'Let your light shine' ... as the Star of Bethlehem."

Suddenly the light disappeared.

Hauge had taken the candle down to snuf it, and when he again put it in the window it shone very brightly.

"Did you see that?" said Roersveen.

"Yes," answered Samson Traa; "the light wins over darkness; but the snuffing of the candle means the cleansing of the Church, that God's Word—the light from heaven—in greater brilliancy may shine throughout the land."

"That's right," said Ole Roersveen, "God's people must look to the future—let the light so shine—from church and home, that everybody, even the worldly, may see the good work of those that fear God, and glorify our Father which is in heaven. We must tell this to our brothers throughout the land."

And while they were watching the light that shone through the prison-bars in the little window, Hauge began to sing Luther's great battle-hymn, "A mighty fortress is our God."

His voice was gaining strength and had its old ring. The listeners outside noticed this and were glad. Hauge was yet his old self, and they had something to tell the neighbors when they came home. Now they heard the words plainly, and when he sang the last line of the last verse, W i t h u s r e- m a i n s t h e k i n g d o m, Samson Traa cried aloud, "That's our slogan, Ole; that last line we must bring our friends, as Hauge's last message to all his friends."

G u d g i d i g e n g l a d j u l, H a n s! both said; and they turned and left; but the message flew in hundreds of letters to all parts of Norway, and thousands of friends read the inspiring words.

CHAPTER LIII

Judge and Magistrate

Three years had passed. Hans Nielsen Hauge was still languishing in the dark and dismal cell in Oslo prison without any hope of relief. Judge Collett had continued the investigation with some results; but the evidence obtained was mostly statements from local officials and clergymen who hated Hauge, and their dispositions were accusations rather than testimony. Hundreds of hearings had been held throughout the land to unearth testimony against Hauge.

The final hearing began October 24, 1807, and concluded December twelfth of the same year. A summary of the hearings was sent to the K a n- c i l l i in Copenhagen, Denmark, on the eighth day of January, 1808. But the K a n c i l l i rested sixteen months, and then ordered a new trial May 5, 1809.

The continued imprisonment had brought on many severe ailments and diseases until Hauge's strong body was broken and his health gone. And

257

not only that. His mind was failing and his soul was full of despair.

His brother Mikkel had tried again and again with the aid of influential neighbors and men of authority and wealth to get Hauge released on bail, but the K a n c i l l i insisted on Hauge staying in prison until his case was settled.

Their attitude was severely criticized and termed barbarous even by some of the king's own officers.

* * *

It was spring again, but Hauge's cell was just as dark as ever. No sunshine penetrated the gloom, and nothing inside gave any evidence that a new and glorious spring was at hand.

Niels Lumholtz, who had just been appointed attorney for Hauge, was seeking advice from Judge Bull as to the handling of the case.

On this glorious spring-day he had induced Judge Bull to go with him to the prison. They found Chief of Police Wulfsberg and he politely accompanied the judge to the prison in person.

The head jailer went with them and opened the door to the cell. Hauge was resting on the hard wooden cot when he heard the jailer rattle the keys, and he wondered if something had turned up at last.

"Good morning, Hauge," said the chief of police; "here I bring Judge Bull, who has come to see you."

"Good morning," answered Hauge, and he turned to look at this tall stranger with the piercing eyes.

Judge Bull was looking at Hauge, intensely interested.

Then he turned abruptly to the chief of police and said very pointedly: "But this man is quite sick!"

The chief made no answer to this charge.

Judge Bull stepped up to Hauge and shook hands, saying, "I was surprised to find a sick man here, but on second thought I do not wonder any more. If I can do something for you to improve your situation I shall gladly do it for you. This is quite inexcusable."

Again he looked at the chief.

Hauge was still holding Judge Bull's hand with both of his own, as he said feebly, "God's blessing I wish you for this. He shall reward you. Once more can I begin to believe in mankind."

Judge Bull placed his hand on Hauge's shoulder and said in his warm-hearted manner, "Believe in God; that is better."

Hauge looked at the judge with the innocent stare of a child.

"Yes, I do believe in God," Hauge answered, and his voice grew strong; "that is why I am here, because I believed, and I wanted others to believe; but it is so hard to keep patient in this long waiting."

Judge Bull was all sympathy as he added in a sad voice, "Faithful unto death, was it not so?"

"Yes," answered Hauge, "if death would come."

The judge nodded and said, "But what of all your friends?"

Hauge heaved a deep sigh. "Oh, if I could reach them to give them a word of cheer," he said, his voice trembling.

It was too much for him. He burst into tears as he continued, "Now I am as a tree in the shade, bearing no fruit, and thus I must remain, a barren tree in God's garden."

Deep silence reigned while Hauge regained his calm.

"Are you never out?" asked the judge. "Don't you get some fresh air occasionally?"

The police chief started to say something, but Hauge began to cough violently so he remained quiet.

When the coughing subsided Hauge explained, "I have not seen the sun for almost four years."

"But," interjected the chief of police, "the order given was 'strictest watch' and 'no communication'."

Judge Bull did not seem to hear this.

He stepped up to Hauge, took his hand and said, "Now listen! Don't lose courage! Something shall be done to remedy this. Now, good-bye!" and he turned and left hurriedly.

The chief of police was already outside. As the judge caught up with him he mumbled to himself, "Nigh unto four years—not sentenced—perhaps an innocent man—in this condition—for the infirmary—."

Turning to the chief he said, "I cannot understand how in conscience you can justify this—this—."

"I have my orders," said the chief of police; "I have no authority to change them or interfere in any way."

"I know," answered the judge, "but you can report."

"That is the duty of the inspector. He has done nothing."

"Well, I am going to look into this; it is a blot upon Norway's administration of justice — farewell!"

And the chief hurried to add, "For God's sake, I—"

But the judge cut him short with, "I know; but now you will help me to have this changed—farewell!"

In the waiting-room he found D e f e n s o r Lumholtz, who immediately asked him how he had found the client.

"He is an honest and innocent man," answered Judge Bull, "but it is a shame that he is persecuted and confined for years in a dungeon on account of his opinions."

"I am glad to hear that," said Lumholtz.

"But I am less glad," said Judge Bull, "that neither the government nor the defense has done anything to relieve the intolerable prison conditions."

Attorney Lumholtz reddened. "Being recently appointed, I must admit that this intricate case has made me forget the client's health," he said.

"But that is preposterous, beginning at the wrong end," expostulated the judge. "Of what avail is it to win for a dead man?"

Herr Lumholtz said no more, and they walked in silence.

"Well, you do your part and I will do mine," said the judge, as they parted. "This man shall not stay entombed in this manner, or it will be a judicial murder."

* * *

The same afternoon Judge Bull called on Count Moltke who was now chief magistrate of the southern districts or counties in Norway. The count took him to his private den, and when seated asked to what he was indebted for the honored visit.

"My dear Count," the judge began, "I have come today to interest you in something that concerns our mutual interests."

"That sounds rather intriguing, and whets my curiosity," said the count; "pray, what may it be?"

"It concerns the man Hans Nielsen Hauge," said the judge, with a solemnity unusual for him.

"Ah! That religious fanatic!" exclaimed the count.

"Maybe so, or maybe not," countered the judge.

"He was tried and sentenced in Trondheim," said the count. "He may have had good intentions, but his doctrines created a number of sects and stirred up a commotion wherever he went."

"That may all be," admitted the judge; "but that is not the question involved just now. As you evidently know, my dear Count, I am strongly opposed to all religious constraint, and I hate persecuting people on account of their opinions; hence if it were up to me I would set this very unfortunate man free today. Admitting that the government has a right to secure his person, that does not concede any judicial or moral right to rob a man of life and health in solitary confinement in a most unhealthy prison cell."

Count Moltke was surprised at this vehement outburst. "You must have been peeved at something," he said.

"Yes," answered the judge, "and you would be too if you would visit this broken-down man in his prison cell. I do not like to use the word 'barbarous', but it does describe the treatment Hauge has received. Its a blot on our prison records."

"Something must be wrong," conceded the count, "when you, my dear Judge, resort to such strong language. I shall investigate this and correct what is wrong."

"Thank you," said the judge, "that is as it should be; and if it were one of us, perhaps circumstances would allow bail to be considered. Few men are more loyal than Hauge. He has spent his life exhorting one and all to obey God and our government."

The count nodded. "That is evidently true, and in accordance with previous knowledge of this man," he admitted.

"Then I would propose," said the judge, "that some relief be given to Hauge now, while it may do him some good."

"And what could that be?" inquired the count.

"Oh," said the judge, "could I, on his word of honor, take him out to my residence to help in the garden?"

Count Moltke's face wrinkled into a smile.

"And," continued the judge, "when he gains a little strength, perhaps you, my dear Count, might find that he could help you with something."

Count Moltke laughed outright. "That's quite original, my noble friend, and does your heart credit; but—I think it can be arranged—on your risk of course; however, be careful."

"Thank you, thank you!" said Judge Bull, as he arose and shook hands.

"And I hope," said the count, "that you will have nothing but joy from this startling venture."

"We'll patch up s o m e of the injustice, anyway," said the judge.

* * *

A few days later Judge Bull's equipage rolled up in front of the prison, and a bent figure was helped into the carriage. It was the once strong and vigorous man, Hans Nielsen Hauge.

CHAPTER LIV

Released for Emergency Service

During the summer 1808 Hauge gained a little in health. He quite frequently was taken out to the residences of Judge Bull or Count Moltke where he was supposed to "help with one thing or another;" but when winter came the king's commission insisted on his staying in prison—for some reason of their own.

The heating and ventilation of the cells were poor. Hauge in his weak condition caught a bad cold and soon began spitting blood. Both of his brothers had been there to visit him; but when they tried to get him out on bail they were met with stern refusal.

Judge Bull and Count Moltke had warmly recommended the efforts of Hauge's brothers, but it was of no avail.

Hauge was spending his fifth Christmas in his dark and dismal cell, in hopeless despondence. No ray of light was seen anywhere, and no answer came from the K a n c i l l i in Copenhagen.

* * *

Meanwhile all Europe was in a turmoil on account of the Napoleonic wars. England was trying to force Denmark into an alliance against Napoleon, and, after the bombardment of Copenhagen in 1807, had blockaded the seaports of Norway.

Hence there was famine in Norway, and a serious shortage of grain and salt. The leading men of Oslo consulted with the provisional administration as to methods of meeting this calamity, but the meetings were barren of results.

Judge Bull had occasionally visited Hauge to cheer him up. One day in February, 1809, he asked Hauge if he knew anything about the manufacturing of salt.

"Yes," Hauge answered, "I experimented with it while curing fish." The judge left abruptly and went to the provisional magistrate to consult about the manufacturing of salt.

A few days later he came to Chief of Police Wulfsberg and surprised him with astonishing news.

"I have found a way," said the judge, "to save Hauge from dying in prison before his case is settled by the courts."

The chief looked at him in wonder and said: "It gladdens me to hear it. I pity that unfortunate man more than I can tell."

"And that gladdens me too," said the judge, "but it is a pity that Collett and Ingstad do not see it that way; he might be a free man."

"Well, they are his judges now," said the chief.

"And supposed to be righteous," added the judge,

"but listen." And he drew his chair up a little closer. "As we all know, this war has brought us close to starvation. Our need of grain is great because of the poor crops in the farm districts; but our need of salt is greater, as we have no efficient salt-works. You are perhaps aware of the fact that our prisoner, Hans Nielsen Hauge, is a genius in practical things. He has started a number of industries in various places. Now I find that he is well posted on the manufacturing of salt, perhaps the best informed in the land. It is really remarkable how this thoroughly religious man is gifted with insight and ability to discern and help forward the material progress of the land. I find something almost perfect in this combination of the spiritual and material."

"Assuredly," the chief joined in, "this is the fifth year he is under my surveillance, and I find him dependable."

"Well," continued the judge; "What would you say about recommending him to build salt-works along the coast? That would relieve the present need, and eventually expand into extended industries. And don't you think that the king and his council would be in favor of it?"

Chief Wulfsberg sat in deep thought, then said, "The plan is good, and I do not think that the provisional magistrate will reject it, but other difficulties—"

"What other difficulties?" interposed the judge.

"For one thing," said the chief, "sufficient bail must be provided to secure a release from the prison."

"And how much will be sufficient bail?" asked the judge.

"Well, at least a thousand dollars," answered the chief.

"That ought to be more than sufficient," said the

judge; "but let it go at that. I'll stand security for a thousand dollars if the government accepts my proposition for building salt-works along the coast."

The chief was surprised. "That may be settled; but suppose there might be more difficulties?"

"What more difficulties?" queried the judge.

"Are you sure that Hauge himself will agree to this?"

This surprised the judge into complete silence.

The chief continued, "A man who has suffered such extreme violation of judicial rights—would he be willing to aid his persecutors and place himself at their disposal? I am afraid not, and it is not human to expect it."

There was a prolonged silence.

At last the judge said, "I believe you are right—and most remarkable; I did not think of that. But we are all human, and human nature is not easily overcome."

"I know it," said the chief, "and in his place I would decline."

"In his present condition, and—after all these years of suffering—all the vain attempts to be let out on bail and the rejected prayers for justice—I must admit," said the judge, "in his place I would myself decline. He sees this war as a judgment of the Lord upon ungodly nations—the severe punishment that had to come upon this wicked and perverse generation."

"But I am going to try him," said the judge, as he held out his hand and bid the chief of police adieu.

"Adieu," said the chief, "and I hope you will succeed."

* * *

February was cold—cold outside and cold inside, too, on days when the stoves were slow and drew poorly.

Hauge huddled down on the wooden cot and drew a blanket over himself; it was hard to keep warm.

Mechanically he folded his hands and mumbled the oft repeated prayer, "Lord, how long?" But thought and reason were almost lost, and he felt himself dying; only his faith in God remained.

Some one unlocked the door. He sat up—was it another false alarm? In came Judge Bull. He had asked the jailer to remain outside, as he wanted to be alone with Hauge. "How are you today?" said the judge, as he shook hands with Hauge.

"Today as every other day," answered Hauge in a weak voice. "Is there any answer from the K a n- c e l l i?"

"No," said the judge; "thirteen months have passed, and it may take another thirteen months before the K a n c e l l i decides anything."

Hauge's heart sank.

"But," the judge continued, "today I have something special which I wish to talk over with you."

Hauge looked up and nodded.

"Today," said the judge, "Norway is facing a famine. The shortage in salt and grain is very serious. There is perhaps some grain left in the farm districts, but salt is very scarce; the government wants a number of salt-works built, and I have concluded that you are the man to do it. What do you say?"

Hauge sat with bowed head, unable to say anything.

The judge began to doubt his mission.

"Do you think I could do that?" whispered Hauge.

Judge Bull stood up. "I understand," he said. "You cannot do this. You feel that these happenings bear their own fruit."

Hauge, astounded beyond words, was silent.

The judge continued slowly: "You have a right

to think that this war is God's judgment upon a frivolous and erring generation."

There was a pause, and then—"It may be unethical to ask this of you, but—it will free you from prison for a while."

Hauge arose and straightened, then turned to the judge, "My dear Judge," said he—slowly and with some difficulties, "give them a message from Hans Nielsen Hauge that the God who returns good for evil is my Master, and Him will I serve. If there is suffering in the land and I can help, I will come. The eternal, loving God be praised who in His grace gives me another chance to do some good."

And from the judge came fervent words, "Truthful and loyal Hauge, you are indeed a man of God and a 'true Israelite in whom there is no guile.'"

* * *

A few days later Hauge was released from prison, and the "most dangerous criminal" was sent out as the king's trusted servant, with subsidy from the government to build factories along the coast for making salt.

He left the prison February 27, 1809, and in the course of six months he had built no less than five salt-works, two at Lillesand, one at Egersund, one near Stavanger and one at Svanø, north of Bergen.

CHAPTER LV

A Series of Trials

On the fifth of May, 1809, the K a n c e l l i in Copenhagen had decided on a new trial; but on account of the war and the blockade by English cruisers the order did not reach Norway until the middle of August.

The same commission for the king (Collett and Ingstad) had been appointed judges in the case.

They called a hearing August 25, and Collett presided.

At the opening session Count Moltke, the provincial magistrate, was announced and admitted.

The presiding judge, Collett, left his seat to receive the guest. "To what are we indebted for the honor of the count's visit?" said Judge Collett, as he shook hands with the count.

The count nodded his cognizance of the members present, and walking to the desk of the presiding judge, saying, "I am informed that the king's commission has arranged for a hearing in the new trial of Hans Nielsen Hauge today."

"The information is correct," answered the judge.

The count bowed to the chair with a smile as he said, "Thank you, my dear Judge; but the defendant should be present."

"Certainly," answered the Judge, "we shall call him this afternoon."

The count smiled indulgently.

"That is good news, as nothing has been done for over a year," he said.

"There have been good reasons for that. The war—"

"Certainly," answered the count; "the war has compelled the authorities to act in extraordinary ways and seize the available forces in the land, to meet the enemy and relieve the increasing wants."

Judge Collett was getting angry. His eyes burned as he said, "We know our duty and will mind our business; the prisoner shall be called immediately."

"That will be quite impossible," said the count calmly, "and for this reason I have the honor of paying you my respects."

The count looked around at the members of the commission as one who is conscious of his authority.

Judge Collett and Ingstad as well as the associate members of the commission were angry, but they said nothing.

"As a magistrate," said the count, "and in behalf of His Highness, Prince Christian August, I have the honor to inform you gentlemen of the commission, that Hans Nielsen Hauge, according to government orders, has been released from prison and is now at Egersund."

Judge Collett turned white and red by turns as he arose from the chair. "Sir Magistrate!" he cried in a voice that almost broke from suppressed rage; "against this overt act of the local government I, as president of this commission, will register my protest."

Count Moltke bowed his acceptance of the protest. "That is your privilege, Judge Collett; but the local government is able to defend their actions."

Judge Collett bowed somewhat stiffly, "Perhaps we may be permitted to hear the reason for such extraordinary proceedings," he inquired.

Count Moltke nodded and said, "There are no secrets about this, my dear Judge. Extraordinary conditions require extraordinary action. The war has caused a famine and a severe shortage in salt; and the man who knew how to make salt is Hauge."

Judge Collett smiled sarcastically, "Aid from the prison!" he exclaimed.

"Yes! Aid from the prisons as well as from the bench," answered the count. "The government has among its functionaries no one more able and honest and loyal and self-sacrificing than Hans Nielsen Hauge; and I want you gentlemen especially to note this and carry it in your mind when you examine into the charges against him. Furthermore, I wish to say that the adherents of Hauge have shown that they are among the best citizens in our land, and I make no great mistake when I mention them as the salt that will keep Norway's people fresh and clean in the great trials that now and in the future will threaten our land."

Judge Collett was furious. He said, sarcastically, "The count makes an admirable plea for the defense."

"Not at all, my dear Judge! Hauge's activities and labor will be his best defense. I do not doubt that he can be convicted on some subtle paragraph in law interpreted a d u s u m j u s t i t i a—but I doubt if the people of Norway will sanction it. Adieu, gentlemen!"

As the count turned to go, Judge Collett arose again and trembling with impotent rage, he almost hissed: "As duly appointed judges we take the full responsibility in this case. However, since the prisoner is not present we may as well adjourn. For this hindrance which obstructs the legal procedure we hold the magistrate responsible."

"Certainly!" answered the count, and bowed his adieu.

* * *

Hauge had returned, and on the eleventh of October another hearing was called. Everything went smoothly and nothing was said about the release.

However, at the end of the session when Hauge was ready to leave with his attorney, Judge Collett rapped the desk with his gavel and announced: "In behalf of the commission we insist that Hans Nielsen Hauge remain in prison until sentence is passed."

There was a painful, oppressive silence.

Hauge turned, walked over to the judge, and said, "The judge is aware of the fact that I have been released on bail and entrusted with a king's charge in the land. The salt-works that I have started need my attention, and I demand my freedom to continue."

Judge Collett cleared his throat and answered, "Such a demand is contrary to the king's will and cannot be granted. According to the king's k o mm i s s o r i u m of May fifth, this year, the king wills that you remain in prison until your case is settled."

Hauge turned to his attorney for advice, but then bethought himself of his loyalty to the king and said, "If this be His royal Majesty's most gracious will I must obey."

Hauge turned to the door where the guards waited to escort him to prison. A little later, as Judge Collett left the court-room, he met Judge Bull who accosted him, "I hear that you have remanded Hauge to prison."

Judge Bull towered as a veritable giant above the little Collett—and the latter shivered as he said, "It was according to the king's order of May fifth."

Judge Bull's dark eyes burned into the very soul of the little man as he continued: "You have remanded Hauge to prison, an innocent man! Maltreated for years with criminal incarceration! And in spite of it all he has sacrificed everything for his country and materially helped to relieve suffering. I am going to tell you something. Your Judgeship is entirely lacking the ennobled and refined sensibility that distinguishes a real judge. What happened here is uncommonly brutal, ungrateful, and unworthy of a civilized nation and an enlightened age."

He turned and left the disconcerted Judge Collett without another word.

Further imprisonment quickly effaced the beneficial results of Hauge's outdoor life during his release from prison. He began to cough again and spit blood. The prison fare did not agree with him at all.

He was worried over the reason for his return to prison. He brooded for weeks and weeks, wondering why nothing more was done with his case. Had he been called in from his work to that perfunctory hearing, October 11, for the purpose of burying him in this prison cell?

Late in November Hauge became so seriously ill that he was taken to the infirmary. His brother Mikkel came to see him, and when Hauge began to improve he obtained, with the aid of Judge Bull and Chief Wulfsberg, a permit for him to visit his aged parents.

A few days before Christmas their brother Ole met them as they landed in Fredrikstad, and towards evening they arrived at the old homestead. The parents cried for joy when Hans appeared.

He was very weak, and they put him to bed. His mother found great pleasure in tucking the blankets around him, as she had done when he was a little boy; it made her feel young again. Father had to come in, too, and talk with him while she brought in some good things to eat.

Hans was tired, however, and soon fell asleep.

After a while he awoke and looked around, bewildered. He turned his head and saw his father, reading the Bible.

"Is that you, father?" he asked in wonder.

"Yes, and you are at home now," his father answered with a happy smile.

"Oh, how glad I am," exclaimed the sick man.

Mother came in from the kitchen.

"And glad to see you, mother," Hans continued.

Glad! She had to embrace him, holding him very close, and kissing him fondly—wasn't he the loved one she had lost and found again?

The evening passed very quickly. Father and mother were so enraptured that afterwards they remembered it almost as a happy dream. Ole and Mikkel kept in the background so the aged parents could have Hans to themselves.

He improved rapidly, and on Christmas day he was able to attend church. He went over to the grave of his sister, Anna. The tears flowed freely as he thought of her. But it was good for her to be resting in peace—and a great longing came upon him to rest with her. Then he remembered her last words and took fresh courage. Perhaps God in His infinite grace would yet find a way for him to do something in the vineyard.

A host of friends had gathered to visit with him, but they were greatly surprised at the great change in his appearance—the sunken eyes, the hollow cheeks, and the sickly, yellow color of his face.

The next day word came that Mikkel had reached his home at Eker, and on the way had obtained permit for Hans to extend his visit with his parents to a full month.

This of course was welcome and contributed greatly to the improvement of his health. He was out a while every day to visit the various places he remembered from his boyhood days, and so lived over again the experiences of youth.

One day he walked as far as Haugebraaten, now converted into a fine meadow. As the journey had tired him he sat down on a stone. He thought of the stump-pulling and stone-breaking he had done to clear this ground. And now it was a delightful, smooth surface covered with snow. He remembered the inspiration for his mission obtained in this work, and wondered if his spiritual stone-breaking would have such fine results.

Then he remembered that after he had cleared the ground, others had done the planting, and—perhaps God wanted others to plant where he had cleared in the spiritual field.

This thought cheered him immensely. In spite of imprisonment his work might not be in vain. Paul has planted, Apollos had watered, but God had given the increase, he remembered.

Then he turned homeward, happy and content,

for God had shown him that even in prison his steadfastness could help others to be steadfast and remain faithful to the end.

It cheered his mother to have him with them, and they spent much time in his room, reading, praying, and talking. He told them of the things that had inspired him to acknowledge God's wisdom, the things that had happened to strengthen his faith in God. Even his prison-life, he thought, would be for some good.

The happy days ended too soon for them. When the time was up it became brother Ole's duty, as sheriff, to return Hans to the prison. The mother cried bitterly, and the father shed tears, too, when they said good-bye. "I shall never see him again!" wailed the bereaved mother.

Some time after Hauge came back to prison he had word from Bergen that his brother-in-law and business partner, J. N. Loose, had died. He had been married to Hauge's sister, Karen.

This was a great shock to Hauge. He could not help brooding over it. One of the best workers in Bergen had been called away, thus weakening the working forces of the Lord at a time when they were most needed.

Later in the winter Hauge had a letter from his sister Karen, stating that their mother was sick. She told that she had decided to leave Bergen and go back to the old farmstead to care for her mother and help the aged father. Thus Hauge felt some relief regarding his parents at this message.

Another year in waiting passed. Then he received word from his father that his mother had died January 30, 1811. Thus Anna had died, Loose had died, and his mother had died—and the longing that he, too, might depart, redoubled within him.

CHAPTER LVI

The Girl Once More

As we begin this chapter we have to go back seven years.

Madam Boes in Bergen had been weakening gradually during the year of 1803, and at Hauge's last visit in July, 1804, he found her abed, weak and failing fast, but her mind was as bright and active as ever. She had sent for Hauge to come and spend an hour with her before he left. When he came he found a goodly number of her friends gathered, too.

Hauge shook hands with her and those present, and Madam Boes spoke up in her quaint way: "When I cannot come to your meetings, you have to come to me and have a meeting here, where I can hear the message."

Hauge did not preach a farewell sermon but rather talked about the bliss and happiness in heaven for God's children who remain faithful here on earth unto the end of their lives. They carry their cross here, but in heaven they exchange it for a crown of life.

After the service they all had to partake of refreshments, and Hauge gave a somewhat extensive table talk.

As the visitors left they shook hands with Hauge and wished him God-speed upon his journey. They urged him to be sure to come back as soon as possible.

Hauge delayed a little longer than usual, for he felt that this was perhaps the last time he should see his benefactress alive. So he sat by her bedside and talked of the labors in God's kingdom.

Finally he took both of her hands in his and fervently thanked her again for the gifts she had bestowed upon him, wishing her the joy and happiness that is promised God's children. Then she said good-bye.

The housemaid managed to have a heart-to-heart talk with him too before he left.

* * *

After Hauge's departure, Madam Boes grew steadily worse. The faithful maid had her hands full caring for her. What gave her most comfort were Hauge's books. But she tired quickly. The maid happened to have a good voice, well-modulated and pleasant, and soon she did all the reading aloud. Thus time dragged on until late in September, when Madam Boes had a stroke. She died a few days later.

There was an unusually large funeral. All the poor people—and there were many that Madam Boes had helped—came to the large cathedral, Korskirken, that day. Bishop Brun preached a sermon on the beautiful life of God's faithful children, a life that spans death and lasts throughout eternity.

The chief mourner was the housemaid. Being an orphan, she had loved Madam Boes as a mother. Now she was left alone.

* * *

The authorities had taken over the estate. The will had been read and approved, and the housemaid, whose proper name was Andrea Nyhus, received a goodly portion for her faithful service. As she had no real home in Bergen, she decided to visit her relatives in Romerike, some of whom she had not seen for years.

She took passage in a sailing vessel from Bergen to Oslo in company with some nurses who were going there for Christmas visiting.

When they came to Oslo she heard that Hauge had been arrested and was lodged in the city prison.

This was a great shock to her. She did not know the reason but concluded that there must be some ungodly people in Oslo, since such a good man as Hauge had been arrested.

She realized more than ever how she sympathized with Hauge and his great work. And now they had put him in jail to stop his good work and bring sorrow to his many friends throughout the land.

She stayed a few days at the capital and finally made up her mind to call on Hauge in the prison, but here she received another shock. For when she arrived at the prison she was informed that Hauge was a dangerous criminal, and that no one was permitted to see or commune with him. Nor would she be allowed even to send a message to him!

This was terrible. Had the world gone crazy? Or was Hauge a criminal? She could not believe it. But, since she found it impossible to see Hauge, she left for her childhood home in Ness parish, Romerike.

Arriving at Ness, she found her aged aunt Karina, still alive, but infirm and sickly. So it was arranged that she should stay and care for her aunt during her illness. That stay was prolonged nearly six years, as the sick woman lingered until the fall of 1810.

Andrea Nyhus was again homeless. She decided to go back to Oslo to find the school that the nurses had been talking about. In this she was unsuccessful, but she did find plenty of work, nursing, after she became acquainted with the doctors. For they found her quite capable as a nurse.

In the summer of 1811 Hauge became so seriously ill that he again was taken to the infirmary. He had been found in his cell unconscious, and for weeks hovered between life and death. It was the nurse Andrea Nyhus, who finally succeeded in bringing him back to life.

Mikkel Hauge came over from Eker (about 50 miles west of Oslo) and found him very weak. Hence he started a campaign among the authorities, and, with the aid of Judge Bull, succeeded in securing a permit to provide for Hans outside of the prison.

Mikkel Hauge then bought a small farmstead, Bakkehaugen, with an antiquated house on it, near Sagene, a manufacturing suburb, and when Hans was stronger he was moved to this quiet retreat. Here the faithful Andrea Nyhus attended him faithfully and soon he was back on his feet again.

When he was able to be outside the sunshine and fresh air gave him the best of tonics, and soon he began to look around for something to do. There was a stretch of rapids in the river running through this piece of land, and he conceived the idea of utilizing it.

He borrowed money and built a dam and a mill for four pairs of stones for meal, and one pair for making groats and pearl barley.

He was fortunate in securing a contract from the government to do the grinding for the soldiers. Thus his mill had work for a night shift, when the water was not too low, and he made money—paid his debts and began to feel himself again, except for the chronic sick spells that came upon him.

During the famine years of 1812 and 1813, "Hauge's Mill" on Bakkehaugen became the center of charities.

Hauge had planted all of his little farm into potatoes and harvested several hundred barrels. His friends in Bergen had clubbed together and sent him an extra shipment of fresh herring besides what he had ordered. Then his friends in the farm districts sent him grain, and thus Hauge was the veritable "Joseph in Oslo."

Poor people came from far and near to get a "hand-out" at "Hauge's Mill," and the number increased until he had to build an extra dining hall outside the kitchen for hungry people.

Those that remained for a time were immediately set to work at odd jobs, for Hauge hated idleness more than anything else.

Faithful Andrea Nyhus was the soul of everything. She was the first one to arise in the morning and the last one to go to bed at night. Still she retained the rosy cheeks and happy smile that brought the dimples Hauge thought so wonderful.

The late task in the evenings was the washing of a stack of dishes, and when Hauge offered to help she would deck him out in one of her big aprons and give him a dish cloth to wipe the dishes that she washed.

Her sweet voice which had charmed Madam Boes made Hauge, too, forget that he was sick—forget his worries and troubles, and that he was a "jailbird." For he was legally still a prisoner.

She reminded him of the time she carried hampers for Madam Boes in Bergen, how she thought then that it was hard work; and yet it did not begin to compare with the work that she had for Hauge. "But," she would say, "I have never been so happy as I am now; and I must agree with you that work is not a curse, but a great blessing."

Sometimes Hans would fret because he was not allowed to go out and preach and talk with people while his case was pending.

Andrea wouldn't listen to such talk. "Aren't we preaching now?" she said. "These bins of potatoes that the Lord gave us, don't they preach? And the consignments of foodstuff that God's Spirit moved your friends to send us, don't they preach? And the 'hand-outs' we are able to give every day, don't they preach? Now don't they, Hans?"

Hans had to admit they did. Actions speak louder than words, and here was action aplenty.

"I hear," said Hans one day, "that the k n e i p-v e r t (ale-house-keeper) near the lumber yard has quit giving free lunches this year."

"Yes," she answered, "now they come to us for free lunch, but you give them a Bible verse or some good advice instead of a stein of beer."

Hans turned red at this sally.

"Oh, but you are funny, Hans," and she laughed so heartily that Hans had to laugh with her.

He was surprised! Why, for seven long years he had not laughed, as far as he could remember, and now it came unbidden. He felt ashamed of himself. Was it right for God's children to laugh?

Reason as he would, he could find nothing wrong in laughing, except in laughing at something sinful. Andrea was carrying away the dishes and did not notice Hauge's reverie. Seven years he had preached almost continuously—had been arrested nine times and freed again—and then had spent seven years in a prison-cell, isolated from the world until health was gone. All this had happened because he, a layman, had preached from the Bible the simple truths of salvation.

Andrea came in and sat down.

"We have no visitors tonight," said Hauge, "so I will ask you to read for me and lead in devotion."

Andrea took down the Bible—found Psalm 146 and read it. Then in her simple way she thanked the Lord for all His blessings and for preserving them in faith. And they both sang:

> *Remember us, dear Lord, we pray,*
> *While burdened in the flesh we stay;*
> *Thou only canst our soul defend;*
> *Be with us, Savior, to the end, Amen!*

CHAPTER LVII

Hauge's Case Concluded

Thus passed the years 1812 and 1813. In spite of his sick spells Hauge was happy because of the extensive charity work and the many friends that incessantly came to see him.

Of course, he could not preach; but his evening devotions were the next thing to it; and many attended them quite regularly. Even Countess Wedell-Jarlsberg came often.

The commission judges, Collett and Ingstad, did not like this and talked of ordering Hauge back to jail, but somehow they did not dare to because of the charity work.

Hauge had gained too many influential friends, and the poor people thought everything of Hauge; hence it was not safe to stir the people, and Hauge was left in peace.

He had been questioned at various hearings in a most abusive and insulting manner for the purpose of angering him and getting him to speak something that could be held against him; but Hauge's even temper and truthfulness baffled all the efforts.

During the years 1810-1812 local hearings had been held in all the districts where Hauge had preached, and testimonies from more than six hundred witnesses had been collected. Not one sustained the twenty-odd charges against Hauge, except that he had preached the Gospel, which was forbidden by the Conventicle Act.

After searching all this testimony and weighing it pro and con, Judge Collett and Ingstad, on the fourth day of December, 1813, sentenced the prisoner to two years of imprisonment at hard labor in the castle at Akershus.

Hauge did not accept this sentence, but appealed his case to the supreme court. The war continued, and Norway had to shift for itself. Denmark was not able to raise the blockade, and Norway was forced to rely on her own resources in everything.

An extraordinary s t o r t i n g (parliament) was called, and after due deliberation declared Norway independent, May 17, 1814. Hauge was still a prisoner, but he rejoiced with the people at the birth of a new nation.

So many things transpired during this momentous year that the supreme court did not find time to take up Hauge's case until just before Christmas.

The members of the supreme court were Andreas Arntzen, Chr. Anker Berg, Christian Diriks, H. Hagerup Talbe, and Triman Omsen. On December twenty-third they reversed the decision of the lower court, as there were no criminal findings, and declared Hauge free from corporal punishment but guilty on the following counts:

"(a) That Hans Nielsen Hauge, against the ordinance of January 13, 1741, had gone about the land preaching.

"(b) That he had encouraged others to do the same.

"(c) That he in his writings had used grievous invectives against the clergy; but they could be tolerantly explained."

Then the decision of the court read, "Therefore is said Hans Nielsen Hauge sentenced to pay a fine of one thousand dollars to the city poor fund, and costs."

A sigh of relief went through the audience as the p r a e c e s read these findings. Hauge's friends came forward to congratulate him. He answered in his quiet, simple way, that he was glad. All the slanderous charges had been refuted and disproved as groundless.

Judge Bull, too, came to shake hands. "Many of us believe you entirely innocent," he said, "and that you have suffered outrageously for a good cause. But be of good cheer; the future will prove I am right. The fine will be provided in some way."

"I have no doubt about that," Hauge answered, "for the Master has said: 'The Lord will provide.' Help will come!"

And help did come.

When the tidings of Hauge's final sentence reached his friends all over the land money came quick and fast, and the fine and costs were soon paid. Hauge wrote a personal letter of thanks to his friends, and reminded them of God's grace to His children. "However dark it may look sometimes," it ran, "the sun is behind the clouds, and God can see us in the dark. What did all these evil accusations amount to? Of what use is the stack of documents that they sweated over and labored on? Of what avail that they worried and tortured me with vicious questions in the hope of convicting me of crime?

"The Lord be praised forever that He saved me from the wicked. I will praise the Lord unto the end of my days, and I salute you in the name of Christ Jesus, our Savior, that ye may remain in grace forever."

* * *

There was great rejoicing among the friends of Hauge all over the land. The next day was Christmas, and many of them had assembled at Bakkehaugen. The spacious dining-hall, where the thousands had been fed, was well-filled, and lighted candles shone from every window by the time evening came. They sang Brorson's well-known Christmas hymn and read the angel's message to the shepherds. One of the guests closed the devotion with prayer.

Hauge's friend, Ole Roersveen, sat next to Hauge at the table, and when they began eating, Hauge asked him if he remembered the Christmas Eve nine years ago.

"Assuredly I do remember that little candle in the prison window, and how it shone when you trimmed it," he responded.

"Yes," Hauge answered, "light has conquered, and instead of one light in the window there are thousands now."

* * *

When all the visitors had left, and Hauge with his faithful Andrea had put the finishing touches to the evening chores in the kitchen, they sat down on a bench to talk.

"I haven't been so happy since I was a little boy playing with my sister Anna, on the home-farm," said Hauge. "Now I am a free man again. How good it feels to be free."

"Yes, I feel it too," said Andrea, and a smile dimpled her cheek.

"And because I am free I want to ask you something," continued Hans, "something that has been on my heart a long time. I do not know about romance—but my heart warms to you more than ever. You have been a joy to me. I am a poor man and have nothing to offer, yet there is a strong urge to ask you, dear one: Will you be my wife?"

Andrea's eyes grew big and dark. She looked upon him admiringly and stammered: "Do you really want me?"

"Want you?" Hans asked, surprised. "I want you more than anything else I ever wanted or ever will want. You have been an inspiration to me; you have called me back to life; you have been the soul of charity and preached with your two hands the best of sermons. But I want your answer; will you marry me?"

Andrea smiled coyly, almost provokingly; then she sobered and suddenly burst into tears.

"Oh, Hans," she whispered, "I am not worthy of you."

Andrea's tears were disconcerting. Hans did not know what to make of it. But he drew her close and said, "Please don't cry."

She snuggled closer and hid her face, saying brokenly, "I am so happy, Hans,—I have to cry—I have loved you ever since the first time I saw you—will love you ever—yes, I will marry you."

A month later they were married.

After the wedding, life continued the same as before at Bakkehaugen, except that it gained in popularity in ever widening circles among the many well-to-do people who came to see Hauge and hear of his extensive charity work.

Although too weak to preach as in former days, he used what strength he could muster to give talks at the evening devotions.

And friends from all parts of the country came to visit and consult him on various questions. They always found a willing ear, an open heart, and a ready will to encourage the laymen's movement.

The hospitality at Bakkehaugen knew no limitations. The company was of the most varied kind. Of course laymen were preeminently dominant. Sometimes the most ragged tramps from the slums came. And the better classes, too. But all were welcome!

* * *

After the Declaration of Independence of the previous year came a period of "Reconstruction." The s t o r t i n g was reorganized and new members came from some districts.

Several of Hauge's friends had been chosen, and as the session of the s t o r t i n g opened they came to visit him and congratulate him upon the happy ending of his trial.

Among these Mikkel Grendahl was one of the most intimate with Hauge. He spent many an evening with him in talking over the problems of the new government.

With Grendahl came other members, and some very lively discussions on the future of Norway took place. The recently established state university presented new problems of religious tolerance.

The university stressed the study of theology to supply the demand for pastors throughout the land. The leading professors were Hersleb and Stenersen, both doctors of theology.

They naturally became interested in Hauge, and Prof. Stenersen often entered into discussions to find if he was sound in doctrine. The professor was surprised to find Hauge remarkably orthodox in doctrine and with a knowledge of the Bible that extended far beyond that of the average clergyman.

After getting better acquainted, Prof. Stenersen found pleasure in talking with this mild-mannered man of most varied experiences. It was like a repetition of John Tauler's story, where the learned man could enrich his knowledge from the experiences of a layman.

These discussions caught the interest of many intelligent people who had come to listen, often out of curiosity. Very often, however, they returned home deeply concerned over their soul's salvation.

Thus the circle of interested people grew, and Bakkehaugen became the center of charity in a new way, that of feeding hungry souls.

At the time of the spring session of the s t o r- t i n g Hauge celebrated his forty--fourth birthday. This festival was graced by the presence of two bishops (Krogh and Bugge), two professors (Hersleb and Stenersen) and fifteen pastors from various districts in southern Norway.

Hauge felt out of place at these demonstrations; but his wife—the faithful Andrea who had been trained by Madam Boes, filled her place as hostess with grace and dignity.

Toward midsummer the session of the s t o r- t i n g closed, and everybody had a vacation. Even at Bakkehaugen there was a respite which gave Hauge and his wife a chance to rest up after a busy season.

Hauge's health had improved so much that he was able to make a journey to Eker to visit his brother Mikkel and see the paper-mill.

It was a happy reunion of the families, and the happy days spent together were like a tonic to Hauge. There were new improvements in the paper-mill that interested him very much; and they began to plan for other industries in connection with the paper-mill.

Then they were invited to visit the old time friends, Kristofer Hoen, Ole Foss and Niels Braaten, who did their utmost to make the stay of Hauge very pleasant. He enjoyed their devotions and table-talks. It showed him how greatly they had gained in Christian knowledge.

At the end of the second month of their stay Hauge was informed that Sheriff Jens Gram had become seriously ill. Hauge was visiting with Kristofer Hoen, and he offered to take Hauge over to Hougsund.

When they came to the residence the sheriff was raving and did not recognize his visitors. Hauge tried to speak to him, but the sheriff did not listen. He apparently did not know anyone.

Hauge felt very sad, but nothing could be done for a raving maniac. He died shortly afterwards, without regaining his reason.

At length the vacation ended, and Hauge with his wife returned to Bakkehaugen to prepare for another winter of extended charity work.

Their many friends helped them in different ways, and Bakkehaugen was as popular as ever. They had hired extra help to have more time for entertaining visitors. Besides, Andrea occasionally felt indisposed. She needed rest and retirement.

* * *

Then came the expected event. A son was born to them on December twelfth, 1815. He was strong and healthy, but the mother suffered from most severe hemorrhages. She weakened from day to day until at last there was no hope for her.

Hans sat by her bedside faithfully and read and sang hymns of faith and devotion. He talked of life here on earth compared with the life beyond.

The end drew near. Evening shadows hid the landscape, and the candles were lit. Andrea slept. Her face was so pale and her breath was so feeble that Hans thought she was dying, and he began to weep.

She awoke and saw his tears. She motioned to him, and bending low over the bed he heard her whisper: "Do not grieve for me, Hans. I have been so happy with you. I knew it could not last. But now I feel that I shall be still happier with the angels, singing the praises of my Lord and Master in Paradise, and you will soon join me."

Then she fell back, murmuring, "Sing to me, Hans." So he sang,

> Lord, Thou hath joined my soul to Thine,
>   In bonds no power can sever;
> Grafted in Thee, the living vine,
>   I shall be Thine forever;
> Lord, when I die, I die in Thee,
> Thy precious death hath won for me
>   A life that endeth never.

Hans took her hand and repeated the last line.

A smile flitted across her face, and her lips moved as if she echoed the last line:

A life that endeth never!

Then she sank into a coma, and toward morning, five days before Christmas, she breathed her last.

Hauge's widowed sister Karen had come to help him. This was very fortunate, as Hauge for weeks and months after his wife's death was unable to concentrate his mind or do any work. He needed someone to care for him.

The year before had been such a glorious time, when so many had come to congratulate him or seek advice. His dining-hall had been filled with people, prelates as well as vagrants and destitutes.

And his wife—faithful Andrea, who had so ably filled her place as hostess, now she was no more.

Bakkehaugen, promising so much, became hateful to him.

Two years later he bought a place called "Bredtvedt" near the Botanical gardens in eastern Aker. Here he lived in quiet retirement the remaining years of his life. The year he left Bakkehaugen he visited his brother Mikkel, at the Eker paper-mill. While here he was married to Marie Olsdatter on January 22, 1817. He needed a mother for his little boy, Andreas, who had been named after the faithful Andrea.

Shortly after his second marriage he was taken sick again—his health was gone. He did not travel any more, nor did he preach; but he wrote books of devotion and a series of sermons that found a wide circulation. He also published his biography.

The printers in Oslo were just as anxious at this time to print his writings as they had been to reject them twenty years before.

Hauge also published a book of hymns, mostly selections from Kingo, and a presentation of the doctrines he had preached.

CHAPTER LVIII

The Closing of a Brief Life

Spring had come, and the song of migrating birds was heard in the parks and nearby woods.

The lawns and fields in the suburbs were turning green, and the buds on the trees were beginning to swell. The glorious sun was warming the air and advancing northward.

A tall man with stooping shoulders and bent back was walking across the greensward. His face was sallow and wan with pain. By his side was a boy seven years old, rather large for his age.

Hans Nielsen Hauge was enjoying the spring with his son Andreas.

"Look, father, the flowers are awake!"

The boy bent over and picked a golden dandelion; then continued: "Father, do you know who waked them?"

"It was God who waked them," answered the father.

The little boy thought a while.

"Where did they have their beds?" asked the boy.

"In the ground," Hauge answered, "and God covered them with a heavy blanket of snow, and they slept very snugly all winter."

The boy pondered—then asked: "Shall we sometime sleep under the snow all winter?" His eyes were big with wonder.

A smile flitted across the man's face.

"Yes, my child," he said, "some time—when we die. God will spread His blanket of snow over us, and we shall sleep."

"And are we going to have a bed in the ground?" the boy asked.

"Yes, we call it the grave."

"But," said the boy, "it must be cold in the winter."

"No, it is snug and sheltered down there."

They walked awhile in silence.

"But when the sun comes back," said the boy, "shall we come up again with the flowers?"

"Oh, yes, like the flowers, fresh and new."

"How can they be new and fresh?" asked the boy.

"Because they have the seed of life in them." Hauge looked tenderly into his boy's blue eyes and thought of the wonder of life's renewal.

They walked on. Hauge explained to his son the wonders of life above, below, and everywhere, as it springs out to testify to the glory of God, the Father in heaven.

The little boy never seemed tire of asking questions, and his father never tired of answering them.

Spring passed into summer, summer into autumn, and autumn into winter—there were always some new things that puzzled the boy, and his father must explain. He tried to pass some of his thoughts and ideas on to the son.

Hauge felt the time for his departure nearing and he wanted to instill his faith in his little son, to be conveyed to future generations.

* * *

Nearly a year had passed. A mild south-wind was causing the snow to melt, and indicated the first signs of another spring. Crows and starlings had begun their scavenger work, but it was too early for the other migrating tribes. Nature was preparing for a grand revival.

Over in the city the rush and bustle of busy people was increased, but the Bredtvedt farmstead in the eastern suburb was very quiet. Death was hovering near, ready to claim its own.

Hans Nielsen Hauge had been ailing since November. His strength was gradually sinking. He knew his time had come, and was prepared.

He had no fear of death, but he feared for those who should survive him. He admonished one and all not to grieve for him, because death would open the gate to heaven for him. But would they follow?—that was the question.

He read and prayed with his family as long as he was able to do so, but toward the last the attacks of pain were so severe that he lost consciousness.

On some nights the spells were unusually severe. Spasms of cramps and shooting pains held him unconscious; then again he had relief and slept for a few hours.

One morning he woke up and said, "What day have we today?"

"It is Sunday," his wife answered.

"Sunday!" he repeated, "and I can't go to church any more to join the congregation in singing."

He folded his hands and prayed. Then he wanted his wife to sing, but she was so weak and exhausted that she did not succeed.

"I am glad I have had some relief today. The Lord's Day has abated my suffering—and soon it will be finished."

"Yes, yes," said his wife, but as she looked upon his pale face she burst into tears. It was so hard for her to lose him. Hauge tried to comfort her, but his voice failed him, and soon he fell into a comatose condition.

Toward evening he awoke. Seeing his wife sitting so quietly, weeping, grieved him also. He managed to say, however, "Do not worry, my dear. You still have our little girl and the little boy to look after. God will take care of you."

Then he closed his eyes and rested.

Opening his eyes again he turned to his wife and said, "My work here on earth is finished, and I long for the peaceful days of rest in the mansions above."

"Yes, yes," his wife answered. "Everything is good. And God is living! He is living and lives forever."

Hans tried to say something, but again lapsed into unconsciousness.

Then he suddenly opened his eyes. Seeing his wife sitting at his bedside, he whispered: "Are you still sitting there? It is night, and you must have your sleep. I am so sleepy myself."

"No, no," said his wife, "it is full daylight yet."

"So it is," he whispered, "it is only within us that there is night—but God's day will last forever."

His eyes closed again, and he slept.

Late in the evening the housemaid brought in the children. They wanted to see papa. The father evidently sensed it. For he opened his eyes.

His wife held up the baby-girl so that he could see her. After the evening prayer the baby was kissed good-night. Then the boy bent over his father and kissed him, saying, "Good-night, papa, soon we'll have spring."

A smile rested on the drawn face. "Good night, my children," he whispered. "God bless you and keep you." Then he held out his hand and laid it upon the boy's head. Lying thus he closed his eyes and rested.

It was very quiet, and he seemed to sleep.

The clock on the wall was ticking and ticking as the minutes and hours crept slowly by. An hour after midnight another severe attack of cramps came upon the sufferer. Breathing became very difficult—he tried to speak, but no words came.

Sometimes he opened his eyes in pain. With a pleading expression on his face he would look at his wife, but he could not say anything. Nor did he moan or wail. Everything was borne in patience. He had the fortitude to hold himself in restraint even to the last.

It was past four in the morning. The pains were less intense. Hauge's lips moved, but he could say nothing, only stare.

"Oh, if I could know what he wants," his wife wailed. But she could do nothing—except watch, and cry. The nurse, however, administered an anesthetic which apparently gave some relief.

The eight-year old boy had awakened and came into the room in his night clothes. He wanted to see papa and sleep with him.

"Papa, papa," he called, as he tried to clamber into the bed.

Then, all at once the strong nature of the father reasserted itself, and his voice came back to him for a moment. Clearly and distinctly came the words: "Follow Jesus!"

"Follow Jesus, my son, follow Jesus, and God will take care of you." Again he laid his hand on the boy's head and blest him in the name of the triune God, adding the wish that the boy would grow up to follow Jesus, and be one of His disciples.

The little boy, who was fully awake now, said in his childish way, "Yes, papa, I will follow Jesus!"

The father's head sank back—a sweet smile illumined his face. His joy reflected the dawn of a new day.

He folded his hands and prayed, "O Thou eternal and loving God, praise and thanks to Thee now and forever more! Now I can die happy."

His eyes began to glaze, but he managed to whisper, "Let us pray," whereas the friends present kneeled around the bed and united in the Lord's Prayer.

And as they prayed the soul left its earthly clay and soared away to the eternal home.

The clock on the wall struck five, and now, on the morning of March 29, 1824, everyone present realized that Hauge was no more. One of them, Ole Roersveen, suggested an hour of devotion.

He prayed, thanking God for the departed friend, what he had done for them all, and, now that he had gone to his reward, that God would send them some one to take his place and continue the work in the true faith.

And he prayed for himself, that God would be gracious and let the Holy Spirit guide and give him strength to remain faithful to the end. After another had continued in prayer and praise they all sang:

> *Despair not, O heart, in thy sorrow,*
> *But hope from God's promises borrow,*
> *Beware, in thy sorrow, of sinning,*
> *For death is of life the beginning.*
>
> *A dearly beloved one has left us;*
> *God has in his wisdom bereft us;*
> *But He will not leave us forsaken—*
> *We know that the dead shall awaken.*
>
> *Then dawneth the glorious morrow,*
> *This body we now view with sorrow,*
> *A glorified form shall be given,*
> *Restored to its spirit in heaven.*
>
> *The seed that in springtime is planted,*
> *Is hid in the ground; but, if granted*
> *A measure of sunshine and showers,*
> *Will spring into fruitage and flowers.*
>
> *A gift to the churchyard we tender,*
> *As dust to the dust we surrender;*
> *Returning the clay to its Maker,*
> *We lay it to rest in God's acre.*

A soul in that body abided,
A soul that in Jesus confided,
A soul that was longing for heaven,
Where mansions in glory are given.

To earth we consign to its keeping
The body with sorrow and weeping;
In peace to await resurrection,
When he shall arise in perfection.*

A noble soul had passed to its reward. Hauge's passing was mourned by thousands of friends throughout the land.

His lifework had been consecrated to the labor in God's vineyard, exhorting people to spiritual awakening, true conversion, and a God-fearing life, and even in death he admonished them to follow Jesus and love Him above all.

Hauge was one of Norway's best and ablest sons, the noblest and most sacrificing—a grand personality of integrity and confidence risen out of common stock of rural people.

He was one of the few truly faithful human beings who stake their lives upon their faith and convictions.

His whole life was a sacrifice for the welfare of others—a sacrifice to bring the noblest and best there was in the Norwegian people to rise in grandeur and prosperity from bondage and servitude to a victorious freedom in Christ Jesus. His slogan was, "Liberated in Christ, ye are indeed free."

In the old cemetery of Østre Aker there is a modest tombstone with the name Hans Nielsen Hauge upon it, indicating the place where he was laid to rest. But he has raised himself a far better monument in the hearts of men—a loving memory of the things he did while here on earth, and the sacrifices

---

* Prudentius, 413; tr. Hegelund (Dan.), 1586; O. T. Sanden (Eng.), 1909.

he made to accomplish his mission and prove the work.

Hauge saw only the beginning—the dawn of the new day in Norway that came with the Declaration of Independence and the establishing of a university—but it was enough to show him that his mission had not been in vain.

If he could have seen the industrial, naval, political, mental, and spiritual progress, and the tremendous results that followed, he would not have believed his own eyes nor understood it.

The theme: "Seek ye first the kingdom of God and His righteousness, and all these things shall be added unto you" (Matt. 6:33) was the keynote of his life.

From this text Hauge had preached more often than any other. It is the favorite text of the Haugians today, and will be the connecting link in true Christianity from generation to generation, even unto the end.

Long live the memory of the true Christian Patriot, H a n s N i e l s e n H a u g e.

THE END

www.ingramcontent.com/pod-product-compliance
Lightning Source LLC
Chambersburg PA
CBHW070304230426
43664CB00014B/2631